Adobe® Acrobat® 3 For Dummies®

W9-CNA-143

Working with Individual Pages

Option	What It Does	Windows Shortcut	Mac Shortcut
Delete Pages	Deletes pages from a PDF	Ctrl+Shift+D	Cmd+Shift+D
Extract Pages	Removes pages from the current PDF and places them in a new PDF	Ctrl+Shift+E	Cmd+Shift+E
Insert Pages	Imports pages from one PDF into another	Ctrl+Shift+I	Cmd+Shift+I
Replace Pages	Replaces pages in current PDF with selected pages from another PDF	Ctrl+Shift+R	Cmd+Shift+R
Rotate Pages	Changes pages from tall to wide	Ctrl+Shift+O	Cmd+Shift+O

Navigation and Views

Option	What It Does	Windows Shortcut	Mac Shortcut
100% View	Displays page in 100% view	Ctrl+H	Cmd+H
Articles	Displays and selects articles	Ctrl+Shift+A	Cmd+Shift+A
Bookmark and Page	Displays bookmarks	Ctrl+7	Cmd+7
Cascade	Stacks all open PDFs for easy access	Shift+F5	no shortcut
Close All	Closes all open PDFs	no shortcut	Cmd+Option+W
Continuous	Goes to continuous page view	Ctrl+Shift+C	Cmd+Shift+C
First Page	Returns to the first page of a PDF	Ctrl+1	Cmd+1
Fit Page	Fits the page in the document window	Ctrl+J	Cmd+J
Fit Visible	Fills the document window with the current page	Ctrl+M	Cmd+M
Fit Width	Fits the page in the width of the document window	Ctrl+K	Cmd+K
Full Screen	Displays the PDF devoid of menus and toolbars	Ctrl+Shift+L	Cmd+Shift+L
Go Back	Goes back to the previous view	Ctrl+-	Cmd+-
Go Forward	Goes to the next view	Ctrl+=	Cmd+=
Go to Page	Displays the Go To Page dialog box to allow you to choose a page	Ctrl+5	Cmd+5
Hide Menu Bar	Toggles the menu bar on and off	Ctrl+Shift+M	Cmd+Shift+B
Hide Toolbar	Toggles the toolbar on and off	Ctrl+Shift+M	Ctrl+Shift+M
Last Page	Goes to last page in a PDF	Ctrl+4	Cmd+4
New Bookmark	Creates a new bookmark	Ctrl+B	Cmd+B
Next	Goes forward one page	Ctrl+3	Cmd+3
Page Only	Displays the page in the window with no bookmarks or thumbnails	Ctrl+6	Cmd+6
Previous Page	Goes back one page	Ctrl+2	Cmd+2
Reset Bookmark Destination	Changes the view to which a bookmark is linked	Ctrl+A	Cmd+R
Single Page	Goes to the single page view	Ctrl+Shift+N	Cmd+Shift+N
Thumbnails and Page	Displays thumbnails	Ctrl+8	Cmd+8
Tile Horizontally	Places open PDFs side-by-side horizontally	Shift+F4	no shortcut
Tile Vertically	Places open PDFs side-by-side vertically	Shift+F3	no shortcut
Zoom To	Opens the Zoom To dialog box to allow you to select a preset view	Ctrl+L	Cmd+L

...For Dummies: #1 Computer Book Series for Beginners

Adobe® Acrobat® 3 For Dummies®

COMPUTER
BOOK SERIES
FROM IDG

Cheat Sheet

Acrobat Exchange and Reader
Shortcut Keys and Tools

Working with Files

Option	What It Does	Windows Shortcut	Mac Shortcut
Close	Closes current PDF	Ctrl+W	Cmd+W
Open	Opens an existing PDF	Ctrl+O	Cmd+O
Page Setup	Allows you to make printer and page settings	no shortcut	Cmd+Shift+P
Print	Prints current PDF	Ctrl+P	Cmd+P
Quit	Closes Acrobat application	Ctrl+Q	Cmd+Q
Save	Saves current PDF	Ctrl+S	Cmd+S
Save As	Allows you to name and save current untitled PDF	Ctrl+S	Cmd+Shift+S

Editing PDFs

Option	What It Does	Windows Shortcut	Mac Shortcut
Copy	Copies object and places it on the Clipboard	Ctrl+C	Cmd+C
Copy File to Clipboard	Copies entire PDF to the Clipboard	Ctrl+Shift+K	no shortcut
Cut	Removes object and places it on the Clipboard	Ctrl+X	Cmd+X
Find First Suspects	Finds first Capture plug-in suspect	no shortcut	Cmd+Tab
Paste	Pastes object from the Clipboard into the current document	Ctrl+V	Cmd+V
Properties	Displays Properties dialog box for selected objects	Ctrl+I	Cmd+I
Select All	Selects all objects on the current page	Ctrl+A	Cmd+A
Undo	Reverses the last action	Ctrl+Z	Cmd+Z

IDG
BOOKS
WORLDWIDE

...For Dummies: #1 Computer Book Series for Beginners

References for the Rest of Us! ®

COMPUTER BOOK SERIES FROM IDG

Are you intimidated and confused by computers? Do you find that traditional manuals are overloaded with technical details you'll never use? Do your friends and family always call you to fix simple problems on their PCs? Then the *...For Dummies*® computer book series from IDG Books Worldwide is for you.

...For Dummies books are written for those frustrated computer users who know they aren't really dumb but find that PC hardware, software, and indeed the unique vocabulary of computing make them feel helpless. *...For Dummies* books use a lighthearted approach, a down-to-earth style, and even cartoons and humorous icons to diffuse computer novices' fears and build their confidence. Lighthearted but not lightweight, these books are a perfect survival guide for anyone forced to use a computer.

> *"I like my copy so much I told friends; now they bought copies."*
>
> **Irene C., Orwell, Ohio**

> *"Quick, concise, nontechnical, and humorous."*
>
> **Jay A., Elburn, Illinois**

> *"Thanks, I needed this book. Now I can sleep at night."*
>
> **Robin F., British Columbia, Canada**

Already, hundreds of thousands of satisfied readers agree. They have made *...For Dummies* books the #1 introductory level computer book series and have written asking for more. So, if you're looking for the most fun and easy way to learn about computers, look to *...For Dummies* books to give you a helping hand.

IDG BOOKS WORLDWIDE

7/96r

ADOBE® ACROBAT® 3
FOR DUMMIES®

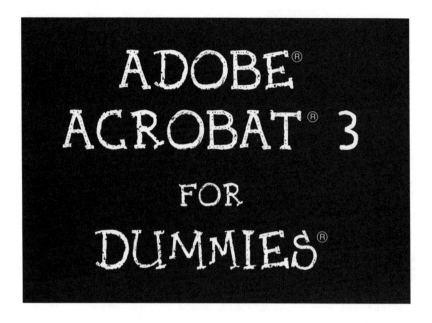

ADOBE® ACROBAT® 3 FOR DUMMIES®

by William Harrel

IDG Books Worldwide, Inc.
An International Data Group Company

Foster City, CA ♦ Chicago, IL ♦ Indianapolis, IN ♦ Southlake, TX

Adobe® Acrobat® 3 For Dummies®

Published by
IDG Books Worldwide, Inc.
An International Data Group Company
919 E. Hillsdale Blvd.
Suite 400
Foster City, CA 94404
http://www.idgbooks.com (IDG Books Worldwide Web Site)
http://www.dummies.com (Dummies Press Web Site)

Library of Congress Catalog Card No.: 97-70728

ISBN: 0-7645-0154-2

Printed in the United States of America

10 9 8 7 6 5 4 3 2 1

1E/TQ/QU/ZX/IN

Distributed in the United States by IDG Books Worldwide, Inc.

Distributed by Macmillan Canada for Canada; by Transworld Publishers Limited in the United Kingdom and Europe; by WoodsLane Pty. Ltd. for Australia; by WoodsLane Enterprises Ltd. for New Zealand; by Longman Singapore Publishers Ltd. for Singapore, Malaysia, Thailand, and Indonesia; by Simron Pty. Ltd. for South Africa; by Toppan Company Ltd. for Japan; by Distribuidora Cuspide for Argentina; by Livraria Cultura for Brazil; by Ediciencia S.A. for Ecuador; by Addison-Wesley Publishing Company for Korea; by Ediciones ZETA S.C.R. Ltda. for Peru; by WS Computer Publishing Company, Inc., for the Philippines; by Unalis Corporation for Taiwan; by Contemporanea de Ediciones for Venezuela. Authorized Sales Agent: Anthony Rudkin Associates for the Middle East and North Africa.

For general information on IDG Books Worldwide's books in the U.S., please call our Consumer Customer Service department at 800-762-2974. For reseller information, including discounts and premium sales, please call our Reseller Customer Service department at 800-434-3422.

For information on where to purchase IDG Books Worldwide's books outside the U.S., please contact our International Sales department at 415-655-3023 or fax 415-655-3299.

For information on foreign language translations, please contact our Foreign & Subsidiary Rights department at 415-655-3021 or fax 415-655-3281.

For sales inquiries and special prices for bulk quantities, please contact our Sales department at 415-655-3200 or write to the address above.

For information on using IDG Books Worldwide's books in the classroom or for ordering examination copies, please contact our Educational Sales department at 800-434-2086 or fax 817-251-8174.

For press review copies, author interviews, or other publicity information, please contact our Public Relations department at 415-655-3000 or fax 415-655-3299.

For authorization to photocopy items for corporate, personal, or educational use, please contact Copyright Clearance Center, 222 Rosewood Drive, Danvers, MA 01923, or fax 508-750-4470.

 is a trademark under exclusive license to IDG Books Worldwide, Inc., from International Data Group, Inc.

About the Author

William Harrel is a graphics designer and freelance writer based in Southern California. His design firm has produced layouts and Web pages for major companies and organizations, such as Executone and Johnson & Johnson, as well as for several states and counties. In addition, he has written hundreds of articles on desktop design for several magazines, including *PC World, Windows Magazine,* and *Publish,* and is a contributing editor for *Home Office Computing.* He has authored or coauthored 18 books, including *CorelDRAW 7 Secrets* and *The Macworld PageMaker 6.5 Bible* (both published by IDG Books Worldwide, Inc.).

ABOUT IDG BOOKS WORLDWIDE

Welcome to the world of IDG Books Worldwide.

IDG Books Worldwide, Inc., is a subsidiary of International Data Group, the world's largest publisher of computer-related information and the leading global provider of information services on information technology. IDG was founded more than 25 years ago and now employs more than 8,500 people worldwide. IDG publishes more than 275 computer publications in over 75 countries (see listing below). More than 60 million people read one or more IDG publications each month.

Launched in 1990, IDG Books Worldwide is today the #1 publisher of best-selling computer books in the United States. We are proud to have received eight awards from the Computer Press Association in recognition of editorial excellence and three from *Computer Currents'* First Annual Readers' Choice Awards. Our best-selling *...For Dummies®* series has more than 30 million copies in print with translations in 30 languages. IDG Books Worldwide, through a joint venture with IDG's Hi-Tech Beijing, became the first U.S. publisher to publish a computer book in the People's Republic of China. In record time, IDG Books Worldwide has become the first choice for millions of readers around the world who want to learn how to better manage their businesses.

Our mission is simple: Every one of our books is designed to bring extra value and skill-building instructions to the reader. Our books are written by experts who understand and care about our readers. The knowledge base of our editorial staff comes from years of experience in publishing, education, and journalism — experience we use to produce books for the '90s. In short, we care about books, so we attract the best people. We devote special attention to details such as audience, interior design, use of icons, and illustrations. And because we use an efficient process of authoring, editing, and desktop publishing our books electronically, we can spend more time ensuring superior content and spend less time on the technicalities of making books.

You can count on our commitment to deliver high-quality books at competitive prices on topics you want to read about. At IDG Books Worldwide, we continue in the IDG tradition of delivering quality for more than 25 years. You'll find no better book on a subject than one from IDG Books Worldwide.

John Kilcullen
CEO
IDG Books Worldwide, Inc.

Steven Berkowitz
President and Publisher
IDG Books Worldwide, Inc.

Eighth Annual Computer Press Awards ≥1992

Ninth Annual Computer Press Awards ≥1993

Tenth Annual Computer Press Awards ≥1994

Eleventh Annual Computer Press Awards ≥1995

Author's Acknowledgments

I would like to thank Susan Pink and the good folks at IDG Books Worldwide for their patience and help during the writing and production of this book. It was not easy boiling down such an immense topic. Thanks also to Jim Alley, the technical reviewer, for his Macintosh expertise.

Publisher's Acknowledgments

We're proud of this book; please send us your comments about it by using the IDG Books Worldwide Registration Card at the back of the book or by e-mailing us at feedback/dummies@idgbooks.com. Some of the people who helped bring this book to market include the following:

Acquisitions, Development, and Editorial

Project Editor: Susan Pink

Acquisitions Editor: Gareth Hancock

Product Development Director: Mary Bednarek

Media Development Manager: Joyce Pepple

Associate Permissions Editor: Heather H. Dismore

Technical Editor: Jim Alley

Editorial Manager: Mary C. Corder

Editorial Assistants: Chris H. Collins, Steven H. Hayes

Production

Project Coordinator: Debbie Stailey

Layout and Graphics: Cameron Booker, Lou Boudreau, J. Tyler Connor, Tom Missler, Drew R. Moore, Kate Snell

Proofreaders: Renee Kelty, Joel K. Draper

Indexer: Sherry Massey

Special Help

Suzanne Packer, Lead Copy Editor; Constance Carlisle, Copy Editor

---

General and Administrative

IDG Books Worldwide, Inc.: John Kilcullen, CEO; Steven Berkowitz, President and Publisher

IDG Books Technology Publishing: Brenda McLaughlin, Senior Vice President and Group Publisher

Dummies Technology Press and Dummies Editorial: Diane Graves Steele, Vice President and Associate Publisher; Judith A. Taylor, Brand Manager; Kristin A. Cocks, Editorial Director

Dummies Trade Press: Kathleen A. Welton, Vice President and Publisher; Stacy S. Collins, Brand Manager

IDG Books Production for Dummies Press: Beth Jenkins, Production Director; Cindy L. Phipps, Supervisor of Project Coordination, Production Proofreading, and Indexing; Kathie S. Schutte, Supervisor of Page Layout; Shelley Lea, Supervisor of Graphics and Design; Debbie J. Gates, Production Systems Specialist; Tony Augsburger, Supervisor of Reprints and Bluelines; Leslie Popplewell, Media Archive Coordinator

Dummies Packaging and Book Design: Patti Sandez, Packaging Specialist; Lance Kayser, Packaging Assistant; Kavish + Kavish, Cover Design

♦

The publisher would like to give special thanks to Patrick J. McGovern, without whom this book would not have been possible.

♦

Contents at a Glance

Cartoons at a Glance

By Rich Tennant • Fax: 508-546-7747 • E-mail: the5wave@tiac.net

page 241

page 281

page 7

page 75

page 169

Table of Contents

Introduction

● ●

*W*ith today's emphasis on the World Wide Web, company networks, CD-ROM titles, and the like, the Information Age is on a steady course to publishing without paper and to the paperless office. Nowadays, more of us perform our work and get information from our computers rather than through conventional printed books, magazines, and manuals. Adobe Acrobat is designed to hasten the process of moving us from the printed page to the computer monitor — in spite of the incompatibility problems that arise when transferring documents between Windows, Mac/OS, and UNIX.

The type of document Acrobat creates, Adobe's Portable Document Format (PDF), is known as an electronic document. The difference between it and many other types of computer documents, such as word processor or desktop publishing layouts, is that PDFs are designed to be viewed and read (or *used*) on any computer, instead of printed on a desktop printer or at a print shop. (You can, however, also print PDFs.)

At first, accessing information from a computer may seem foreign. It's hard to get used to going from page to page by clicking buttons instead of by turning pages. We are all programmed in school to find information by first flipping back and forth between tables of contents and indexes, and then scanning pages for pertinent subheads or relevant text. PDFs provide an all-new, more efficient way to find the information we need through hyperlinked text and graphics or by searching for keywords and phrases. When used properly and created effectively, PDFs enable you to find information more quickly and are easier to use than conventional paper documents.

Hundreds of companies and organizations are using PDFs to distribute information and documents, such as forms and training manuals, over company networks and on the Internet. And hundreds more are making the transition from the traditional reams of paper media they print and distribute to the more efficient implementation of PDF libraries.

Acrobat performs its magic by allowing you to convert virtually any computer document — a word processor file, a desktop publishing layout, a presentation — to PDF. Then the document can be enhanced by adding links to material in the document itself, to other PDFs, and even to HTML documents on the World Wide Web. Users of the PDF can find quickly the information they need and skip around in vast libraries of information for related topics.

Today, we all need information fast — now, if not sooner. Acrobat is designed to allow you, the purveyor of the information, to provide information in an efficient and time-saving manner. You can use Acrobat to create marketing material and multimedia titles, to convey information over a network or the Internet, and more. And you find all the information you need in this book to design the electronic document application just right for your needs.

About This Book

If you sit down and read any computer book from cover to cover, let's face it: You need to get a life! Most of us need information to solve the problem at hand. We pick up a book like this only when the solution is not self-evident.

So, I haven't deluded myself into thinking that you'll sit up one night enthralled, enthusiastically flipping through this book as you would your favorite novel. *Adobe Acrobat 3 For Dummies* is not *Of Mice and Men*. I know you'll pick it up only when you need to work through a problem with Acrobat. I'm glad to be of help.

How to Use This Book

This book is designed to be a painless reference. You should use it when you have a problem to solve. Open the book, find the solution, and then get back to work.

I've designed this book by procedures. How to do this. How to do that. Why you should do it my way. And so on. You'll find hundreds of step-by-step procedures, along with design tips and other tidbits to make your life easier.

Use the table of contents to find specific topics and procedures. If you want to narrow the search, try the index.

You can find information easier if you read the next section, "How This Book Is Organized," which provides an overview of how the information in this book flows.

How This Book Is Organized

This book is divided into five parts. Each part is divided into chapters. As much as I could, I tried to make each chapter a stand-alone module. In the few instances where you need information covered in another chapter, I refer you to the place in the book where you can find the information.

Part I: Getting to Know Acrobat

This part familiarizes you with Adobe Acrobat. Chapter 1 provides an overview of Acrobat and what you can do with the program. Then basic concepts, such as how to use PDFs to display and find information with Acrobat Reader (the viewer with which most users access and navigate PDFs), are discussed. After all, you can't design an effective document if you don't know the procedures that your audience uses. This part ends with information on how to convert your documents to PDF with Acrobat Distiller.

Part II: Enhancing PDFs in Exchange

Acrobat Exchange is the application in the Acrobat package that you use to enhance and optimize your PDFs. With it, you can create navigational links, edit text and graphics, add multimedia files (movies and sound), and perform a bunch of other functions that make your PDFs more functional and interesting. Part II walks you through the basics of creating links, editing text, adding and deleting pages to and from your PDFs, creating interactive indexes and tables of contents, using and creating Acrobat forms, and even using the Scan and Capture plug-ins to scan documents and turn the scanned text into editable PDF text. Much of the information you need to create PDFs is in this part.

Part III: Bringing PDFs to Life

Part III covers the advanced features of Exchange, such as adding multimedia sound and movie files to your PDFs. You also find information on how to create searchable indexes that your users can use to find information by searching for terms and phrases. Use these features to make your PDFs easier to use and exciting to view.

Part IV: Distributing PDFs on the Internet and Other Networks

Okay, so now you have a bunch of PDFs and you're wondering what's the best way to distribute them to your users. In Part IV, you find the answers. I discuss how to optimize PDFs for quick downloading over modems on the World Wide Web, as well as how to prepare and organize your PDFs for use on a corporate network or intranet.

Part V: The Part of Tens

No *...For Dummies* book would be complete without "The Part of Tens." This part is a collection of useful tidbits to make working with Acrobat easier. The topics are ten useful types of PDF applications and ten ways to troubleshoot problems.

Icons Used in This Book

What would a *...For Dummies* book be without its share of goofy little pictures in the margins? I've used my share of them. Here's a list of the pictures, or icons, used in this book and the types of information you find beside them.

All computer books have tips — those bits of information that the writer couldn't logically squeeze into the main text. This book has a bunch of them. Whenever you see a tip, you find a little trick or technique designed to make your life easier.

Acrobat is in some ways a document design program. I haven't assumed that you know how to create PDFs or that you are a graphics artist. So, whenever I thought of a nifty way to spruce up your PDFs, I passed it along to you as a design tip.

Here's an easy one to figure out. It means simply: Don't try this. I already have and can tell you from my own experience that it can be disastrous (or at least cause problems). When you see a warning, read it; it could save you some time and grief.

Most often, a note signifies an exception or contains additional information. For example, some procedures won't always work the way I explain in the text, depending on various software settings. A note might point out these exceptions.

Nerdy stuff appears beside this icon. You can skip it without feeling guilty.

Acrobat is a cross-platform application, which means you can use it on any type of computer. Some dialog boxes and procedures, however, are slightly different on Macintosh systems and on Windows machines. This icon flags the places in the text where the discussion is specific to Macs making the information easier to find.

Where to Go from Here

If you're familiar with Acrobat Reader and how to use it to access and navigate PDFs, you can skip Chapters 1 through 3 and go straight to Chapter 4 to see how documents are converted to PDFs. If you're not familiar with Acrobat at all, start at Chapter 1.

Acrobat is a great, easy-to-use, and hassle-free program. So have fun!

Part I
Getting to Know Acrobat

The 5th Wave — By Rich Tennant

In this part . . .

This part begins with an introduction to Acrobat —
what it is and what you can do with it. It then covers
accessing and navigating Acrobat documents with
Acrobat Reader, which is the viewer most people use with
PDFs. Reader is covered from two perspectives: accessing
and navigating PDFs on a local computer, and then using
Reader on the World Wide Web. This part ends with
instructions on how to convert regular computer documents to PDFs.

Chapter 1

Publishing without Paper

• •

In This Chapter

▶ Discovering electronic documents

▶ Examining Adobe Acrobat

▶ Understanding how Acrobat can help me and my company rein in the paper blizzard

▶ Figuring out what kind of computer I need to run Acrobat

• •

A few years ago we all heard a lot of talk about the "paperless office." The term buzzed from office to office, and across radio, television, and print media. Soon we'd all be free from stacks of memos, reports, and forms — and save a few trees. Oh, happy days.

In reality, since the advent of the personal computer and desktop printers, we use more paper (and cut down more trees) than ever before. Why? One reason is that as versatile as computers are, it's often not that easy to access files generated on computers other than our own.

Computers come in various flavors, such as Windows PCs, Macs, and UNIX systems. And to make matters worse, folks use different applications — word processors, spreadsheets, presentation programs, desktop publishing software — the list goes on and on. Folks also use different types of programs, such as Microsoft Word and WordPerfect. You get the idea.

If things weren't bad enough, now we have to contend with the Internet and a whole new medium for distributing computer files between all these different types of computers. What the computer document world needs is an equalizer. Hence, the invention of Adobe Acrobat and programs like it.

Acrobat makes juggling those different computer files easier. By converting electronic documents to a common *portable document format,* or *PDF,* Acrobat makes it possible for anyone using any computer to access files created on any other computer by any other program. At the risk of being ridiculously obvious, that's what *portable document* means. The file can be moved from computer to computer — with ease.

Sound like magic? Well it's not. Surely you've seen circus acts where acrobats nimbly jump through hoops, tumble, and contort themselves. You know it's not magic, but they make it seem so easy. In theory and in practice, PDFs perform very simple tricks, all the while making documents easier to read and to navigate than conventional paper. And they do so with a distinct grace and suppleness, as you'll soon see.

What Is an Electronic Document?

I can hear your mind churning. "Electronic document? Wait a minute, everything you create on a computer is an electronic document, right? It's all digitized."

And right you are. But we computer nerds (or propeller-heads, if you prefer) have a compulsion to assign fancy terms to everything. For the purpose of discussing Acrobat and other programs that create documents designed primarily to be viewed on a computer, *electronic document* has a special meaning. It means (you guessed it) a document designed to be viewed on a computer, rather than on conventional medium, such as paper, slides, overhead transparencies, or film.

As you move through this discussion of electronic documents, and Acrobat's Portable Document Format in general, I should bring you up to speed on industry terminology. A *document* is just about any file created with an application, such as word processor documents or desktop publishing documents. A *PDF* is a document created by Acrobat. It is common practice in the computer world, and especially on the World Wide Web, to refer to an Acrobat document as a PDF, and more than one PDF as *PDFs*. It is also common in the computer world to call any file created with a software application a *document*. To avoid monotony, I use these terms interchangeably throughout this book.

PDFs created by Acrobat are just one of the many types of electronic documents. Others include multimedia titles, such as courseware, "edutainment," and games; electronic presentations, such as those you create with Microsoft PowerPoint or SPC Harvard Graphics; and application Help files (those often not-so-helpful items you find on the Help menu of most programs).

What is a portable document?

Well, now. What is a portable telephone? A portable television? A portable computer? These are devices designed to be taken from place to place. A *portable document* is designed to be taken from computer to computer, regardless of platform (PC, Mac, or UNIX) and regardless of the application that created it (Word, WordPerfect, PageMaker, QuarkXPress, you name it). It's that simple.

In Figures 1-1 and 1-2, for instance, you see a PDF that looks the same in Windows 95 and on a Mac. Acrobat's PDF files are designed to transcend the limitations placed on traditional computer files by platform incompatibilities. You look more closely at how this works later in this chapter and throughout this book.

Common PDF applications

With PDFs, you can create electronic catalogs, manuals, training material, documents for viewing on the World Wide Web — you name it. You can even create multimedia titles, as discussed in the next section. Here are a few possibilities. (Also see Chapter 18 for ten more.)

PDFs as sales material

Suppose your company needs a full-color brochure or catalog. Reproducing (printing) these kinds of documents can be expensive, especially if you have to update them regularly.

Figure 1-1:
Portable documents display the same across platforms, regardless of configuration. Here's a PDF in Windows 95.

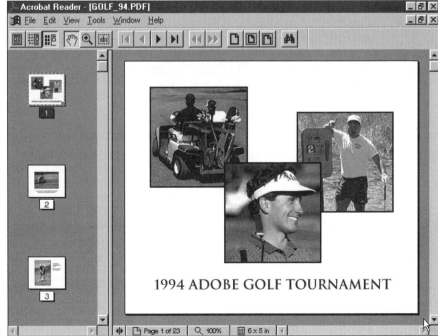

1994 ADOBE GOLF TOURNAMENT

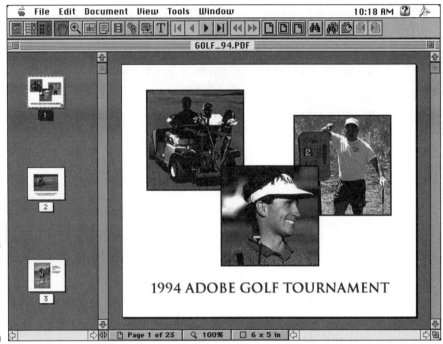

Figure 1-2:
And here's
the same
PDF on a
Mac.

Instead of printing hundreds of copies of the sales material for mailing or distribution through your sales people, you could produce the document as a PDF that can be mailed on a floppy disk, e-mailed, distributed over the Internet, and kept on your salespeople's portable computers. Customers (or your salespeople) can then print the portions of the document they're interested in or browse and search the document on their computers. You also can make changes quickly, such as adding products or changing prices — eliminating the need to throw away expensive, obsolete documents and print new ones.

Network document libraries

Popular uses for Acrobat are corporate network and Internet libraries. In both scenarios, you create and maintain a collection of PDFs that users can easily find and access by searching for keywords and phrases with Acrobat Search or another search engine. Both applications are discussed in Chapters 9 and 15.

Acrobat multimedia titles

There I go again, trying to impress you with 50-cent terms. *Multimedia* means more than one medium. Technically, any computer document that contains more than one type of medium, such as text and graphics, is a multimedia document. Traditionally, however, when we nerds let the term *multimedia* roll from our lips, we mean documents that contain digitized sound, animation, and video. So, a multimedia title is a computer document that contains these three elements. It is a publication, much the same way that books are often referred to as *titles*.

Multimedia documents come in a bunch of flavors. If you bought your computer recently, it probably included several multimedia documents, such as a multimedia encyclopedia (for example, Microsoft Encarta), games, and music video samplers. Figure 1-3 shows a multimedia title, just to give you a clearer idea about what I mean.

And yes, we have fancy terms for different types of multimedia titles, including edutainment, courseware, point-of-sale kiosks, business presentations, and electronic sales and marketing demos. The beauty of Acrobat 3.0 is that you can use it to create almost all these types of documents, in addition to standard PDFs. The following sections look at each of these multimedia types in more detail.

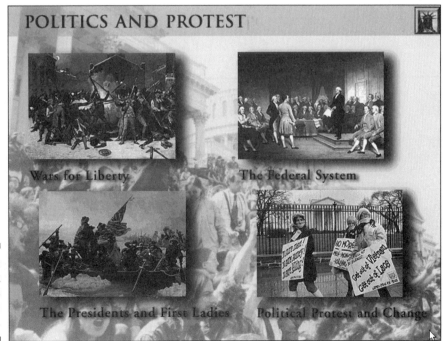

Figure 1-3: Check out this multimedia encyclopedia.

Edutainment

Edutainment — don't you just love it when technonerds murder our language this way? If you haven't guessed by now, I'm the kind of guy who loves these types of terms. *Edutainment* is the marriage of education and entertainment — a form of education that has been going on for years. The concept behind edutainment is that students learn more if the mode of instruction is entertaining and engaging (instead of a stodgy old teacher).

This idea has been going on in kindergarten classes for some time. Television realized that students, especially young students, learn more from entertaining content — which resulted in programming such as *Mr. Wizard* and *Sesame Street*. And the good folks at IDG Books Worldwide, Inc. have made a fortune with these books that demystify computers in a tongue-and-cheek, entertaining manner.

Multimedia edutainment titles — complete with sites and sounds — make learning on a computer lively and interesting. The interactivity provides instant gratification, something needed by young and old alike. Some of the more successful titles include Grolier Multimedia Encyclopedia (shown in Figure 1-4) and Microsoft Bookshelf. The good news is that you can create these types of electronic documents in Acrobat. You can find out more in Part 3.

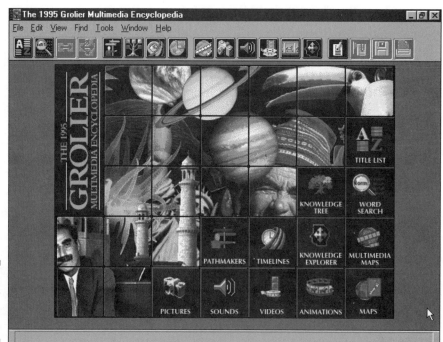

Figure 1-4:
Grolier
Multimedia
Encyclopedia.

Courseware

Ah. Courseware. That's another great marriage of words. You've probably already figured this out, but *courseware* is software that teaches or trains. The first implementations were corporate training courses. Chain restaurants, for example, use courseware to train new employees and to instruct them in company rules, the menu, and work procedures. Large corporations often use courseware to train people for new positions.

Today's courseware is sophisticated, often providing reading material, multimedia descriptions and demonstrations, workbooks, and even the kudos (immediate gratification) in one package. Good courseware also controls the students' rate of advancement by restricting movement to advanced topics until students have mastered the current lessons and by providing additional material to reinforce students weak areas.

Courseware is mostly restricted to use among mid-sized and large companies. These companies often make the courses available over a network, allowing employees to train in their spare time. Although you can create some rudimentary courseware titles in Acrobat, it lacks features necessary to make it a major player in creating this type of application. For example, Acrobat cannot create applications that tally scores and measure user responses, nor can it make calls to databases of information. Full-fledged multimedia authoring programs, such as Macromedia Director, are more suited to this use.

I know. Just when you were beginning to think that Acrobat could do everything. . . .

Point-of-sale kiosks

Point-of-sale kiosks are becoming popular in shopping malls, discount warehouses, and government centers. The three basic types of point-of-sale kiosks are self-running kiosks, kiosks with buttons next to the monitor, and touch-screen kiosks.

Some kiosks display product information or provide directions. Others let you order products or services. The ones popping up in government installations let you fill out forms, such as business license applications, divorce papers, and income tax forms. A common kiosk is one that enables you to reserve and purchase wedding gifts. The computer displays each product and tells you whether somebody else has already purchased it for the soon-to-be newlyweds.

Most kiosks are simple, displaying text and graphics based on user interactivity. Acrobat can create many types of kiosks, although it does not directly support touch-screen and button interfaces. Unless your kiosk utilizes standard keyboard and mouse (pointer) interaction, you may have better luck with software designed for this purpose.

Business presentations

When people think of business presentations, the image usually consists of a presenter — or narrator — operating some type of device, usually a slide projector or an overhead projector. As he or she speaks, supporting data and graphics are displayed on a screen. The screen presentation serves two purposes. One, it increases interest for the audience (making the information more palatable) by adding visual reinforcement. Two, it helps guide the presenter during the presentation.

Typically, this type of presentation is built around a slide metaphor, or one static screen of information followed by another. Ho-hum. Computers, however, are rapidly changing the nature of presentations. Now many business people deliver their presentations from a computer, complete with animated objects (such as bullet points that flow from various directions), charts and graphs with elements such as bars and lines that grow and shrink, as well as movie and sound files.

Typically, these extravaganzas are created in presentation programs such as Microsoft PowerPoint. But you can create some sophisticated presentations in Acrobat, as shown in Part 3. You can also create standalone viewer-interactive presentations, self-running presentations, and cross-platform electronic slide shows from existing presentations created in your favorite presentation program.

Viewer-interactive presentations

Viewer-interactive presentations are also built around the slide metaphor (or pages, in PDFs). The difference is that instead of sitting in an audience with a narrator controlling the flow of information, the viewer (or user) sits in front of a computer and navigates the presentation, aided by hyperlinks, or "hot" text and graphics buttons that let the viewer decide which part of the document to go to next. (Great for us control freaks, huh?)

As you see throughout this book, Acrobat is ideal for creating this type of electronic document. And this type of presentation is ideal for delivering information over the Internet. A viewer-interactive presentation is much handier and is more efficient for the audience than a linear video tape or a conventional presentation.

Self-running presentations

Another type of electronic document made popular by presentation programs is the self-running presentation. This is simply a presentation that
runs unassisted, one screen of information after another, usually continuously
(in a loop). The Acrobat capability to create PDFs with built-in automatic
screen advancement makes it adept at creating self-running presentations.

Electronic sales and marketing demos

Electronic sales and marketing demos are all over the place. Perhaps the
most common are demos that run on display models in computer and
electronic stores. Software companies also distribute demos of their
products. Figure 1-5, for example, shows an Adobe Photoshop demo.
The computer (and Acrobat) is ideal for creating and displaying this type
of electronic document.

Computers and software are not the only products advertised through
electronic marketing demos. You also can create PDFs that describe and
display just about anything you can think of, from jet skis to Ninjitsu. With
so many people buying computers, you can easily mass produce CD-ROM
brochures or deliver impressive demos and marketing material with PDFs
over the Internet.

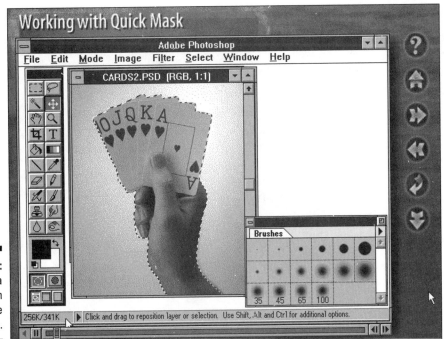

Figure 1-5:
Here's a
demo from
Adobe
Photoshop.

Okay, I'm Convinced. So What Is Acrobat?

I'm tempted to say "Acrobat is a suite of applications for creating, distributing, viewing, and printing PDFs." But my editors won't let me off the hook that easily. So, in this section, I break Acrobat down into its various components: Acrobat Reader, Acrobat Distiller, Acrobat Exchange, Acrobat Catalog, and the Acrobat Capture plug-in.

Acrobat Reader

Acrobat Reader is the most widely distributed portion of the Acrobat suite. It does just what its name says; it reads Acrobat documents, or PDFs. You use it to display, navigate, and print PDFs. It's that simple.

Acrobat Reader also doubles as a Web browser plug-in. A *plug-in* is a small piece of software that enhances a larger application's features and functionality. Web browsers, such as Netscape Navigator and Microsoft Internet Exchange, use plug-ins to display (or play, in the case of sound and movies) files that they cannot access on their own. Acrobat Reader lets you access PDFs from a Web browser, as shown in Figure 1-6.

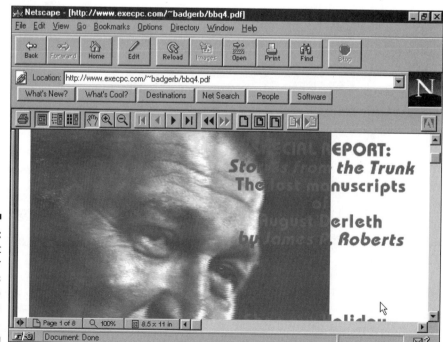

Figure 1-6:
Acrobat
Reader
working as
a plug-in to
Netscape
Navigator.

In addition to providing Reader with the Acrobat suite (which, by the way, you can freely distribute with virtually no restrictions), Adobe provides it free on its Web site (http://www.adobe.com), and with most of its other software applications, such as Photoshop, Illustrator, PageMaker, and Premiere. It is also distributed with many other software applications, especially those that provide product documentation in PDF documents.

Chapter 2 looks at using Reader as a standard PDF viewer, and Chapter 3 covers using Reader as a browser plug-in on the Internet. These chapters also cover how to obtain and install Reader.

Acrobat Distiller

PDFs are usually created from existing documents. The typical process is to print the document to a PostScript print file and then open it in Distiller to turn it into a PDF. Another method is to use Acrobat PDFWriter, which is a printer driver that does the work of Distiller automatically.

Don't get hung up on this *PostScript print file* thing. It's not complicated — I promise. I cover it in detail in Chapter 4, where you look into Distiller and PDFWriter.

Acrobat Exchange

The real magic of Acrobat takes place in Acrobat Exchange. Most of this book deals with Acrobat Exchange, the part of the suite that lets you enhance your PDFs. You use Exchange to create navigation hot links, embed movies and sounds, edit PDFs, and a whole bunch of other nifty stuff. In essence, learning Acrobat means learning Exchange. Compared to most other software programs with this much power, Exchange is remarkably easy to use.

Any PDFs that you may want to create from scratch (by scanning or importing images) rather than from existing documents are created in Exchange. It is truly the meat and potatoes of Acrobat (or the tofu and rice, if you prefer).

Adobe Catalog

Catalog is the most difficult part of the suite. But if all software programs were as complicated as Catalog, there wouldn't be a need for so many aftermarket computer books.

Put most simply, Catalog allows you to work with multiple PDFs simultaneously. You use it to create catalogs, or collections, of PDFs. After you catalog a bunch of PDFs, you can create indexes, tables of contents, and other types of lists based on the contents of all the PDFs in the catalog. Cataloging a group of PDFs also enables you to create search criteria across the entire catalog, so you can search for information in related PDFs from any PDF in the collection.

The applications for cataloged PDFs are immense, including distributing a document base over a corporate network or intranet, distributing multiple documents over the Internet, and creating sophisticated CD-ROM titles. You can discover how to perform this magic with Catalog in Chapter 14.

Adobe Capture

As mentioned, a plug-in enhances a program's features. The Adobe Capture plug-in adds scanning features — image scanning and optical character recognition (OCR) — to Exchange. You already know about image scanning, but you may not know about OCR.

OCR is the process of scanning text documents and converting them into editable text files. After using OCR for some time, I'm convinced that the software engineers who created and developed this technology are truly wizards. Capture allows you to scan text and graphics to enhance your PDFs. You find out how to use Capture in Chapter 8.

Why Do I Need Acrobat?

If you don't plan to publish documents to be read on multiple computers or across a network or the Internet, you don't need the full Acrobat application. You can get by fine with Reader. And, hey, it's free. But if you do plan on publishing documents for distribution on multiple computers — no matter how you distribute them — Acrobat is a foolproof and simple method for doing so. This section looks at some of the reasons why you may need Acrobat.

Leaping documents across platforms

From the beginning of the information age, it's been nothing short of a hassle to transport documents from one computer platform to another. Just as people who speak different languages have trouble communicating, so do computers that use different chips and operating systems. PCs speak Windows, Macs talk System 7, UNIX systems use Sun Spark — and it's all Greek between them.

We have some relief in the migration from character-based interfaces, such as the boring and unfriendly DOS prompt to the graphical user interface (GUI, pronounced "gooey") of late. Since the advent of Windows on the PC and UNIX GUIs, software developers have been able to produce cross-platform applications that behave similarly and can read files generated on different types of systems. Back in Figures 1-1 and 1-2, for instance, Adobe PageMaker is running in Windows 95 and on a Mac, respectively. Notice that both are displaying the same document.

But this is only half the battle. (I know, you didn't even know we were at war.) Other differences between the two platforms make this type of file transfer problematic. A major consideration is cost. For example, to send a Macintosh PageMaker file to a client to review on his or her Windows machine, the client must have PageMaker, a several hundred-dollar computer program. Ouch! Then the client must also have the same fonts installed on his or her computer that I used in the document, which constitutes an even greater expense.

Not so bad, you say? Well, fonts on one platform often have different names from fonts on another. Even if the client does have my fonts, PageMaker may not know to use them because the names don't match. What do I do? Design the document beforehand with the client's computer configuration in mind? No way, José. I won't let a measly configuration difference dampen my designing spirit. I'll use Acrobat, thank you.

Tumbling documents from computer to computer

It's less of a problem opening a document created on another computer of the same type, or platform. You can, however, still experience problems with things such as font matches. Different designers prefer different fonts; some use Type 1 PostScript fonts while others use TrueType. (You can look into the different types of fonts in Chapter 4.)

Sometimes font differences can be resolved by the applications. PageMaker and CorelDRAW!, for example, come with a utility called PANOSE that tries to match fonts based on name and characteristics. PANOSE and similar utilities however, are inadequate. There are tens of thousands of fonts from many vendors. And even fonts from different manufacturers that are supposedly the same design can have different spacing and character widths. When this occurs, the application must reformat the document; this can change text line lengths and placement, and play havoc with a meticulously designed layout. Also, when PANOSE does match a font, it guesses and is seldom right — giving you an entirely different font and a new look to your document, and making a mess of your text and graphic placement.

Another frequent mismatch when porting documents from one computer to another is application version differences. Some users upgrade their software religiously; others do not. Suppose that I e-mail to you a document formatted in Microsoft Word 7 but you're using Version 3. The document won't look and print the way I designed it because your version doesn't support many of the features that mine does. I hate it when that happens.

This mismatch can be worse depending on the application. Some programs, such as PageMaker, support only the preceding version. PageMaker 6.5, for example, can't open Version 4 without running it through a conversion utility. The conversion is seldom foolproof, and it's a bit much to ask your client (or boss) to go through all this hassle just to review your document.

What did I do with that copy of Acrobat?

Juggling documents from application to application

Nowadays, many programs claim to support files from like applications. Word, for instance, saves and opens files created in WordPerfect, and vice versa. CorelDRAW! opens documents created in Adobe Illustrator. Harvard Graphics lets you open and edit Microsoft PowerPoint. You get the idea.

Sometimes this exchange works fine — especially when documents are simple; for example, text flowing from line to line without graphics or advanced features such as tables and columns. But often it doesn't work fine. This is especially true of graphics and page layout programs, such as Corel Ventura, PageMaker, and QuarkXPress. Just about anything can happen, such as different text line breaks or incorrectly placed graphics. These things happen because the programs work differently and support different features. In addition, all the other problems discussed in the previous section also apply to juggling documents from application to application.

What Do I Need to Run Acrobat?

Acrobat is one of the few applications available that runs on all three major computer platforms. With some minimal limitations, discussed on a case-by-case basis as they arise throughout this book, you can run most of the applications in the suite on any platform. This means you can view, edit, and enhance Acrobat files on almost any computer. This section looks at each platform separately and discusses the system requirements for each one.

Running Acrobat in Windows

Acrobat applications run under Windows 3.1, Windows 95, and Windows NT. Table 1-1 shows the system requirements for each application in the suite on each platform.

Table 1-1 System Requirements for Running Acrobat in Windows		
Operating System	*Acrobat Application*	*System Requirements*
Windows 3.1 and 95	All applications	386, 486, or Pentium
	Reader	8MB RAM
	Exchange	8MB RAM
	Catalog	8MB RAM
	Distiller	16MB RAM
	Capture	16MB RAM; 486 or Pentium
Windows NT 3.5.1 and later	Reader	16MB RAM
	Exchange	16MB RAM
	Catalog	16MB RAM
	Distiller	24MB RAM
	Capture	24MB RAM; 486 or Pentium runs on NT 3.5.1 or later

In addition to the requirements in Table 1-1, Acrobat requires from 1.5MB to about 45MB of hard disk space, depending on the options you installed. To use the Capture plug-in, you also need a desktop scanner.

Running Acrobat on a Mac

Acrobat originated on the Mac, as did most Adobe graphics and layout applications. At the risk of ruffling some feathers, let me say that Mac is superior to Windows and UNIX systems for page layout and graphics applications, and it runs Acrobat wonderfully. This is not to say that you won't have great luck running Acrobat on Windows and UNIX systems.

Note that some slight differences exist in using Exchange, Distiller, and Catalog in Windows versus on a Mac. I'll point out these differences as they come up.

Table 1-2 shows the system requirements for running Acrobat on a Macintosh or Power Macintosh. Keep in mind when reading this table that Macs use memory differently than Windows. Depending on the extensions (INITs) that load when you start your system and the applications you have running, more or less of your system RAM is available. Acrobat's RAM requirements are measured by available RAM, rather than overall system RAM.

Table 1-2	System Requirements for Running Acrobat on a Macintosh	
Mac Type	*Application*	*System Requirements*
Mac 68020 – 60840	All applications	System 7.0 or later
	Reader	3.5MB available
	Exchange	6MB available
	Catalog	6MB available
	Distiller	6MB available
	Capture	Not available on the Mac
Power Macintosh	All applications	System 7.0 or later
	Reader	5MB available
	Exchange	6MB available
	Catalog	8MB available
	Distiller	8MB available
	Capture	16MB available

Running Acrobat on a UNIX system

UNIX is primarily a networking platform, in which applications are typically run from a workstation. In this scenario, most UNIX computers can run Acrobat, with the exception of the Capture plug-in, which is unavailable. The following is a list of UNIX operating systems on which Acrobat will run:

- X Windows v.11 (releases 4.5 and 6, including Sun-3, Sun-4, Sun 386I, and Sun SPARCStation)
- Generic 386/486/Pentium computer running Linux 386/ix, FreeBSD, ISC UNIX, or Solaris; HP 900/300 and 9000/800; DECStation 2100 and 3100
- VAX running Ultrix and OSF/1
- Sequent Symmetry

✔ Convex C1 and C2

✔ Tektronix 4300

✔ SGI Iris indigo

✔ 4.4bsd UNIX systems (FreeBSD, NetBSD, Sparc, M68k), Apple, Amiga, Sun, Hewlett-Packard, VAX, and 386BSD

Which Web browser do I need?

A *Web browser* is an application that lets you navigate and view hypertext markup language (HTML) documents on the World Wide Web. To create PDFs, you don't need a Web browser. To test your PDF creations and view other PDFs on the Web, however, you do need a Web browser.

If you spend time on the Web, you already have some sort of Web browser. To get the most from Acrobat 3, though, you should have a browser that supports plug-ins, such as Netscape Navigator 3 or Microsoft Internet Explorer 3.

Before going into Web browsers, take a brief look at how Acrobat works on the Internet. To navigate and view PDFs on the World Wide Web, you use Acrobat Reader. Reader can interact with your Web browser in two ways, either as a helper application or as a plug-in. A *helper application* works differently from a plug-in in that it opens, or *spawns,* as a separate application to display a file, instead of displaying the file inside the Web browser.

Sound confusing? Check out Figures 1-7 and 1-8. They show the difference between Acrobat Reader acting as a plug-in and as a helper application. (You can find out about the advantages and disadvantages to both methods in Chapter 3.) Almost any application can serve as a helper application, but only specially designed applications can act as browser plug-ins. Acrobat Reader is designed to double as a plug-in. (Technically, it's a *viewer application,* but you read about all that in Chapter 3.)

To use Reader as a plug-in, you need Netscape Navigator 3 or Microsoft Internet Explorer 3. Most other browsers can use Reader as a helper application. Chapter 3 describes how to use Reader to view documents on the Internet. In the meantime, you can download Navigator at

```
http://home.netscape.com
```

You can get Microsoft Internet Explorer at

```
http://www.microsoft.com.
```

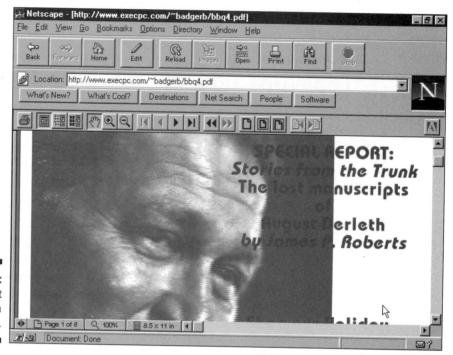

Figure 1-7:
Acrobat
Reader as a
plug-in.

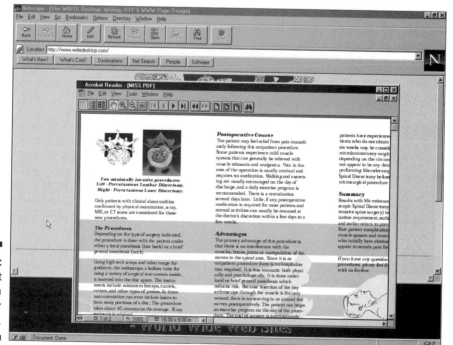

Figure 1-8:
Acrobat
Reader as a
helper
application.

Chapter 2

Viewing and Navigating PDFs on Your Computer

*W*elcome to the 21st century, where there is no more disease or poverty and — best of all — we no longer need paper. All documents are distributed online. You talk to your computer, and it talks back.

Sound like *Star Trek?* Acrobat is certainly a step in that direction. One thing that's holding us back is that we are steeped in the use of paper documents. We feel comfortable poring over tables of contents and indexes, and then flipping pages to find the information we're after.

But as you'll see after reading this chapter, PDFs are a more efficient way to use documents. Not only is it easier to find material by searching for keywords and topics, but well-designed PDFs let you effortlessly jump from page to page and topic to topic, getting definitions and elaborations. Then, if you really need to, printing a page or two is easy to do.

Rather than continue this shameless exuberance, I'll just jump right into the ways to obtain, install, and use Acrobat Reader. After you get into using PDFs, you gain an appreciation for just how Neanderthal conventional printed material really is.

How Do I Get and Install Acrobat Reader?

Acrobat Reader, or Reader for short, is the utility used to view and print the Acrobat portable document format, or PDF. Anybody with a computer running Windows, Windows NT, Macintosh System 7.x, or most UNIX operating systems can use Reader. And the best part is that it's free!

If you've purchased any software lately, you may already have Reader. If you've already purchased the Acrobat package, look no further. You have Reader.

Adobe distributes Reader at no cost to anybody who wants it. The point is that if everybody has Reader, Web designers, software manufacturers, network administrators, and the like will purchase Acrobat Pro for creating PDFs. Great marketing, don't you think? Wouldn't it be great if music CD manufacturers gave away stereo systems so you could listen to their CDs?

You can obtain a copy of Reader in several ways:

- ✔ It is distributed free with many software applications.
- ✔ You can download it from Adobe's site on the World Wide Web.
- ✔ You can get it from a friend or an associate, and you can distribute it yourself, with a few restrictions
- ✔ You can get Reader from your network administrator or from the company network. (Talk to your administrator about this one.)
- ✔ It comes as a toy surprise in Cracker Jacks and with McDonald's Happy Meals — well, maybe someday.

This section looks at each method of obtaining Reader.

Software application

Many software vendors now distribute their product documentation (manuals and such) in PDF format. This is much cheaper than printing up hundreds of thousands of big, bulky manuals. It makes producing the software less expensive — saving you and the software company money, right? (In theory. But so far I haven't seen these companies drop their prices.)

Finding Acrobat Reader

If you distribute PDF documents with your products, you need to provide a way for your customers to access them. Hence, Reader is included on the installation disks or CD-ROM. If you have any recent Adobe products —

PageMaker, Photoshop, Illustrator, PageMill, and several others — Reader is on the disk. Reader also comes with numerous other programs, more than I can mention here. Many application boxes list it as free software.

To determine whether Reader is on an installation disk, simply load the disk into the computer. Open Windows Explorer and look for a folder called Acroread, as shown in Figure 2-1. On a Mac, open the disk while in Finder; look in the Acrobat Reader 3.0 folder.

Figure 2-1:
To deter-
mine
whether
Acrobat
Reader is
on a
software
disk, simply
look for the
Acroread
folder (or
Acrobat
Reader 3.0
on a
Macintosh).

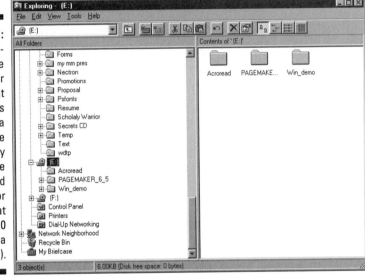

Installing Acrobat Reader

Okay. So you have Acrobat reader on one of your software installation disks. Your quest is over! Now all you have to do is install it.

Wait! Before installing Reader with the following method, make sure that you are installing Version 3.0. To find out which version is on the disk, double-click the Readme.txt file in the Acroread folder (or Reader — Reader on a Mac). It tells you which version you are using. (On a Mac, you know because the installation file resides in a folder called Acrobat Reader 3.0.) If you can't find Version 3.0 on one of your software installation disks, try downloading it from the World Wide Web, as described in the next section. (If you are installing from a network, talk to your system administrator before deviating from company-issued software.)

Here's how to install Reader:

1. **In Windows Explorer (or Macintosh Finder), double-click on the Acroread folder (Acrobat Reader 3.0 on a Macintosh).**
2. **Find and double-click on the Setup.exe file (or Install Acrobat Reader on a Mac).**
3. **Follow the directions to install the program.**

That's it. You're finished. You are now ready to use Reader.

The World Wide Web

Almost everybody with a computer has access to the Web these days. If you do, you can get the latest version of Reader from the Adobe Web site. Here's how:

1. **Point your Web browser to** http://www.adobe.com.

   The Adobe home page changes frequently, but it invariably has a button leading to the Acrobat Reader download page. On the day I wrote this, adobe.com looked like Figure 2-2.

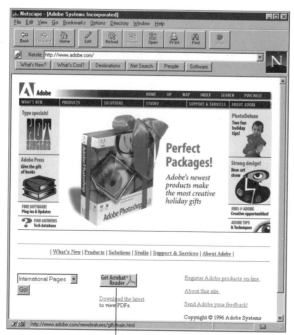

Figure 2-2:
Go to the
Adobe
home page
to get a
copy of
Reader.

Click here to download Acrobat.

2. **Simply click on the Get Acrobat Reader button.**

3. **Follow the steps for downloading the software.**

   Remember where on your computer your browser saves the file, as well as the name of the file.

4. **After the download is complete, close your browser.**

5. **From Windows Explorer (or Macintosh Finder), double-click on the icon for the file you downloaded.**

6. **Simply follow the directions on-screen.**

   The installation program does the rest.

 While you're in the Acrobat Reader pages on the Adobe site, look for a link that says, "How to freely distribute Adobe Acrobat Reader," and click on it. You get a page that tells you about Adobe's liberal distribution policy. Basically, it's this: Give Reader to anybody you want as often as you want. Can't beat that.

Becoming Familiar with Acrobat Reader

With Reader installed (make sure it is before reading on), you're ready to open and check out some PDFs. The information in this section serves two purposes. First, it familiarizes you with reading and navigating PDFs. Second, by helping you understand how Reader handles PDFs, this section helps prepare you for the time when you create your own electronic documents. After all, how many movie directors exist that haven't seen any movies?

Identifying PDF files

 How can you open PDFs with Reader if you don't know what they look like, right? In Windows 95 and on a Mac, identifying PDFs is simple. They show up in Windows Explorer and Finder as distinctive icons, as shown in the margin. They look similar on both platforms. To open a PDF from Windows Explorer or Finder, simply double-click on the icon.

You also can tell which files are PDFs from the Acrobat Reader Open dialog box (File➪Open) from inside Reader, as shown in Figure 2-3. The list in the Open dialog box displays only PDFs, ignoring other files. This makes sense because PDFs are the only type of file that Reader can open. To open a file from here, select the file name and then click Open.

Where did I put that PDF?

Okay. So the description on how to find PDFs is simple. Bet you wish all tasks on a computer were this easy. Well, if it sounds too good to be true. . . . You know the rest.

In Windows 95, for the Reader Open dialog box or Windows Explorer to identify PDFs as Acrobat files, the file names must include a .pdf extension. Otherwise, they show up as generic computer files, or they won't show up at all in the Open dialog box. When you save a file from Distiller or Exchange, the program automatically tacks on the .pdf. If you or somebody else changes the file name, removing or modifying the extension, your PDFs are not easily located and identified.

This is also true in Windows 3.x, which uses the same file naming conventions to associate files with applications. This does not mean that simply tacking a .pdf extension on any file name will automatically convert it to a PDF. Only PDFs created from Distiller or Exchange can be PDFs, period. The good news for Mac users is that System 7 uses a different method for identifying files and associating them with the host application. On a Mac, you can name a file anything you want (apple pie, cheese, file). Both Finder and Reader are able to recognize it as an Acrobat file.

Figure 2-3:
From the Acrobat Reader Open dialog box, you can identify PDFs because they are the only files displayed.

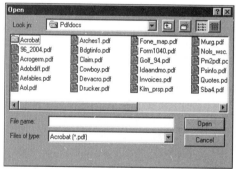

A quick tour of the Acrobat Reader interface

It's time to introduce you to the Reader interface. Should I just point out all the menus and buttons and tell you what each item does, or should I walk you through using the application? Both approaches have merit.

Rather than worrying about which type of reader will get the most from which method, I like to use them both. In this section, I describe each button and menu. Then, in the next section, I give you a blow-by-blow on the easiest ways to get around in a PDF with Reader. Begin by taking a look at Figure 2-4.

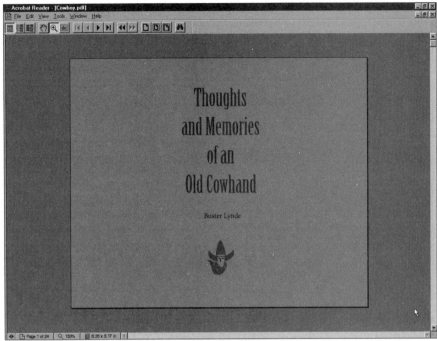

Figure 2-4:
The
Acrobat
Reader
interface.

Toolbars

Now, if there's anything in Figure 2-4 that you don't recognize, check out the following descriptions:

 Page Only: Use this option to display only the document page in the document window. This makes more sense if you read about the next two bullets, Bookmarks and Page and Thumbnails and Page.

 Bookmarks and Page: *Bookmarks* are table of contents-like hyperlinks to pages and views in the document. Clicking on them takes you to predefined places in the document. Note, though, that not all PDFs have bookmarks. To see how bookmarks are created, read Chapter 6.

 Thumbnails and Page: *Thumbnails* are small pictures of the pages in a PDF. Clicking on them takes you to specific pages in the file. The pictures help you decide which page to go to. Not all PDFs have thumbnails. Chapter 6 shows you how to create thumbnails in your PDFs.

 Hand: Use the Hand tool to move the page around in the document window. This tool works only when you are zoomed in on a portion of the page, rather than in a full-page view. To move the page in one direction or another, simply click on the page and drag in the desired direction.

Zoom: Use this tool to zoom in and out on specific portions of a page. The Zoom tool is discussed in detail later in this chapter.

Select Text: This tool allows you to select text in a PDF, which you can then copy with the Copy command on the Edit menu and paste into another Acrobat Exchange or Windows document. A similar command for selecting graphics is Tools⇨Select Graphics.

First Page: Use this option to return to the first page of a document, no matter where you are in the document. When you are already on the first page, this option appears dimmed.

Previous Page: Use this option to go to the page preceding the current page. For example, if you are on page 4, this option sends you to page 3.

Next Page: Use this option to go to the next page after the current page. If you are on page 4, for example, this option sends you to page 5.

Last Page: Use this option to go to the last page in the document, no matter where you are in the document. When you are already on the last page, this option appears dimmed.

Previous View: Use this option to go to the most recent page. For example, if you were on page 6 and then went to page 10, clicking this button returns you to page 6. Clicking again returns you to the page you were on prior to page 6, and so on.

Next View: Use this option to return to the page before the current view. This option works when you have already used Previous View to make a view change. It takes you in the opposite direction from Previous View.

100% View: Many computer programs have a 100% View, or Actual Size, command. And I think this size is supposed to correspond with the actual printed size of the page. The 100% View, however, is actually dependent on the resolution and size of your computer's display system. Frankly, I find this command superfluous and useless.

Fit Window: Fit Window is much more useful than Actual Size. This option forces the page to fill the window, regardless of the display size and resolution. This is the most efficient way to get a view of the entire page in the largest size for your monitor.

Fit Width: This option forces the display of the current page to fill the viewing area from the left page border to the right page border, providing you with the widest view of the page without having to scroll left or right. To see upper and lower portions of the page, you can use the Hand tool or scroll bars to scroll up or down.

Find: Use this option to search for specific text in a document. When you search in a document that belongs to a catalog, you can also search for a text string in all other documents in the catalog. (Catalogs are discussed in Chapter 14.)

Clicking this button brings up the Find dialog box. Simply type the text string and click Find. If you don't select Match Whole Word Only, Reader finds a text string even if it is part of a larger word. The letters *in,* for example, would stop on every word containing those two letters. To find the next occurrence of a word, press Ctrl+G (Cmd+G on the Mac).

 Split Window: Use this button to adjust the size of the bookmarks and thumbnails pane. The most common use for this option is to make all your bookmarks readable or to view more thumbnails at once. Simply drag the Split Window icon left or right to adjust the size of the window.

 Go To Page: Use this option to go to a specific page based on the page number. Simply click the button and type the new page number in the Go To Page dialog box.

 Zoom To: Use this option to set the magnification level. Clicking this button brings up the Zoom To dialog box. Simply type a magnification level by percentage or select a preset level from the list. Holding this button displays a pop-up menu containing zoom levels.

 Page Layout: Use this option to tell Reader to display pages either continuously or in a facing pages view, rather than one page at a time. This view simply lets you see more pages at once, depending on the zoom level and resolution of your monitor. The options are Single Page, Continuous Page, Continuous — Facing Pages.

File menu

Reader's File menu is simple and complies to the conventions used by most other Windows and Mac File menus. Here you find commands for opening, closing, and printing documents. Open the menu, however, and you notice that something is missing: Reader has no Save or Save As commands. You can't save documents from Reader. It is solely a viewer.

The Document Info command provides three types of information about the current document: General information, such as who created the document and when it was created, Font information, or which fonts are contained in the document, and Security information, such as whether the document can be printed or changed. Document Info is provided by Exchange during the PDF creation process, as discussed in Chapter 7.

Changing how Acrobat Reader works

Out of the box, computer programs are designed to do things in a specific way. You tell the program "do this," and it does it in a specific manner. When you open a file in Reader, for example, it always opens in a 100 percent view, page units are always displayed in inches, and so on. These are called the program's *defaults,* or *default preferences. Default* means, "If I don't tell you differently, always do it this way."

Most of Reader's defaults work well enough for most PDFs. But sometimes you may want to change them. Maybe you prefer a continuous page view, rather than a single page view. Maybe you prefer millimeters to inches. You change Reader's defaults from the Preferences menu (File⇨Preferences).

I will not drag you through a lengthy discussion of all the preference settings and what they do. Instead, I want to let you know that you have the ability to change them. Then, as you become more familiar with Reader and Acrobat PDFs in general, you may find times when you want to change the preference settings.

The Reader preferences are split into four categories: General, Notes, Full Screen, and Weblink. (See the accompanying figure.) Most General preferences, controlled from the General Preferences dialog box, control how documents are displayed in Reader. If you read

the section in this chapter on the Reader interface, most of the options in the dialog box make sense to you. You can get a full description of the General Preferences dialog box in the Acrobat Help PDF. Just search for *preferences.* Throughout the book, I point out where it is helpful to adjust preferences.

The Notes and Full Screen options are discussed in the section "Getting around in Acrobat Reader." The Weblink option is discussed in Chapter 3.

For now, though, just be aware that you can control several aspects of the Reader interface with options on the Preferences menu.

Edit menu

There's nothing new in Reader's Edit menu. It is standard Edit menu stuff: Copy, Paste, Cut. If you use Windows or System 7, you know how to do this stuff.

View menu

In the View menu, you find many navigational and zoom tools. Most of the options on this menu match the navigational tools on the button bars, which are discussed later in this section.

Tools menu

The Tools menu is where you find some more navigational tools, such as Find and Find Again, which let you search for specific text. Many of these tools also match the navigational tools on the button bars.

Window menu

Reader's Window menu is another standard Windows menu, allowing you to navigate between your open documents as well as display and hide elements of the Reader interface, such as button bars and the menu bar.

Help menu

Look on the Help menu to find the documentation provided with Reader. The difference between Acrobat help and that provided by other applications is that it comes in PDF files, rather than standard Help files. Check out these files — they're quite helpful.

Getting around in Acrobat Reader

Few programs provide more navigation options than Acrobat Reader. We've already discussed several. If the options discussed in the preceding section — bookmarks, thumbnails, Hand, Zoom, the First Page, Previous Page, Next Page, Last Page, Previous View, Next View, Go To Page buttons and commands, and Page Layout — were the only way to get around in a PDF, you'd get along fine. Many PDFs also provide built-in navigational tools, such as hypertext tables of contents and hyperlink text and graphics buttons.

In this section, you take a brief look at how to use Reader's built-in options. Then you look at the ways some PDF designers provide even greater navigational tools. I won't expend any more ink on the page advancement (Next Page, First Page, and so on) and the view advancement (Next View, Previous View) buttons and commands, because they speak for themselves.

Moving around with bookmarks and thumbnails

If you've ever used Microsoft Encarta or the Windows Help system, you may be familiar with bookmarks. There's a difference between those bookmarks and PDF bookmarks. In Encarta and Help, you, the user, create bookmarks to help you get back to important or frequently needed information. In PDFs, the creator of the document creates bookmarks.

Bookmarks in PDFs not only can take you to specific pages, but they also include specific views. In Figure 2-5, which is a PDF version of a manual, you can navigate to specific portions of the brochure, and then zoom in on the portion of the page containing the information corresponding to the bookmark, as shown in Figure 2-6.

The success with which a bookmark displays information depends on the designer, which is something you should consider when designing your own PDFs. You can find out how to create bookmarks in Chapter 9.

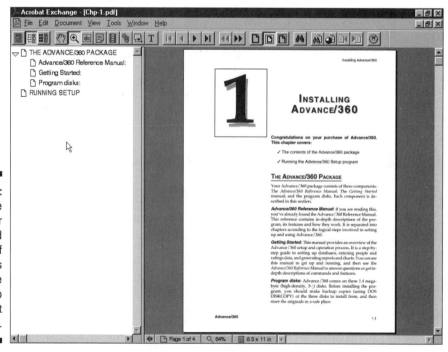

Figure 2-5: The designer has created plenty of bookmarks to lead the reader to important sections.

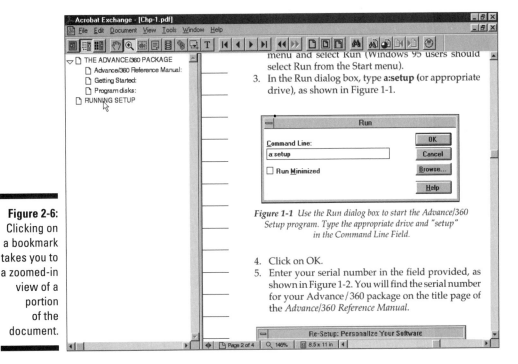

Figure 2-6:
Clicking on
a bookmark
takes you to
a zoomed-in
view of a
portion
of the
document.

One more thing to know about navigating with bookmarks is that designers can arrange them in groups of heads and subheads, as shown in Figure 2-7. The small triangle to the left of a bookmark means there are additional bookmarks, or subheadings. To see them, you simply click on the triangle, as shown in Figure 2-8. The most obvious use of this arrangement is creating bookmarks based on chapter titles, headings, and subheadings.

Thumbnails are another story. They simply allow you to go to a specific page, which is useful if you don't know what specific information you're looking for, when a specific page icon looks interesting or useful. Thumbnails also help you navigate documents that don't contain bookmarks.

Figure 2-7:
The triangle
to the left of
a bookmark
denotes the
presence
of sub-
bookmarks.

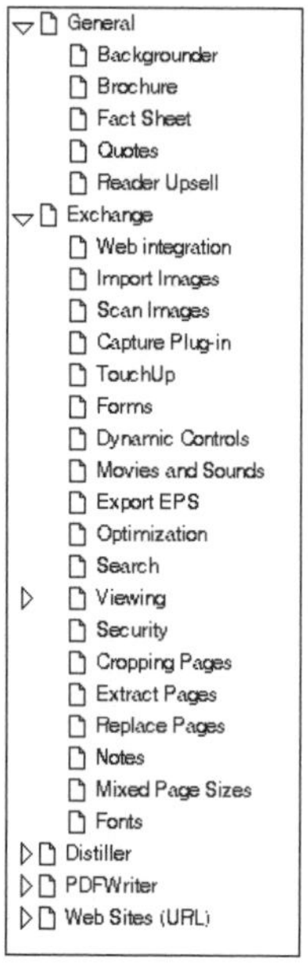

```
▽ 🗋 General
     🗋 Backgrounder
     🗋 Brochure
     🗋 Fact Sheet
     🗋 Quotes
     🗋 Reader Upsell
▽ 🗋 Exchange
     🗋 Web integration
     🗋 Import Images
     🗋 Scan Images
     🗋 Capture Plug-in
     🗋 TouchUp
     🗋 Forms
     🗋 Dynamic Controls
     🗋 Movies and Sounds
     🗋 Export EPS
     🗋 Optimization
     🗋 Search
  ▷  🗋 Viewing
     🗋 Security
     🗋 Cropping Pages
     🗋 Extract Pages
     🗋 Replace Pages
     🗋 Notes
     🗋 Mixed Page Sizes
     🗋 Fonts
▷ 🗋 Distiller
▷ 🗋 PDFWriter
▷ 🗋 Web Sites (URL)
```

Figure 2-8:
Clicking on
the triangle
opens the
major
bookmark,
displaying
minor
bookmarks.

Moving around with hyperlinks

A *hyperlink* is a hot spot in a document or on a page that allows you to jump to another portion of the PDF. If you spend any time on the Web or in multimedia titles, you're familiar with these. Like bookmarks, hyperlinks are created by the creator of the PDF. They can consist of text or graphics buttons.

A good example of the use of hyperlinks is the *Adobe Acrobat PDF Guide,* a sample of which is shown in Figure 2-9. As with any well-designed PDF, the creators of this document provide a page describing how to get around in the file.

Anywhere throughout the PDF, clicking on one of these objects takes you to another part of the document. The top two in the list are buttons on the button bar. The others are elements you might find on any page, such as the one in Figure 2-10.

You know from looking at Figure 2-9 what the hot elements in Figure 2-10 do. You also can tell whether an element is hot by hovering your mouse cursor over it. If the cursor turns into a pointing hand, you know that clicking on it will jump you to another spot in the PDF.

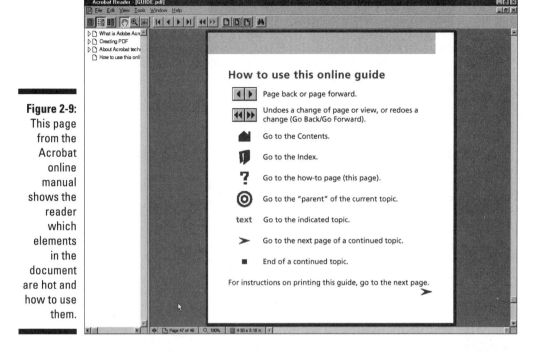

Figure 2-9:
This page
from the
Acrobat
online
manual
shows the
reader
which
elements
in the
document
are hot and
how to use
them.

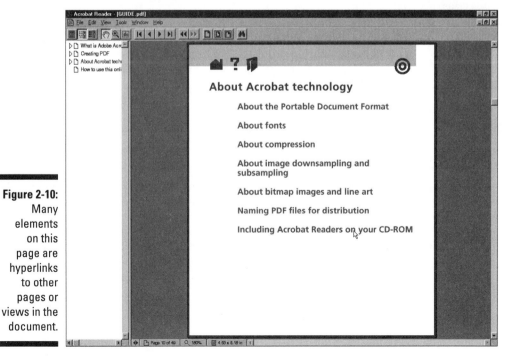

Figure 2-10:
Many
elements
on this
page are
hyperlinks
to other
pages or
views in the
document.

A common practice of designers is to place hyperlinks in a block of text. For example, suppose you're reading about anteaters and come across a passage that mentions the creatures' diet. The word *diet* shows up in a different color (or underlined, italicized, and so on). Generally, this means the text is hot. In this case, it means you can get to another section of the document describing the diet of the anteater (perhaps a picture of ants). After reading the section, you can click on the Previous View button on the button bar to return to the page you were reading when you clicked on *diet.* Make sense?

Other types of navigational controls

In addition to bookmarks, thumbnails, and text and graphics hyperlinks, PDFs can contain image maps similar to those you find on Web pages. You click on specific portions of the image and go to another page. What these images do when you click on them depends greatly on how well designed they are. In Figure 2-11, for example, you have a pretty clear idea where you wind up if you click on a portion of this image. The usefulness of this type of link depends on who designed it.

Figure 2-11:
Watch for image maps that allow you to navigate by clicking on a specific portion of the image.

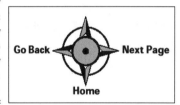

Multimedia links

Two other types of navigational links invoke multimedia events, such as playing a sound file or a movie. These links may not look different than other types. (Again, what they look like depends on the designer.) Rather than jump you to another part of the document, however, they play a file. You can tell whether a link leads to a movie or a sound file: When you hover your mouse over it, the cursor turns into a small movie film icon.

Movies and sound files can play in PDFs in many ways. Often the how and when depends on the designer of the document. Some movies even start automatically when you display a specific page. Some designers provide the reader with multiple types of controls. Chapters 11 and 12 describe multimedia files in PDFs, including how they behave in Reader. In the meantime, if you have the CD-ROM version of Acrobat 3.0 Review (available from Adobe), check out the PDFs in the Movies folder. You get a good idea about how movies work in PDFs.

Notes

Some PDFs contain notes created by the designer. Notes can be attached to any page. You can recognize them by the little note icon shown in Figure 2-12. Simply double-click on the icon to see the note, as shown in Figure 2-13.

You can navigate a PDF by searching for notes with Find Next Note command (Ctrl+Shift+T) on the Tools menu. This option takes you from note to note.

One of the more common uses for notes is to annotate a PDF during the design process. A designer may add notes directly to the layout people, notes to editors, and so on.

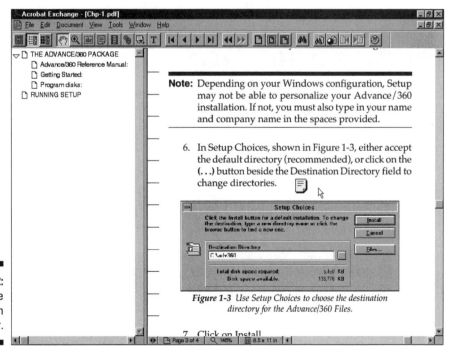

Figure 2-12: An example of a note in Reader.

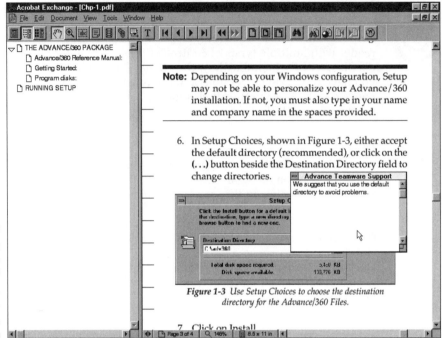

Figure 2-13:
To see the
contents of
a note,
double-
click on it.

Getting a Better View

You've seen how to get to specific places in a PDF. This section looks at how to get a better view of the pages themselves. Previously in this chapter, you found out about the basics of using Actual Size, Fit Page, and Zoom To. These are straightforward, as are the standard buttons and bars at the bottom and right side of the Reader window. Therefore, I won't go over them again here. Instead, take a brief look at two buttons on the top button bar: the Zoom and Hand buttons.

Zooming in and out interactively

By far, the most accurate way to zoom in and out on a page is with the Zoom tool, which you can access by clicking on the magnifying glass on the top button bar. You can zoom in on a specific area in two ways. Simply click on the area of the page you want to zoom in on, or for a more precise zoom, drag the Zoom tool around the specific area you want to zoom in on. The latter method brings the area that you drag around into full view.

In Figure 2-14, for example, I dragged the Zoom tool around the graphic and caption to bring them into full view. The smaller the area you drag around, the larger the information appears in the window.

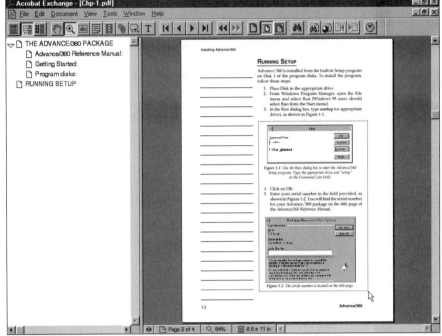

Figure 2-14:
To zoom in
on a
specific
portion of a
page, drag
the Zoom
tool around
the area.

You can also use the Zoom tool to zoom out. Simply hold down the Ctrl key as you click the Zoom tool. (On a Mac, use the Option key.)

Using the Hand tool to move the page into view

When you're zoomed in on a specific portion of a page, you may need to see an area that's not displayed. One way to handle this is to zoom out, and then zoom back in again on the desired area. Another, sometimes more efficient way is to use the Hand tool to drag the page and bring the desired portion into view.

This procedure is simple. Select the Hand tool, and then click and drag the page. To see an area on the right side of the page, drag to the left. To see an area lower on the page, drag upward. You get the idea.

Printing PDFs

Printing PDFs is so easy that I thought about leaving it out altogether. You print PDFs like you print all other Windows documents. Simply choose File⇨Print. You can use the Print Range option to specify whether to print all pages, the current page, or a range of pages. And, when printing over-sized pages (pages larger than the paper size your printer supports), you can force them to fit on the paper. To do so, simply select Shrink to Fit in the Print dialog box.

Getting a Full-Screen View

You can also view PDFs in a full-screen view, similar to a presentation. This view shows the PDF page without the application window, menus, and buttons, as shown in Figure 2-15.

You can still use all the navigation tools discussed in this chapter, such as Zoom, Hand, and Zoom To. But to do so you must use keyboard shortcuts to select the tools. And you can move from page to page with the PageUp and PageDown keys.

You can also set up the presentation to be self-running, with transition effects between each page similar to a PowerPoint presentation. These controls are in the Full-Screen Preferences dialog box (File⇨Preferences⇨Full Screen). You look at creating presentations with Acrobat in Chapter 7.

You covered a lot of ground here. Now you know how to get around in a PDF. (You can learn a lot more about navigating PDFs in Part 2.) Keep in mind, though, that with a PDF, ease of use often depends on how well the PDF was designed.

Figure 2-15:
An example
of a PDF in
full-screen
mode,
devoid of
application
window
elements.

Chapter 3

Viewing and Navigating PDFs on the Web

● ●

In This Chapter

▶ Finding out about PDFs and the Web

▶ Getting and installing Acrobat Reader for use with your Web browser

▶ Using your Web browser to view and navigate PDFs

● ●

*W*hat is all this talk about PDFs and the World Wide Web? Everybody knows that Web pages are created with HTML (hypertext markup language). What does Acrobat have to do with my Web browser?

The answer — a lot. HTML is a limited page description language suited only for simple documents. PDF, on the other hand, can handle all types of documents of just about any size quickly and efficiently.

If you've spent time on the World Wide Web, you've run into sites sporting PDF files for downloading. Acrobat 3 brings this exciting application to life. But don't take my word for it. Read on.

Acrobat Reader and Your Web Browser

PDFs have been scattered over the World Wide Web for a while. What's new is the implementation of PDFs through exciting innovations of Acrobat 3. To see how far this technology has come, you need to first look at how it worked in the past.

In the Dark Ages

Not long ago, before full-fledged Web browsers such as Netscape Navigator and Microsoft Internet Exchange came into being, files were typically downloaded to your computer's hard disk and then opened in separate applications, such as a word processor or a spreadsheet. PDFs were distributed in this way, too. PDFs were handier than most other file formats, however, because you needed only Adobe's free Acrobat Reader to view them.

In those days modems were slow (yes, much slower than they seem today), so getting and viewing a file required a lot of fuss. Most people just didn't bother. Besides, PDFs were large because of the crude compression techniques of yesteryear. These limitations — and the general impatience of the modern Information Age inhabitant — relegated the Acrobat-PDF thing to publishers, designers, and networking types. The rest of you were too smart to fool around with such cumbersome nonsense.

Somersaulting into the Middle Ages

We propeller heads eventually figure out when something is too difficult and time consuming. (We got rid of DOS, didn't we? So what if it took five or six years.) There had to be a better way.

About the time that the World Wide Web began to ascend from its infancy, innovative companies such as Netscape came up with a new kind of Web browser technology known as a helper application. A *helper application* allows you to download and view documents in formats other than HTML from the Internet.

After the file is downloaded, the browser *spawns* (a fancy word for *launches*) the helper application, which in turn opens the downloaded file so you can view or print it. Figure 3-1 shows Reader 2.0 serving as a helper application.

This may sound complicated and cumbersome, but it was much better than the previous method. At least helper applications automated the process. Most applications could serve as helper applications, although some were more suited than others. Huge programs, such as Microsoft Word, Excel, and PageMaker, were not great helper applications because they took too long to load and gobbled up too much memory.

By this time, Adobe had released Acrobat 2, which included Acrobat Reader 2 — a small, memory-efficient utility that loaded fast. Also, advanced compression schemes, especially graphics compression, had rendered PDFs much smaller. In short, PDFs and Reader were the perfect file format and helper application, respectively.

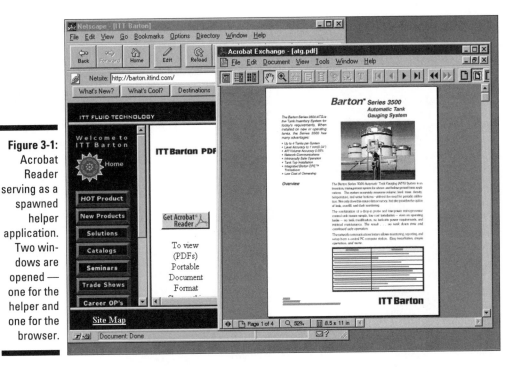

Figure 3-1:
Acrobat
Reader
serving as a
spawned
helper
application.
Two win-
dows are
opened —
one for the
helper and
one for the
browser.

But helper applications have problems. For example, if you're cruising around the Web opening PDF after PDF, you wind up with a bunch of open windows (unless you close the window after viewing each PDF). In addition, the browser and the PDF have no interaction. You cannot link information in a PDF to other PDFs on the same site (or anywhere else on the Web) or to Web pages themselves. You can navigate only within the current PDF.

Worse still is that for a PDF to load into Reader when running as a helper application, you have to download the entire file to see any portion of it. Eh!

Coming of age with Acrobat 3

Acrobat 3 addresses all of the problems listed in the preceding section, and then some. First, Reader is no longer a helper application. Instead, Reader 3 acts as a *viewer application,* with the help of the PDFViewer plug-in. (PDFViewer is discussed in the next section.)

A plug-in enhances the functionality of the host application. Rather than launch as a separate application, the PDF shows up in the browser itself, much like a standard HTML page, as shown in Figure 3-2. Plug-in technology also works with other types of file formats, such as sound and QuickTime movies.

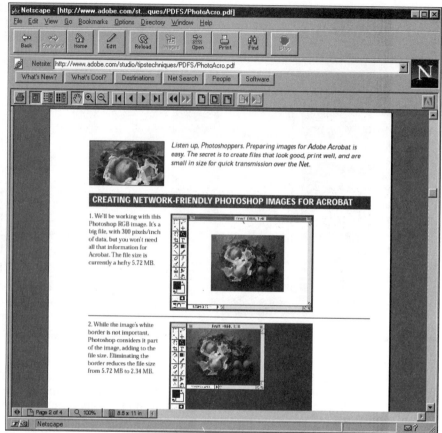

Figure 3-2:
A PDF
displayed in
Netscape
Navigator,
with
Acrobat
Reader 3.0
acting as a
viewer
application
through the
PDFViewer
plug-in.

Notice in Figure 3-2 that the Reader navigation buttons are displayed in the Netscape Navigator window. With this configuration, you can view and browse the PDF right in the browser. (If you don't know what all those buttons and gadgets mean, check out Chapter 2.)

This may look like a cosmetic improvement, but more is going on than meets the eye. In addition to using the Reader buttons and tools, you can also use the standard PDF thumbnails and bookmarks to navigate the document (again, as discussed in Chapter 2). But here's the real magic: If the PDF is configured properly, you can download only the pages in the PDF you need, rather than the entire file.

This means you, the Web surfer, have to download perhaps 20 to 60 kilobytes per page (depending on the content of the page) rather than several hundred thousand or even several megabytes (depending on the size of the PDF).

You can't wait to get some of these super cool PDFs on your company Web site, right? This stuff is discussed in Chapter 16. But check out the rest of this chapter before jumping over there — you need to know a few more things.

Today's Reader can also contain links (on the pages themselves) to other PDFs on the current site or on another site on the Web, as well as links to HTML pages anywhere on the Web. So, you can jump around from PDF to HTML and back until your heart's content. Just don't get dizzy.

Making Acrobat Reader 3 Work with Your Web Browser

You're probably eager to get started using Reader with your browser, so this section tells you what you need to get all this magic working for you. To get Reader to behave the way I described in the preceding section, you need

- ✔ Acrobat Reader 3.0
- ✔ An Acrobat Reader 3-aware Web browser, such as Netscape Navigator 3 or Microsoft Internet Explorer 3

Without these two components, you are confined to running Reader as a helper application. Bummer. For information on getting Reader, see Chapter 2. If you don't have Navigator 3 or Internet Explorer 3, you can download them for free from the manufacturers' Web sites at the following URLs:

Netscape Navigator: http://home.netscape.com

Internet Explorer: http://www.microsoft.com

After you download the file, simply double-click on the icon to start the installation program. The rest is simply a matter of following the directions.

At this point, the author usually makes a recommendation as to which program is better. You know, "I use so-and-so and it slices, it dices, it juliennes." Here's the simple truth about these two Web browsers: They're both great and comparable in performance, including bells and whistles. I have a bunch of computers around here and each has a different browser.

As I write this book, the America Online browser doesn't support Reader 3; that is, it's not Reader 3-aware. Be on the lookout for upgrades to the AOL interface software.

If you've already installed Reader, it's probably installed to work with your Web browser — providing that your browser is Acrobat 3-aware. When you run the Acrobat Reader Setup program, as discussed in Chapter 2, it seeks out your browser and places the PDFViewer plug-in in the correct folder. Just fire up your browser and cruise to a site with some PDFs. Adobe's site (http://www.adobe.com) has a bunch of PDFs as well as links to hundreds of other sites that use them.

If your browser is not configured properly to work with Netscape Navigator or Internet Explorer, you can follow the steps on page 88 of the *Reader Online Guide.* (From Reader, choose Help➪Reader Online Guide.)

Navigating PDFs on the World Wide Web

Here's some more good news. You don't have to learn a new application to navigate PDFs on the Web. The process is similar to using Reader to navigate PDFs on your computer or over a network, which is covered in detail in Chapter 2. Following are a few differences:

- ✔ You don't get any menus. To navigate PDFs from your browser, you must rely on the buttons. Therefore, many commands available in Reader, such as Find and Find Again, are not available when you're in your browser.

- ✔ Speaking of Find and Find Again, you can't perform a search in a PDF from your browser. To search a PDF, use your browser's Save As command to save the file, and then open the file in Reader.

- ✔ You can't copy text and graphics to the Clipboard for pasting into other applications.

- ✔ PDFs in a browser can contain links to other PDFs anywhere on the Web as well as to HTML pages on the Web.

Happy surfing.

Chapter 4

Converting Your Documents to PDF

● ●

In This Chapter

▶ An overview of the PDF conversion process

▶ A little bit about a big subject — PostScript

▶ Printing to a PostScript print file

▶ Converting files using PDFWriter

▶ Converting a PostScript print file to PDF

▶ Speeding up the conversion process with Distiller Assistant

▶ The benefits of using PDF-savvy applications or PDF plug-ins and XTensions

▶ What you should know about converting PDFs in print-on-demand environments

● ●

*T*his chapter boils down a huge subject — creating PDFs — into a digestible, easy-to-swallow soup. You can create PDFs in many ways, depending on your application. The process of turning a standard application document file into a PDF is easy and often foolproof.

Sometimes, such as when you're creating electronic documents for both viewing on a computer and high-quality printing, you need to know a little (and sometimes a lot) about both types of media. This book covers creating electronic documents for viewing and navigating. I suggest you find a good book on offset printing conventions if you will be using Acrobat in a print-on-demand environment.

This chapter shows you how to get from a proprietary document format, such as a word processing document, a spreadsheet, or a presentation, to a PDF. The quality of your results, however, may depend on variables beyond the scope of simple document conversion. So, in addition to telling you how to create PDFs, I also point out when additional information will be helpful and where you can find it.

The Journey from Plain Ol' Computer Document to PDF

Partaking of this magical file format called PDF is easy. Depending on which programs you use and whether you own Acrobat, getting from a plain ol' computer document to a PDF usually requires only a few steps.

Acrobat uses Adobe's PostScript printer language to render, or draw, a document to be viewed on-screen in Exchange or Reader. PostScript is a page description language that tells the printer how to print a page (which fonts to use, where to put graphics, and so on). Acrobat converts the page description into a rendering for the computer monitor.

Sounds simple. Well, the concept is simple, but a lot goes on behind the scenes. Luckily, you don't need to know most of what's going on to be successful in PDF publishing.

Between Acrobat and PostScript, you get a document ideal for on-screen viewing and navigation. The process for getting a document from application to PDF goes something like this:

1. Create the document in an application, such as Microsoft Word or Excel.

2. Print the document to a PostScript print file.

3. Process the document in Acrobat Distiller.

4. Open the document in Acrobat Exchange to add links and other navigational enhancements as well as sounds, movies, and the like.

And that's it! The PDF is now ready for distribution.

The process can vary, however, depending on several factors. For example, if you don't have the full version of Acrobat, you may use PDFWriter, which comes with applications such as PageMaker and Illustrator. Or if you use QuarkXPress, you may use a Quark XTension to create links and other enhancements before processing the document in Distiller. You look at some different scenarios later in this chapter.

What You Should Know about PostScript

I could write an entire book on PostScript — and several authors have. A strong knowledge of PostScript is not essential for most PDF applications. It becomes necessary, however, in print-on-demand environments where your

PDFs are used to print high-quality documents for reproduction at a print shop. This application is beyond the scope of this book, but you can read the "Using Distiller in Print-On-Demand Settings" section later in this chapter for more information.

As mentioned, PostScript is a page description language that tells PostScript printers how to print a page. (PostScript is also used in offset printing *prepress* applications to create high-resolution output, such as camera-ready artwork or negatives for creating press plates. *Prepress* means before the printing press; it's the process of preparing a document for a print run.)

PostScript files also contain a wealth of other data; for example, graphics resolution data, color data, and font adjustment data, such as letter and word spacing. PostScript is so powerful that it even provides information required for printing color separations to create full-color images, such as those used in magazine covers. A PostScript print file, which we discuss in the next section, can even contain embedded fonts, so that the computer you use to print the document doesn't need the same fonts as the machine from which the document originated.

Acrobat takes all the information destined for the printer and reinterprets it for the computer screen. You end up with a document that is universal, or viewable and printable across several platforms, regardless of configuration.

Printing to a PostScript File

The road from creator application document (that is, the word processor, DTP, or presentation file) to PDF begins by printing your document to a PostScript print file. Acrobat Distiller then uses the file to create a PDF. Essentially, printing to a PostScript file is the same whether you're using a Mac or working in Windows. The process can vary, however, from application to application and depending on the printer driver for your printer. And because PostScript was developed on the Mac, PostScript printing options tend to be more advanced on that platform. This section looks at printing to a PostScript file on both platforms.

Printing to a PostScript file in Windows

When working in Windows, you usually have two options for printing to a PostScript file. You can print from the application directly, which is the method to consider if you don't print to a file often. You can also set up a separate printer definition specifically for printing to a file. This is the method to consider if you do print to a file frequently.

The applications you'll be printing from is another consideration. Some applications, such as desktop publishing and draw applications (for example, CorelDRAW! or Illustrator), include powerful controls for printing to a PostScript file. Other programs usually do not.

Whether you should define your PostScript file from an application or from the Windows Printers Control Panel depends largely on your application. Each of the hundreds of Windows applications handles printing to a PostScript file in a slightly different way.

Printing to a PostScript file on a Mac

For the most part, printing to a PostScript file is similar on a Mac and in Windows. The primary difference is that on a Mac you must first select a PostScript printer from the Chooser (choose Apple Menu⇨Chooser).

Then, in most applications, you set up your print file in the application's Print dialog box. Some Mac applications, however, do not provide controls for printing to a file. In these cases, you can use File⇨Page Setup to change the printer's settings so that it prints to a file. After installing Acrobat 3, however, the standard Print dialog box has bulleted choices for Destination: Printer, File, or PDF. This procedure *should* be standard in all Mac applications, but I haven't seen them all.

Walking through printing to a file

In this section, you look at two different, but typical, applications: Microsoft Word and Adobe PageMaker. Figure 4-1 shows the Print to File option for Word, and Figure 4-2 shows the same option for PageMaker.

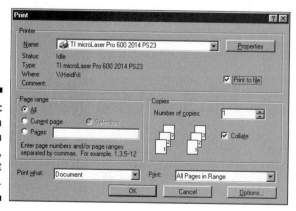

Figure 4-1: To print to a file from Word, select Print to file.

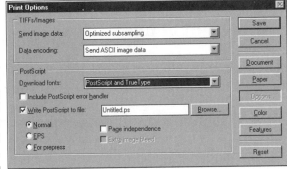

Figure 4-2:
To print to a
file from
PageMaker,
select Write
PostScript
to File, and
then select
the print
options.

As you can see from the two figures, the controls for printing to a PostScript file are more extensive in the desktop publishing program than in the word processor. This is because desktop publishers often create print files for transporting to a service bureau, which provides high-resolution output.

When you print to a file in PageMaker and programs like it, you can control several aspects of the process, including the downloading of fonts to the file. This is an important issue when creating PostScript files for the purpose of creating PDFs. When you print to a file in Word, whether it downloads fonts to a file depends on the type of PostScript printer installed and its *native,* or built-in, fonts.

I can hear your deductive reasoning churning. You're thinking that the capability to control font downloading in desktop publishing and graphics applications makes them superior to word processors for creating PDFs. Well, yes and no. Desktop publishing applications tend to contain more fancy fonts and sophisticated formatting, so they benefit more when the fonts used in creating the document are built into the PostScript file. Word processing documents usually do not contain a lot of formatting that depends on precise spacing and line-break information built into specific fonts, making font embedding less critical. Acrobat has its own font-matching technology that does a reasonably good job of compensating for missing fonts.

Creating PDFs with PDFWriter

PDFWriter does just what its name implies — it writes documents to a PDF. It is, in effect, a printer driver. You use PDFWriter as you would any other printer driver, by selecting it from the Print dialog box in your application and letting 'er rip. Instead of sending the print data to a printer, PDFWriter creates a PDF on your hard disk. You can then open the new PDF in Reader or Exchange.

More about fonts

If you've ever swapped documents with a friend or a colleague, or sent something to the service bureau for processing, you know that the font issue can be a pain. I've mentioned that Acrobat doesn't care about trivia such as which fonts you used to create a document. Well, that's mostly true.

Acrobat uses a technology known as ATM to render fonts for the screen and printer. (No, ATM doesn't refer to the machine that spits out money. It stands for Adobe Type Manager.) ATM uses a built-in font database with information on most fonts. Through a process called *substitution,* ATM uses the information in the database to draw fonts for the screen and printer. This routine is not perfect, however, and ATM doesn't contain information on each of the thousands of available fonts.

So what can you do? You thought Acrobat was supposed to take care of font mismatching. Relax. If you embed a font during the PostScript file printing process, it is available to Acrobat. But embedding fonts is not always necessary. You should embed them only when they are critical to how the document is formatted, or when you use highly decorative fonts and you want the look maintained in the PDF.

Embedding fonts in a PostScript file makes the file larger and could result in a larger PDF.

New font compression routines built into Acrobat 3, however, have greatly reduced the increase in PDF file size caused by embedding fonts.

In addition to embedding fonts in PostScript files, you can also control how and when certain types of fonts, namely Type 1 PostScript fonts, are embedded in a PDF with Distiller (and PDFWriter), as you see later in this chapter.

Unless you're creating PDFs in a print-on-demand environment, the issue of fonts and PDFs is the most complicated in the PDF creation process. Have no fear, though, because Acrobat 3 makes it much easier. All it really comes down to is a tightrope balancing act between file size and accurate screen representation. I'll show you how not to fall.

For Distiller to use TrueType fonts when creating your PDFs, the fonts must be downloaded to the PostScript files. So, when your documents include TrueType fonts that you want included in the PDF, be sure to tell the printer driver to download them. Depending on the printer driver you use, the controls for downloading (or embedding) fonts in a file are in slightly different locations. Most often, you find them by clicking on the Properties or Option button in the Print dialog box.

This PDFWriter business sounds easy — too easy. You're probably wondering why you wouldn't always use this method. Here's why. PDFWriter creates low-resolution, low-quality versions of the graphics in your files. They do not display as nicely and print even worse. When quality, rather than convenience, is the look you're after, use Distiller. (This method is described in the next section.) Distiller provides a wider range of controls over the PDF. PDFWriter works satisfactorily for documents that are primarily text-based, such as memos and reports.

Okay. You've decided to use PDFWriter to create your PDFs. Let's take a quick tour through the process:

1. **If you're using a Mac, choose PDFWriter from the Chooser first:**

   a. **Click on the Apple menu in the upper-left portion of the screen.**

   b. **Select Chooser.**

   c. **Select PDFWriter in the Chooser dialog box.**

   d. **Click the Close button (upper-left corner of dialog box).**

2. **Decide which document you want to use to create a PDF. Open that document using the application in which the document was created.**

3. **Choose File⇨Print.**

   The Acrobat PDFWriter print dialog box appears, as shown in Figure 4-3.

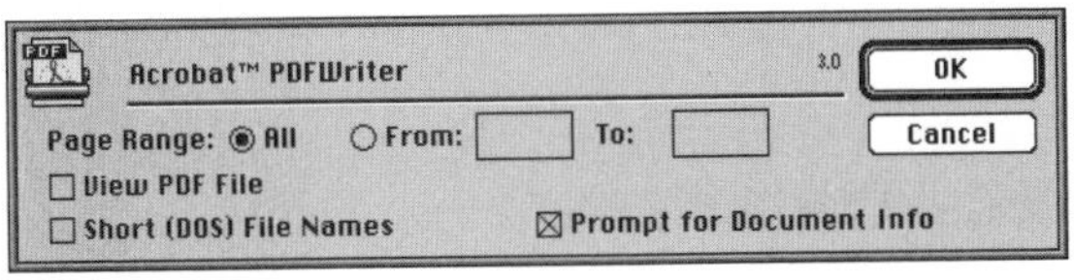

Figure 4-3:
Here's the Acrobat PDFWriter print dialog box on a Mac.

> **Acrobat™ PDFWriter**   3.0   [**OK**]
>
> Page Range: ⦿ All   ○ From: [   ]   To: [   ]   [**Cancel**]
> ☐ View PDF File
> ☐ Short (DOS) File Names   ☒ Prompt for Document Info

4. **Click OK.**

5. **Click the Properties button.**

   The Acrobat PDFWriter on LPT1 dialog box appears, as shown in Figure 4-4. From here you set font and graphics settings, as well as control paper size, resolution, scaling, paper orientation, and several other aspects of the new PDF document. In most cases, you won't need to change these settings.

Figure 4-4:
From this dialog box you control the properties of your PDF.

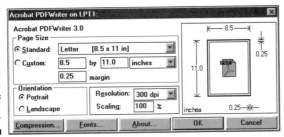

Paper Size: Changing the paper size could cause some of your documents not to fit on the page properly.

Orientation: Changing a page that is Portrait (tall) in the original document to Landscape (wide) would surely play havoc with the original formatting.

Scaling: To make your pages smaller or larger, use Scaling to resize by a percentage.

Resolution: Setting this option does not affect how well the document displays on-screen, but instead how well the PDF will print. In most cases, you should set this option to the resolution of the printer that the document will be printed on, which is usually about 300 dpi. If you're sure the document will always be viewed on-screen, choose the Screen option in the Resolution list.

6. **After you change the properties you want, click Compression.**

   The Acrobat PDFWriter Compression Options dialog shown in Figure 4-5 appears. You use this dialog box to make adjustments to your graphics compression and quality. The settings control the compatibility of your PDF and the quality and size of your graphics.

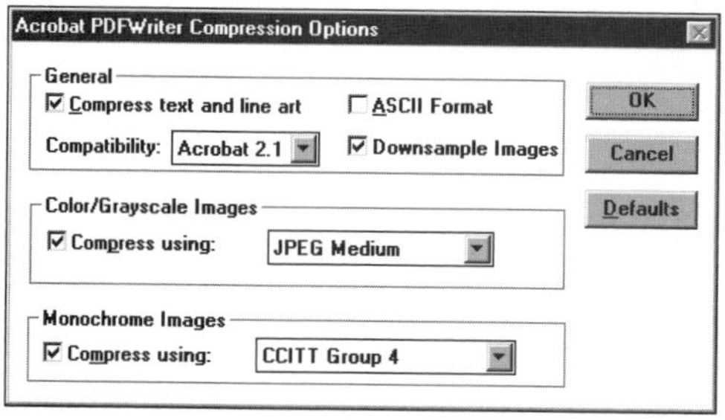

Figure 4-5:
This dialog box is used to control the size and quality of your PDF files.

Compatibility: This option refers to the version(s) of PDF. In other words, if you make your PDF Acrobat 2.1 compatible, Versions 2.1 and later (Versions 2, 2.1, and 3) of Acrobat Reader can access the document. However, the file will be larger in these versions than in Version 3. Only Acrobat 3 and later support Acrobat 3 files. (And files with compatibility settings earlier than Version 3 will not support advanced Internet features, such as the capability to download only the desired pages, as discussed in Chapter 15.)

Compress text and line art: This feature controls how text and black-and-white images are treated. You should almost always use this option because the *ASCII Format* option creates huge files. For information on compressing graphics, see the "Grappling with gigantic graphics" sidebar in this chapter.

7. **After you set your compression options, click OK.**

   The screen returns to the Acrobat PDFWriter on LPT1 dialog box.

8. **Click Fonts.**

   The Font Embedding dialog box shown in Figure 4-6 appears.

Figure 4-6:
Use this
dialog
box to
determine
which
fonts are
embedded
in your
PDFs.

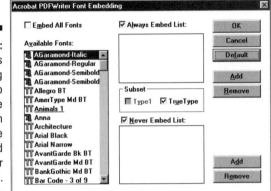

Whether you embed fonts in PDF depends on two factors: How critical the fonts are to the formatting and look of the document and how you plan to distribute the document. If your documents contain conventional Time (Times New Roman in TrueType) and Helvetica (Arial in TrueType) fonts, you don't need to embed fonts because ATM can simulate these and similar looking fonts. I usually embed only fonts that ATM does not handle well, for example, highly decorative fonts such as Brush Script or Park Avenue.

Embed All Fonts: Select this option to include all the fonts in your document in the PDF.

Available Fonts: To add only certain fonts, select fonts from this list and then click the first Add button on the right. If you make a mistake or change your mind, select the *Always Embed List* option. (The second set of Add and Remove buttons are for the Never Embed List option.)

Always Embed List: Use this option to tell PDFWriter which fonts to always install in your PDFs.

Never Embed List: Use this option to tell the program which fonts to never install in your PDFs.

Subset: This option tells PDFWriter to download only the characters you use in your document. Suppose you use a decorative font for a 10-character headline. If you choose Subset, PDFWriter downloads only the ten characters rather than the entire font set; this reduces the size of the PDF.

When you set the Compatibility option in the Compression Options dialog box to Acrobat 2.1, only TrueType fonts can be subsetted. If you use the Acrobat 3 setting, both TrueType and Type 1 fonts can be subsetted.

9. After you set all your font embedding settings, click OK.

The screen returns to the Acrobat PDFWriter LPT1 on dialog box.

10. Click OK.

You are then presented with a dialog box asking you to name and choose a location to save the PDF, as shown in Figure 4-7.

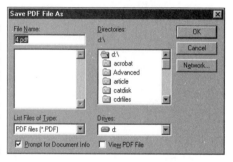

Figure 4-7:
Use this dialog box to name and save your new PDF.

Prompt for Document Info: This option displays the dialog box shown in Figure 4-8. From here you can define information about the PDF, such as the subject of the document, who created it, and keywords that viewers can use in a catalog to find the document.

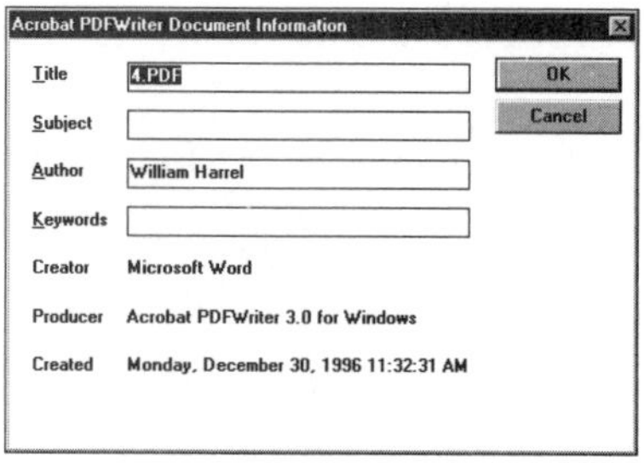

Figure 4-8:
Use this dialog box to modify and add information about your PDF.

View PDF File: If you choose this option, Acrobat Reader opens (after PDF Writer has completed the conversion) and displays the new PDF.

11. Name the file and click Save.

You're finished. Easy, huh?

Grappling with gigantic graphics

Graphics files, especially bitmapped, paint-type images, such as photographs, can make your PDFs huge. This is especially true if you are creating a PDF from a document originally created for offset printing. Color photographs in these files can be gigantic, easily 10 megabytes and beyond.

Acrobat handles these files by compressing them. Compressing images means dropping data. In most types of graphics, more data means higher quality in terms of more colors and greater detail. When converting a document from a format designed for printing to a format designed for viewing on-screen, you usually don't need much of the data in the former format. The typical resolution for a graphic designed to be printed, for instance, is between 200 and 300 dpi. Computer monitors, on the other hand, display between about 70 and 100 dpi.

PDFWriter has default settings that usually work fine for graphics compression. However, you can control the image size and quality, especially color and grayscale, by adjusting the level of compression in the Compression Options dialog box. Acrobat uses JPEG compression, an industry standard. You can choose between five levels of compression.

Low settings give you smaller file sizes with greater quality degradation, and high settings provide opposite results. This is a balancing act. In most situations, JPEG Medium is fine. If you need smaller file sizes or higher quality, you can experiment with the other settings. The results depend on the images you're working with—period. Each image is different.

The other setting in the Compression Options dialog box under Color/Grayscale Images is LZW. This is a TIFF compression routine you use if your PDFs are print-on-demand documents, discussed later in this chapter. Don't change the setting under Monochrome Images unless you are working in a print-on-demand environment.

If you're working on a Mac (lucky you) ATM must be installed for font embedding to work from PDFWriter (or Distiller, as discussed in the next section). TrueType embedding, on the other hand, works the same on either platform.

Creating PDFs with Distiller

As mentioned, to create a PDF with Distiller, you must first print your document to a PostScript file. Although this procedure is a little more cumbersome than using PDFWriter, it is preferable because Distiller provides a much wider range of options for controlling the size and quality of your PDFs. Distiller's options are so thorough, in fact, that I won't try to cover them all here. If you need additional information, you can find everything you need in the *Distiller Online Guide*. (From Distiller, choose Help↩ Distiller Online Guide.)

Fellow techno-geeks can find more ways to tweak PDFs in the *Distiller Parameters Guide,* also on the Help menu. But be forewarned, the *Parameters Guide* is not for the fainthearted.

Setting up Distiller

In many instances, Distiller's default settings will work just fine for your PDFs. All you do is open your PostScript file in Distiller. (If you've installed Acrobat 3 in Windows 95, you find Acrobat Distiller 3.0 on the Adobe Acrobat submenu on the Start menu. On a Mac, you find Acrobat Distiller 3.0 in the Adobe Acrobat 3.0 folder on your hard disk.)

Distiller begins the conversion process by providing you with a dialog box for naming and saving the PDF file. Then after the file is named and saved, Distiller converts the PostScript file to a PDF — just like that. Figure 4-9 shows the Distiller opening screen.

Figure 4-9:
The Distiller opening screen. To process a PostScript file quickly, simply open the file. Distiller will do the rest.

I forgot to mention that when you first open Distiller, it asks whether you want your PDFs to be Acrobat 2.1 or Acrobat 3.0 compatible. Remember that 3.0 files are smaller and support advanced Internet features, but you can't open them in earlier versions of Reader or Exchange.

Sometimes, based on your application, you need to make changes to how Distiller treats aspects of your PDF, such as fonts and images. This section takes a quick look at these options.

Changing Distiller job options

If you read the earlier discussion of PDFWriter, many of the Distiller options will already be familiar to you. If you didn't read the section on PDFWriter, perhaps you should. It will be helpful in understanding the information here.

Distiller's job options are set before you open the PostScript file. To change job options, choose Job Options from the Distiller menu. This displays the dialog box shown in Figure 4-10. Similar to the Acrobat PDFWriter on LPT1 dialog box, from here you control several aspects of your PDF conversion.

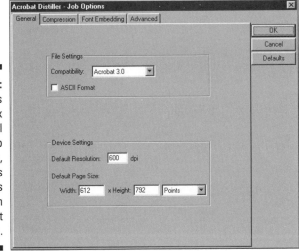

Figure 4-10:
Use this dialog box to control the PDF job options, such as graphics compression and font embedding.

General options

Use the General tab of the Job Options dialog box to change compatibility, resolution and page size. These issues are discussed in the PDFWriter section earlier in this chapter. The primary difference is the way Distiller displays paper sizes. The default page size is 612-by-792 points (8^1/$_2$-by-11 inches). If the PostScript file contains a different page size, Distiller uses the page size in the file.

In most cases, you need to choose a page size only if you are processing Encapsulated PostScript (EPS) files, for example, those created with draw programs such as CorelDRAW! or Illustrator. These types of PostScript files do not contain page dimension information. The minimum page size is 1-by-1 inch. The maximum is 45-by-45 inches.

If using points or pixels to display page sizes is confusing to you, you can change it to inches by simply selecting Inches from the Default Page Size list. Remember, though, that you need to set the page size only when you are working with Encapsulated PostScript files.

Compression options

The items in the Compression tab of the Job Options dialog box, shown in Figure 4-11, allow you to control the compression of images. Remember from the discussion in the PDFWriter section earlier in this chapter that compressing images is a balancing act between quality and file size. In most cases, the default settings work fine, because they are optimized to work well with most of the world's computer monitors, without undue overload on processors and display systems.

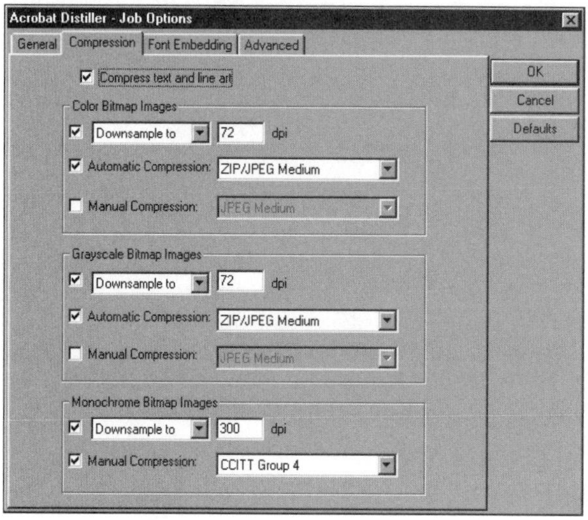

Figure 4-11:
Use this portion of the Job Options dialog box to control image compression.

Notice that the primary difference between the controls here and the same controls in PDFWriter is that Distiller lets you control image resolution, but PDFWriter does not.

If you plan to distribute your PDFs to an unknown audience, such as public Internet users or on CD-ROM products, the default settings work great. If you know exactly where your PDFs will be displayed, you can tweak the image compression. For example, I created a bunch of PDF training manuals for a graphics design firm with really fast Macs and high-resolution monitors. So, I kicked image quality and resolution up for optimal display on that particular network. By the same token, if you are distributing to a bunch of slow workstations with mediocre monitors, you gain little from creating high-quality, high-resolution images.

Everything you never wanted to know about image compression

Working with digital video requires the use of compression techniques to control quality and file size. The two compression methods in common use are the lossless method and the lossy method. Acrobat Distiller supports both. The lossless method of compression keeps all the data intact. The method is called lossless because when the file is decompressed for displaying on a monitor, all data in the file is still there.

Typically, lossless data compression can make a file as much as half its original size. A 50 percent reduction does not always solve the image size dilemma, however, because even small full-color images can eat up several megabytes of disk space. Lossless is preferable when creating PDFs for large storage mediums, such as CD-ROM.

The lossy data compression method uses compression algorithms to eliminate specific data from the image file. The image quality of the resulting digital file may be degraded, but the file size is greatly reduced.

Hold on now. This is not as bad as it sounds. Many images contain far more data than needed to display well on a computer display system. For example, 24-bit images contain a lot of unnecessary repeated data, and display a lot of subtle color differences people cannot perceive. Dropping this data from the file does little to the image quality but helps tremendously in terms of file size manageability.

Unlike lossless, lossy data compression is capable of compression rates as high as 100 to 1. In other words, you can compress a 5MB file down to 50K. The extent to which an image can be compressed depends on the image and the level of degradation you can live with.

The compression methods available through Distiller are LZW, LZW 4-bit, LZW 8-bit, ZIP, ZIP 4-bit, ZIP 8-bit, and JPEG. LZW and ZIP are lossless compression methods. JPEG, LZW 4-bit, LZW 8-bit, ZIP 4-bit, and ZIP 8-bit are lossy compression methods.

If you don't understand all the options in this dialog box, go back in this chapter to read the section on PDFWriter and the sidebar entitled "Grappling with gigantic graphics."

Font embedding options

You've already looked at font embedding extensively in the PDFWriter section earlier in this chapter, so now you can take a brief look at how Distiller differs from PDFWriter. Font embedding in Distiller is controlled from the Font Embedding tab of the Job Options dialog box, shown in Figure 4-12. Essentially, Distiller handles fonts in much the same way as PDFWriter, except Distiller does not display TrueType fonts. Remember that your TrueType fonts must be embedded in the PostScript file.

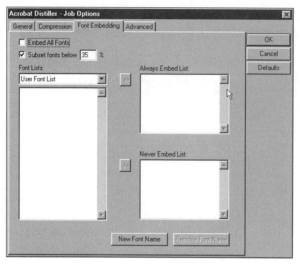

Figure 4-12:
Use this
dialog box
to control
font
embedding.

From Distiller, you can embed fonts from a user-defined list or from specific directories containing Type 1 fonts on your hard disk (or another hard disk on your network). In most cases, the Type 1 fonts on your hard disk are saved in the C:\Acrobat\Distiller\fonts folder. In addition, if Adobe Type Manager is installed on your system, you will probably have additional Type 1 fonts installed the C:\psfonts folder. On a Mac, your fonts are most likely in the System:Fonts folder, with additional fonts in the Adobe Acrobat 3.0:Fonts folder.

Confused yet? Unless you have saved fonts in unusual places, Acrobat and Distiller know where your fonts are. You don't have to know.

All you do is select a folder name from Font Lists. For example, in Figure 4-13, I choose the PSFONTS folder on my hard disk and behold: A list of the Type 1 fonts installed on my system appears. Now I can choose which ones to download. Fonts are embedded in a manner similar to the one described in the PDFWriter section earlier in this chapter.

The User Font List selection in the Font Lists option is used to embed fonts contained in PostScript files that are not on the system from which you are running Distiller. For detailed information on this option, open the Acrobat *Distiller Online Guide* (distillr.pdf) in Reader and go to page 92.

Although you can embed the fonts that were installed with Acrobat in your PDF, there's not much point. These are the fonts Distiller uses to create the PDF. In other words, these are the fonts Distiller uses as substitutes, unless you choose to embed other fonts on your system.

Figure 4-13:
To see a list
of Type 1
fonts on
your
system,
simply
select the
folder in
which your
fonts are
stored from
the Font
Lists.

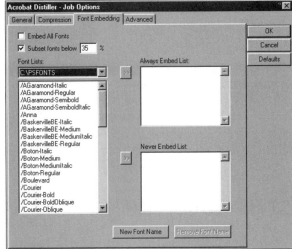

Defining font locations

If you have Type 1 fonts on your system in directories where Distiller does
not expect to find them, you can tell Distiller where they are with the Font
Locations command on the Distiller menu:

1. **Choose Distiller⇨Font Locations.**

   The Font Locations dialog box appears, as shown in Figure 4-14.

Figure 4-14:
Use this
dialog box
to add font
folders
to the
Distiller font
location list.

2. **Click Add Folder.**

3. **Go to the folder in which your fonts are kept, and select the folder.**

4. **Click OK.**

5. Click OK again to return to Distiller.

The fonts are now available on the Font Embedding tab of the Job Options dialog box.

To remove a font folder, select it in the Font Folders List in the Font Locations dialog box. Then click Remove Folder.

If you look on the Distiller menu, you notice a command called Watched Folders. For now, don't worry about this command. You use it when running Acrobat on a network, which you look at in Chapter 17.

Creating PDFs in One Step with Distiller Assistant

You can save a step or two by using Distiller Assistant to process your PDFs. Like PDFWriter, Distiller Assistant works like a printer driver. You select it like you would any printer, from the Print dialog box.

By default, Distiller Assistant is installed as a startup application on your system (or as an extension on a Mac). Each time you start your computer, Distiller Assistant also starts. In Windows, you have three basic options when using Distiller Assistant:

View PDF File	This option launches Reader so that you can see the results of the conversion.
Exit Distiller When Idle	If Distiller sits idle for a short time after it has processed your files, Distiller Assistant closes it automatically, freeing up computer memory.
Ask For PDF Destination	Before launching Distiller, Distiller Assistant asks where you want the ensuing PDF to be stored. If you turn this option off, the PDFs are saved in the root directory on the hard disk containing Distiller.

In Windows 95 and Windows NT 4.0, these three options are turned on and off by right-clicking on the Distiller Assistant icon on the taskbar. In Windows 3.1 and earlier, you control these options by clicking on the minimized Distiller Assistant at the bottom of your screen.

If Distiller Assistant does not start automatically when you start Windows, you can launch it at any time by clicking on the distasst.exe (or distasst) icon in the Acrobat3/Distillr folder from Windows Explorer (Windows 95 and NT 4.0) or File Manager (Windows 3.1).

Distiller Assistant does not require setup on a Mac. It works with the PSPrinter 8.3 (or later) printer driver. Simply choose File⇨Print from the originating application, and then select PDF from the Destination box. Click Distill, tell Distiller where to save the PDF in the ensuing Save As dialog box, and then click Save to let 'er rip. You can create a PostScript file at the same time as the PDF by choosing Save PostScript File in the Save As dialog box. Another option in the Save As dialog box, View PDF File, lets you see the ensuing PDF in Reader immediately after distilling it.

LaserWriter 8.4 does not support Acrobat Distiller Assistant. You must use Adobe PSPrinter, which comes with Acrobat, to have the PDF option available when printing.

Creating PDFs Using PDF-Savvy Applications

Some applications, such as PageMaker, FreeHand, and Illustrator are PDF-savvy, which means they have the capability to create built-in PDFs. Others, such as QuarkXPress, support extensions or plug-ins (Quark calls them XTensions) that provide added PDF support.

In PageMaker, for example, you can save any PageMaker document as a PDF by choosing File⇨Export⇨Adobe PDF. This displays the dialog box shown in Figure 4-15. After you select the settings in this and the other embedded dialog boxes (indicated by the various buttons), when you click Export, Distiller launches and creates your PDFs.

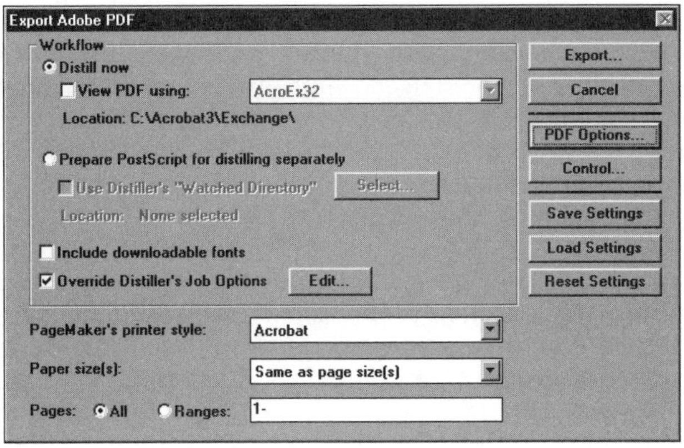

Figure 4-15: PageMaker's PDF export feature lets you create PDFs directly from the program.

PageMaker's PDF export feature may seem like another version of Distiller Assistant, but it's not. When you use Export PDF, all table of contents, index, internal, and external links are preserved. If you don't know PageMaker, this may not make sense to you. If you do know PageMaker, you're probably salivating. You can save hours of prep work in Exchange. For example, if set up properly in PageMaker, all headings and subheads (when you set Include in Table of Contents in your paragraph styles) automatically become bookmarks in your PDF files. Index entries automatically contain hyperlinks to the section of the document they refer to. (Bookmarks and hyperlinks are discussed in Chapter 2.)

If you use QuarkXPress and need similar export capabilities, check out the XTensions from Cascade Systems: Story Threads, Picture Compression, Setting Annotations, and Bookmarks. You can get more information at Cascade Systems, 508-794-8000, or `http://www.cascadeinc.com`.

Using Distiller in Print-on-Demand Settings

Print-on-demand means different things to different people — everything from high-resolution offset printing to desktop printers, even slides and transparencies. The two most common types of applications are print-on-demand for desktop applications and print-on-demand for offset prepress. In the first application, you simply print to your desktop printer when you need a few copies of your document. In the latter, you print new camera-ready art or negatives for processing at the printing press.

Unfortunately, in many settings, optimizing a PDF for printing and for the computer screen is not possible. The differences in the way printers print and monitors display usually mean you set image color and resolution differently for each. You would use low-resolution images for the monitor and higher resolution images for printing. In addition, when preparing images for prepress, you would also use different color models. Monitors use a red, green, and blue subtractive color model, and printing presses use a cyan, magenta, yellow, and black additive color model.

If you're not a desktop publisher or designer, the preceding paragraph may be confusing. Concepts such as prepress and getting optimal performance from desktop printers is beyond the scope of this book. May I suggest my *Macworld PageMaker 6.0 Bible* or *CorelDRAW 7 Secrets* (both published by IDG Books Worldwide, Inc.)? They contain detailed information about printing and prepress. In the meantime, you can find most of the settings you need for optimal printing on the General and Advanced tabs of Distiller's Job Options dialog box (Distiller⇨Job Options).

Part II
Enhancing PDFs in Exchange

The 5th Wave   By Rich Tennant

AND TO COMPLETE THE MULTIMEDIA EXPERIENCE, WE WANT TO SHIP EACH WORKSTATION WITH THIS SCRATCH 'N SNIFF MOUSE PAD AND A SCENT-RESIDENT RAM CARD.

In this part . . .

This part covers the basics of Acrobat Exchange, the application used to add links, edit text, and perform other basic PDF editing and enhancing. You also look at scanning and performing optical character recognition (OCR) to convert hard copy documents to PDFs. The Part ends with an explanation of PDF forms and how to use them.

Chapter 5

Getting to Know Acrobat Exchange

· ·

In This Chapter

▶ Understanding Exchange

▶ Checking out the Exchange interface

▶ Opening and navigating PDFs in Exchange

▶ Changing Exchange defaults

· ·

*I*n this chapter, you find out how to make your PDFs presentable to users. You look at the meat and potatoes of Acrobat: Acrobat Exchange. This is the application you use to add bookmarks, thumbnails, and hyperlinks. (If any of those terms are unfamiliar, check out Chapter 2.) You also can use Exchange to edit the text and graphics in your PDFs, as well as to create interactive tables of contents, indices, and multimedia events, such as movies and sounds.

First, though, take a brief tour of Exchange by finding out how to open PDFs, navigate them, change defaults, and so on.

What Can You Do with Exchange?

The question isn't really "What can you do with Exchange?" It's "What can't you do with Exchange?" Exchange allows you to edit and enhance PDFs. You could even create entire PDF documents from scratch, but other applications are better suited for that.

Basically, Exchange takes the PDFs you create with Distiller or PDFWriter and turns them into interactive electronic documents by adding bookmarks, thumbnails, hyperlinks, and several other interactive or multimedia features. The following is a list of the functions you can perform with Exchange:

✔ View and navigate PDFs much like you do in Reader

✔ Print PDFs much like you do in Reader

✔ Add interactivity through bookmarks, thumbnails, and hyperlinks

✔ Edit text, or copy text to the Clipboard for pasting into other PDFs or other documents

✔ Resize or move graphics in a PDF, or copy graphics to the Clipboard for pasting into other PDFs or other documents

✔ Create interactive forms

✔ Add movies and sounds

✔ Add embedded notes similar to annotations in a word processor

✔ Search across several cataloged PDF indexes to add interactivity between individual PDFs (As you find out in Chapter 14, this isn't as complicated as it sounds.)

You can do all these things and many others, and you can do them in several creative and useful ways. The remainder of this book shows you how.

Acrobat Exchange: A Brief Tour

If you're coming to this section cold, without any Acrobat experience, I suggest that you first take a look at Chapter 2, which discusses viewing and navigating PDFs in Acrobat Reader. Exchange is similar to Reader, so I won't spend a lot of space here rehashing the same material.

You can see the similarities between Exchange and Reader by looking at Figure 5-1. The Exchange toolbar is nearly identical to the one in Reader. Even the menu structure looks similar. This is a good thing. You don't have to learn a new interface for enhancing the PDFs your users will view in Reader.

Now take a closer look. Many of the view and navigational buttons are the same. You zoom in and go to pages in much the same manner. But Exchange also has a few buttons you haven't seen before: the buttons between the Zoom tool (magnifying glass) and the page navigation tools (right- and left-pointing arrows) and the tools to the right of the Find tool (binoculars). You use these tools in the remaining chapters to edit and enhance your PDFs.

I could list the names of these new buttons, but it's not necessary. Simply hover your mouse cursor over each button, and Exchange displays a message telling you what the button does.

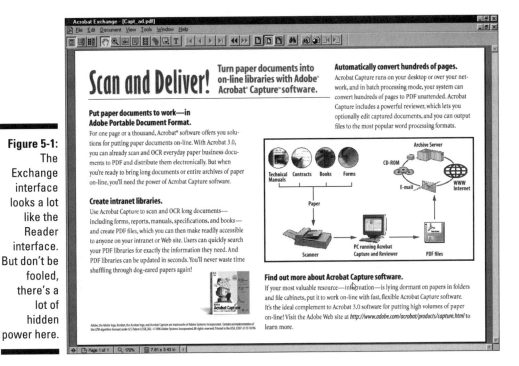

Figure 5-1:
The
Exchange
interface
looks a lot
like the
Reader
interface.
But don't be
fooled,
there's a
lot of
hidden
power here.

Opening PDFs in Exchange

You probably already know how to open a PDF in Exchange. You open a PDF in the same way you open any other document in any other program. Simply follow these steps:

1. **Choose File⇨Open.**

2. **Go to the folder on your system or network containing the PDF.**

3. **Select the PDF and click Open.**

You can use the other file opening methods on your system, such as double-clicking on the file icon in Windows Explorer, File Manager, or Macintosh Finder. In Windows 95, NT 4.0, or Macintosh System 7.x, you can open a PDF also by dragging the document icon onto the program icon in Windows Explorer or Finder or on the Windows or Macintosh desktop. All these procedures launch Exchange and then display the document on which you double-clicked or dragged and dropped.

You can also open several files at once and work on them simultaneously, which is a great way to create hyperlinks in cataloged documents as well as copy and paste elements from one PDF to another.

Sound easy? It is — no hidden buttons, dialog boxes, or caveats for me to show off with. (But there are many later in the book!)

Navigating PDFs in Exchange

Once again, before going into this discussion of navigating PDFs in Exchange, I refer you to Chapter 2. In most cases, you navigate PDFs in Exchange exactly as you do in Reader, with bookmarks, thumbnails, hyper-links, Go To Page, the Zoom tool, and so on. In this section, we look at the few notable differences.

Navigating cataloged PDFs

The primary difference in the navigational prowess of Exchange over Reader is the capability to search across indexes in cataloged PDFs. This is controlled from the four buttons on the far right of the toolbar, shown in Figure 5-2. These buttons, Search, Search Results, Search Previous, and Search Next, allow you to search indexes created with Acrobat Catalog.

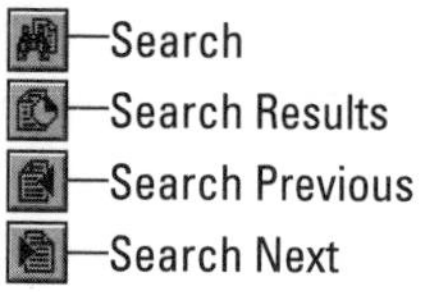

Figure 5-2:
These four Exchange navigation buttons let you search entire catalogs for keywords and phrases.

—Search
—Search Results
—Search Previous
—Search Next

You look at cataloging, indexing, and working with multiple PDFs in Chapter 13. For now, I wanted to point out these navigational tools in case you're the curious type.

Browsing the Web from a PDF

Another navigational option in Exchange is the capability to use a Web browser from inside Exchange on the Internet. By default, the button for this option, shown in Figure 5-3, is not displayed. To turn it on, choose File⇨ Preferences⇨Weblink, and then select Show on Toolbar. You look at using Acrobat on the Web in Chapters 15 and 16.

Figure 5-3:
Use this
button to
open your
browser for
navigating
the Web.

Weblink

Changing How Exchange Behaves

Like Reader, Exchange allows you to change several aspects of how the program works. Exchange, however, has several more options than Reader.

As you can see in Figure 5-4, most of the menu items pertain to particular aspects of creating PDFs, such as how Acrobat Capture or Acrobat Catalog works. These preferences are described in their respective chapters.

Figure 5-4:
Use this
submenu to
change
Exchange's
defaults.

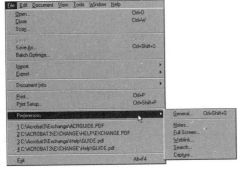

For now, you'll look at some of the General preferences, found in the General Preferences dialog box, shown in Figure 5-5. (Choose File⇨Preferences⇨ General.) Keep in mind during this discussion that this dialog box is similar to the one in Reader, and that the changes you make here have the same results.

Figure 5-5:
Use this
dialog box
to change
the general
preferences
of Acrobat
Exchange,
such as
which
fonts are
substituted
and the
default
page size.

Getting a better view when you open a PDF

When you open Exchange, the program determines at what size to display the page, whether to show single or facing pages, and so on. These are the defaults. They are set for optimal performance on what Adobe figures is the average computer display system, which means they're not always just right for everyone.

On my high-resolution, large-screen graphics display system, for example, the default 100 percent magnification causes the page to open too small. The first thing I have to do when opening either Exchange or Reader is click the Fit Window button to get a good view of the page. To make Fit Window the default (the way the document always opens), I simply changed the Default Magnification setting in General Preferences to Fit in Window.

Here's a way to make sure that pages always open as you want. Click the Zoom tool to bring the page to the level you like. Note the magnification level indicator (the one with the magnifying glass) in the lower-left portion of the screen. Choose File⇨Preferences⇨General, and set the Default Magnification to that level. Now, each time you open a PDF in Exchange, it opens at that zoom level.

You can also choose whether pages display singly, continuously, or as facing pages. These options are discussed in detail in Chapter 2.

Making Exchange work faster

All Acrobat applications are pretty fast. If you use an older, slow computer, however, you may want to make some changes in General Preferences to speed things up. Two options, Display Large Images and Greek Text Below, can give you some relief.

Display Large Images simply tells Exchange not to display images that could slow down the display of a page. Instead, the program displays a gray box where the image is placed.

The second option, Greek Text Below (which is Greek to me), tells Exchange when to stop drawing text and replace it with gray bars, as shown in Figure 5-6. Many of the computer's display system resources are required to redraw text. If the text is too small to read, why take the time and resources to redraw it? This is the idea behind greeking.

The settings you use here depend primarily on the size and resolution of your monitor. On my monitor, for example, I can read 2-point text comfortably. So I set the Greek Text option to 2. If I needed to speed up the redrawing of my display, I would use a larger number.

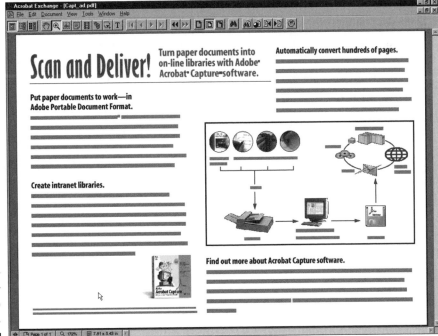

Figure 5-6: An example of greeked text, which is much easier for a computer display system to redraw.

You also can speed up the redrawing of your display by turning off Smooth Text and Monotone Images, but doing so can greatly affect the quality of the display. I suggest you turn this option off while working on the document, and then turn it back on to see how things are shaping up. You can also turn off Use Calibrated Color for Display. Calibrated color tries to ensure that colored images look the same from monitor to monitor.

Chapter 6

Making Your PDFs Interactive

In This Chapter

▶ Finding out how to create bookmarks and thumbnails

▶ Discovering the secrets behind creating text hyperlinks

▶ Enhancing your hyperlinks with graphics

*I*nteractivity. Now there's an interesting buzz word. You hear it all over the place, especially in reference to computer programs. Now we're all waiting for interactive TV. *Interactive* simply means that the viewer, or user, has the ability to control aspects of the viewing experience.

He or she can, perhaps, control the flow of the material, such as decide when to move from screen to screen. A common means of interactivity is allowing the user to choose from a menu to determine what information is displayed next. More sophisticated forms of interactivity include filling out and submitting forms, or answering questions and getting responses. Computer games, multimedia encyclopedias, and many other types of computer applications are interactive.

In this chapter, you find out about the basics of interactivity. You also find ways to go beyond the use of the Page Ahead and Page Back buttons to let users navigate the information in your PDFs.

You can create other, more sophisticated forms of interactivity with Exchange, such as forms, multimedia events, and hypertext tables of contents and indexes. These topics are saved for later chapters. For instance, creating interactive forms is discussed in Chapter 10, and adding multimedia events to your PDFs is discussed in Chapters 11 and 12.

Creating Bookmarks

Bookmarks provide a highly useful way for users of your PDF to navigate the document. They work as an ever-present means for users to find specific information, without having to go from page to page scanning the document.

Bookmarks display on the left side of the window, as shown in Figure 6-1. You can reveal bookmarks by clicking on the Bookmarks button (second from the left) on the toolbar, or by choosing View⇨Bookmarks and Page. Creating them is easy.

To create a bookmark:

1. **Go to the page and view for which you want to create a bookmark.**

   In Figure 6-2, for example, I want users to see a blowup of the picture when they click on the bookmark. So I go to the page containing the image and then use the Zoom tool to magnify the picture.

2. **Choose Document⇨New Bookmark.**

   This places an untitled bookmark in the list of bookmarks.

3. **Type the name of the bookmark.**

   Make the text as descriptive as possible, without making it too long. Although bookmarks can be up to 128 characters, that's way too long. Long names take up too much space in the bookmark window. Balance between short and informative.

4. **Press Enter to accept the new bookmark.**

   That's all there is to it!

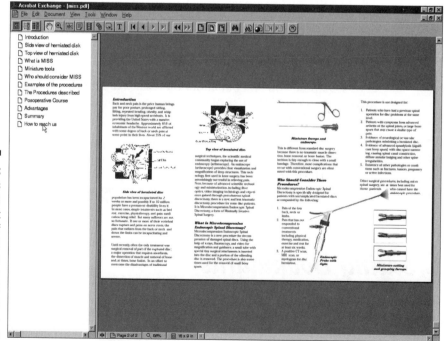

Figure 6-1:
Bookmarks (displayed on the left portion of the screen) allow users of your PDFs to find information quickly.

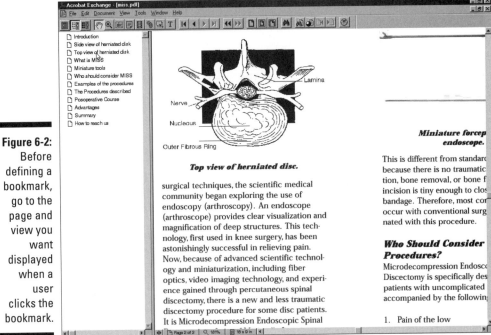

Top view of herniated disc.

Miniature forceps endoscope.

Figure 6-2:
Before defining a bookmark, go to the page and view you want displayed when a user clicks the bookmark.

surgical techniques, the scientific medical community began exploring the use of endoscopy (arthroscopy). An endoscope (arthroscope) provides clear visualization and magnification of deep structures. This technology, first used in knee surgery, has been astonishingly successful in relieving pain. Now, because of advanced scientific technology and miniaturization, including fiber optics, video imaging technology, and experience gained through percutaneous spinal discectomy, there is a new and less traumatic discectomy procedure for some disc patients. It is Microdecompression Endoscopic Spinal

This is different from standard because there is no traumatic tion, bone removal, or bone f incision is tiny enough to clos bandage. Therefore, most cor occur with conventional surg nated with this procedure.

Who Should Consider Procedures?
Microdecompression Endosco Discectomy is specifically des patients with uncomplicated accompanied by the followin

1. Pain of the low

When you make a new bookmark, Exchange places it at the bottom of the list by default. You can insert a bookmark anywhere in the list by selecting an existing bookmark directly above where you want the new one inserted — before you create the new bookmark. Be careful, though, to click on the page icon next to the bookmark text, rather than the text itself. Clicking on the text takes you to the page and view defined in the bookmark, which means you have to define the view for the new bookmark all over again. I hate doing things twice!

You can save yourself some typing and ensure the accuracy of your bookmarks by selecting a snippet of text in the view before you choose New Bookmark. As a result, the selected text becomes the text in the bookmark. This is helpful if you are defining bookmarks based on chapter titles, headings, and subheads.

Editing existing bookmarks

If you have second thoughts about a bookmark (or your boss or client tells you that you're all wet), you can change it easily. You can edit the following:

✔ The bookmark text

✔ The bookmark destination

✔ The bookmark action

Bookmark text and bookmark destination are discussed here. Acrobat supports several types of actions (destinations, movies, sounds, and so on), and a bookmark is just one way to invoke them. You look at creating actions in several chapters in this book.

Editing bookmark text

It doesn't get much easier than editing bookmark text. To do so, simply select the bookmark by clicking the page icon, hover the Text tool over the text, click and type new text:

1. **Click the page icon next to the bookmark you want to edit.**

   This action selects the bookmark.

2. **Hover (hold) the Text tool over the text of the bookmark itself.**

   The Text tool is the one with the uppercase A.

3. **Click on the text to select it.**

4. **Type the new text.**

Editing bookmark destinations

The *bookmark destination* is the place in the document that is displayed when the bookmark is clicked. Exchange allows several types of destinations and various actions, such as starting a movie, opening another Acrobat file, or invoking a menu command. Throughout the book, many of these actions are discussed when they are relevant to the topic. (Movies, for example, are discussed in Chapter 12.) In this section, the focus is on bookmark destination pages and views.

The easiest and most fundamental bookmark destination change is to change the page, the view, or both. The procedure is simple:

1. **Select the bookmark you want to change.**

   Make sure you click on the page icon, not the text.

2. **Go to the new page and view.**

3. **Choose Reset Bookmark Destination.**

   Exchange asks whether you're sure you want to change the destination.

4. **Click OK.**

You can also change the view to one of Exchange's built-in zoom levels, such as Fit In Window, Fit Width, or Fit Height. To do so, follow these steps:

1. **Select the bookmark.**

   Again, make sure that you click on the page icon, not the text.

2. **Right-click on the bookmark and then choose Properties from the pop-up menu. On a Mac, choose Edit⟹Properties.**

   This displays the dialog box shown in Figure 6-3.

Figure 6-3:
Going to a
specific
view, or
destination,
will be the
bookmark's
action
in this
example.

3. **Click Edit Destination.**

   The dialog box changes to the one shown in Figure 6-4.

Figure 6-4:
Use this
dialog
box to
change the
magnification
level for the
bookmark.

4. **In the Magnification list, choose a view.**

   The Fixed entry (shown in Figure 6-4) refers to a view you set manually by page and zoom level. When you select a view from the list, a message appears below the list telling you what the view does. (These views are also described in Chapter 2.)

Deleting bookmarks

You can remove bookmarks from the list in several ways. Here are two ways. You can do the following:

1. **Select the bookmark you want to delete (or hold down the Shift key as you click on multiple bookmarks).**

2. **Right-click on the bookmark. (On a Mac, choose Edit⇨Clear.)**

3. **Choose Clear from the ensuing pop-up menu.**

Another way to remove bookmarks is to select the bookmark and then choose Edit⇨Clear.

Creating subordinate bookmarks

Subordinate — now there's a fancy term. I like sub-bookmarks or bookmark groups better, but Adobe didn't ask me. Subordinate bookmarks are similar to subheads in an article or book chapter. You can also create sub-subordinates, sub-sub-subordinates, and so on.

Creating subordinates is genuinely easy. Before I show you how, though, look at Figure 6-5 so you can get an idea of what subordinates are.

Figure 6-5:
The
indented
bookmarks
are
subordinate
bookmarks
(or sub-
bookmarks).

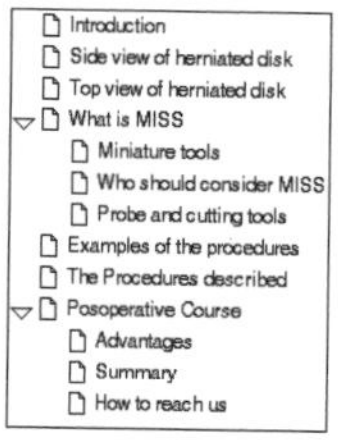

You can open and close the display of subordinates by clicking on the triangle to the left of the parent bookmark. When the point of the triangle faces the bookmark, the subordinates are closed. When the triangle points downward, the subordinates are open.

To create a subordinate, simply click on the page icon for the bookmark you want to de-elevate and drag it to the right. When a small, bold line appears below the first letter in the bookmark directly above the one you are moving, release the mouse button. That's it.

To create a group of subordinates, click on the first one, then Shift-click on the others until you've selected all the ones you want. Now drag the bookmarks to the right. To elevate a subordinate, simply drag it to the left.

If you think this is a wonderful tool, here's something even more wonderful. If your document was created in PageMaker or another PDF-savvy application, you can create your list of bookmarks and subordinates automatically by giving them the proper style definitions. In PageMaker, for example, you would use the Based On option in the Define Styles dialog box.

Creating Thumbnails

Users can navigate your PDF also through the use of little pictures, or *thumbnails,* of the pages. When users click on a thumbnail, they go to the page that the thumbnail represents. Also, when in a zoomed-in view, the user can zoom in on a portion of the thumbnail to move around on the page. In Figure 6-6, for example, I clicked on the page 7 icon to go to page 7.

To display thumbnails in a document, click on the third button from the left on the toolbar. If the document does not contain thumbnails, you see blank, gray pages, rather than little pictures.

Figure 6-6: Thumbnails, the small pictures in the left column, provide a way for users to navigate pages.

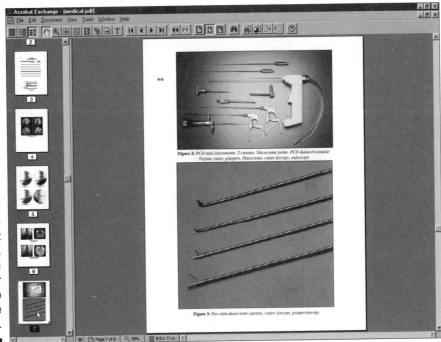

To create the thumbnails, choose Document⇨Create All Thumbnails. A dialog box appears showing you the progress of the creation process.

You can also remove thumbnails by choosing Document⇨Delete All Thumbnails.

Controlling which views are displayed in Reader

When designing PDFs, sometimes you may want to control how the Reader interface and the PDF itself appear to the user. For example, you may want to present users with bookmarks, making it easy for them to find subjects by topic. Or perhaps you want them to start on a specific page at a specific view.

Exchange provides a variety of ways to control the interface users see when they open your PDF. (What more could a control freak ask for?) These options are configured from the Open Info dialog box (File⇨Document Info⇨Open), shown in the figure.

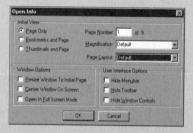

The Open Info dialog box lets you control the way your PDF opens in three ways: Initial View, Window Options, and User Interface Options. Here's a description of each and why you may want to use them.

Initial View: These options control whether the user is greeted with thumbnails or bookmarks, to what page the document opens, the magnification (or zoom) level, and the page layout (single page, facing pages, and so on).

You set these options to make the initial navigation of the PDF easier. Not everybody intuitively knows how to get around in a PDF. Use these options to make it easier for them. One trick I like to use is to have the PDF open already zoomed in on a page containing a menu.

Window Options: Rather than controlling how the document itself is displayed, these options control the Reader application window itself. You can open it full screen, force it to open just large enough to fit the view options you set in Initial View (with Resize Window To Initial Page), and tell Reader to center the page on the screen. Which options you use will depend on the document. Sometimes it's helpful to make the Reader window smaller so that the user can see other applications on the screen. One of my clients embeds in database data-entry forms the PDF documents that provide help for employees on how to use the forms.

User Interface Options: Initially, when Reader displays a document, it displays all its menus and toolbars too. To the user, it seems like he or she is using an application rather than an interactive document. If you build all your navigation tools into the document (thumbnails, bookmarks, hyperlinks, and so on), you can use User Interactive Options to hide the menus, toolbar, and window controls, allowing the PDF to stand on its own as an interactive publication.

Adding Text Hyperlinks

Another term for *hypertext* is *text hyperlinks*. (You know how propeller heads like to rewrite the language.) Hyperlinks are similar to bookmarks, except they are text in the PDF itself, rather than a table of contents off to the side of the document. If you've spent any time on the World Wide Web, you understand the concept of hyperlinks.

Hypertext links can be highlighted text directly in the body of the document, menus, or tables of contents — that is, any text anywhere in the document. Figures 6-7 and 6-8 show examples of hypertext links.

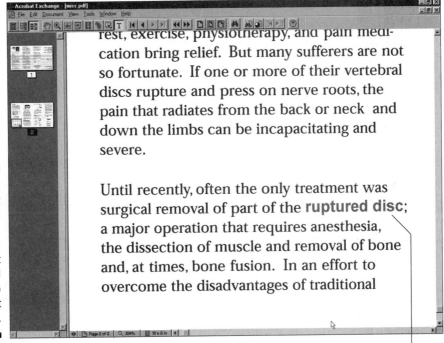

Figure 6-7:
A hypertext link in the text body. The link is a different font and color to make it stand out.

Hyperlink

Hyperlinks

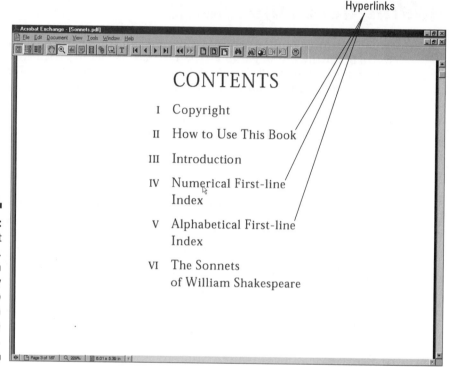

Figure 6-8:
A hypertext
menu.
Clicking on
an entry
takes you to
that portion
of the
document.

Creating a link

Creating the link itself is easy. Before going into that, I should point out that hypertext links can have all the properties of bookmarks. You can configure specific pages, views, and magnification levels, as well as execute menu items, invoke multimedia events, and a bunch of other options. If you don't recognize all these options, read the section on creating bookmarks earlier in this chapter.

This section deals only with creating navigational links, or links that take you to specific pages and views. Invoking other types of events is discussed throughout the book in the relevant sections. Invoking sound, for example, is discussed in Chapter 11.

Links are created with the Link tool. The procedure is as follows:

1. Go to the section of the document where you want to create the link.

Don't go to the destination of the link.

2. Click on the Link tool.

The Link tool looks like a chain.

3. **Begin drawing a rectangle around the text that you want to make into a hypertext link (hot).**

4. **Finish drawing the rectangle.**

   Exchange automatically displays the Create Link dialog box shown in Figure 6-9. From here you define the appearance, action, and magnification of the link. The appearance options from this dialog box are Visible Rectangle and Invisible Rectangle, which you select from the Type list. Visible Rectangle places a visible box (makes sense, right?) around the rectangle you drew in the preceding step. You can then use the Highlight, Width, Color, and Style options to change the appearance of the box.

   I prefer to change the appearance of the text itself. (I show you how in the next section.) So the only thing I usually change here is to set the Type to Invisible Rectangle.

Figure 6-9: Use this dialog box to begin creating your link.

5. **Without closing the Create Link dialog box, go to the page and view of the destination.**

   You define the destination that the link jumps to when the user clicks it.

6. **Use the Zoom tool and the Hand tool to center the page as you want it to appear.**

7. **In the Create Link dialog box, click on Set Link.**

   You're finished.

Editing a link

After you create and set your links you may want to edit them. For example, you may want to change a view or change the type of action the link invokes. The good news is that changing links is almost as easy as creating them. Here's how:

1. **Go to the page and view that contains the hypertext links you want to change.**

2. **Select the Link tool.**

   All the rectangles for the links in the displayed area appear, as shown in Figure 6-10.

3. **Double-click in the rectangle for the link you want to change.**

   The Link Properties dialog box appears.

4. **You can change the link's appearance, change the type of action invoked by the link, or edit the link's destination, page, or view:**

   a. **To change the appearance of the link, make the appropriate selections in the Type and Highlight lists.**

   b. **To set the new action type, select a new action in the Type list.**

      Remember that actions are discussed in this book where they are relevant to the subject at hand.

   c. **To change the destination of the link, click the Edit Destination button. When the destination view and page are defined to your satisfaction, click Set Link.**

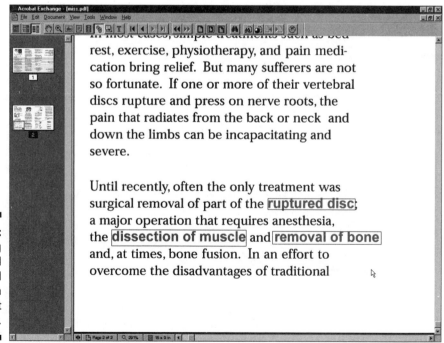

Figure 6-10: Selecting the Link tool displays all the links in the current view.

You can use the methods you've learned in this chapter and in Chapter 2 to navigate to a new destination.

5. Click OK in the Link Properties dialog box when you're finished.

That's it!

Removing a link

If you decide you don't want to keep a link, you can easily delete it as follows:

1. Click on the Link tool.

2. Click on the link rectangle to select it.

3. Right-click on the rectangle. (On a Mac, choose Edit⇨Clear.)

4. Choose Clear from the pop-up menu.

Exchange will ask whether you're sure you want to delete the link.

5. Click OK, and the link is gone.

Making hypertext links distinctive

It does no good to create a bunch of nifty hypertext links if your users can't tell them from the rest of the text in your document. You can't expect your users to run the cursor over the entire document looking for links. Therefore, you need to make the text discernible by changing the font, the color, or both. (Another option is to use a visible rectangle. You choose Visible Rectangle from the Create Link or Link Properties dialog box while creating or editing the link. This approach, however, looks clumsy.)

To change the font, color, and appearance of text in your PDFs, you use the Text Attributes dialog box. Follow these steps:

1. Click the TouchUp tool from the toolbar.

The TouchUp tool has an uppercase T on it.

2. Hold the Ctrl key and drag the text cursor (which now looks like an I-beam) over the text whose attributes you want to change.

In this case, drag the cursor over the text inside the link rectangle.

Holding Ctrl is necessary to override the link inside the rectangle. If you try selecting the text inside the rectangle without holding Ctrl, you activate the link and jump to the destination.

3. Choose Edit⇨Text Attributes.

The dialog box in Figure 6-11 appears. Use it to change the font, color, and other attributes of the text.

4. Click the Font tab.

You use the Font tab to change the typeface, type size, type color, and the outline color of the text.

5. From the first list box, select a typeface.

6. In the first box on the bottom, select a type size.

7. In the middle box on the bottom, select a text color.

8. In the last box on the bottom, select a text outline.

The other tabs in this dialog box are described in the next chapter.

In Exchange, unlike your word processor and most other applications, you change text weights (normal, bold, and so on) by choosing the specific font for that typeface. To make text Arial Bold, for example, you select Arial, Bold from the list, instead of choosing Arial and then clicking on a button to change the type from normal to bold. Most typefaces have four weights: normal (or Roman), bold, italic (sometimes called oblique), and bold-italic.

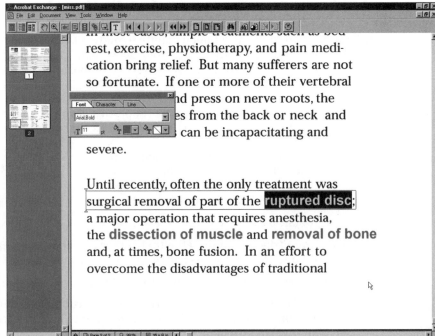

Figure 6-11:
Use this
dialog
box to
change the
attributes of
your linked
text.

When working in Exchange, the Text Attributes typeface list shows all the fonts on the system you're working on. When changing fonts, make sure that you choose fonts embedded in the PDF or fonts that are available on your PDF user's system. For a list of fonts in the PDF, choose File⇨Document Info⇨Fonts. If you don't understand how fonts work in a PDF, check out Chapter 4.

To avoid having to go back to the link after you set the destination, change your text attributes before you go to the destination page and view. I like to change text attributes before I even begin the link creation process.

Creating Hyperlink Graphics

Hyperlinked graphics are similar to hypertext links in that users click on them to go to other places in the PDF. You create them in much the same way, with the Link tool. Simply draw a rectangle around the image you want to make hot, and then use the Create Link dialog box to define the destination of the link.

You can create links from entire images, which is a great way to create buttons. See Figure 6-12. You also can create links from portions of images to create image maps. This is shown in Figure 6-13.

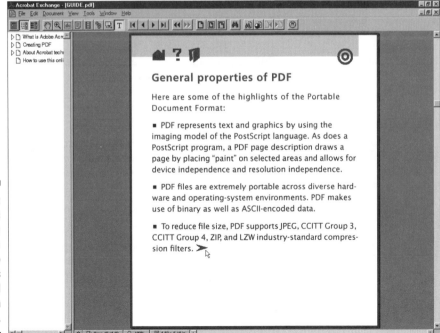

Figure 6-12: The icons on this page contain links to various pages and views in the PDF.

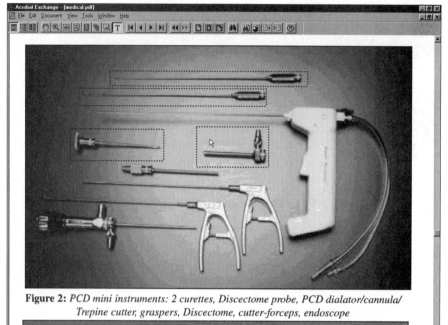

Figure 2: *PCD mini instruments: 2 curettes, Discectome probe, PCD dialator/cannula/ Trepine cutter, graspers, Discectome, cutter-forceps, endoscope*

Again, the procedure for creating graphics hyperlinks is the same as the procedure for creating text hyperlinks discussed previously in this chapter.

Here's a list of tips for using graphics links:

- ✔ Use graphics links to create a series of blow-up maps or diagrams. For example, you may start with an image of the United States with a series of links on each state or region. When users click on a link, they go to another blow-up map of that region. When they click again, they zoom in further.

- ✔ Use graphics links on pictures to invoke descriptions. On an image of a computer, for example, you can link description of various components, such as the monitor, CD-ROM drive, keyboard, and mouse. This works with all types of images.

- ✔ Use graphics links such as icons to invoke sound or movie files. (Sounds and movies are discussed in Chapters 11 and 12, respectively.)

- ✔ Create a series of icons as navigational links, such as arrows to go to the next page, the previous page, and the main menu. You can also find how to add graphics to your PDFs in the next chapter.

With that last tip in mind, when you add hyperlinks such as hypertext and graphics buttons to your documents, don't assume that your users will intuitively know how to use them. Create a "How to Use This Document" section in the PDF explaining the navigational elements. You can be of further help by setting the Document Info⇨Open options (described earlier in this chapter) so that the help page is displayed when the PDF opens.

Chapter 7

Editing Your PDFs

● ●

● ●

*I*f you're reading this book chapter by chapter, you already know that Acrobat is designed to convert existing documents — documents you create in other applications — to PDFs. Acrobat is not designed to create documents on its own, although it does have some limited document creation capabilities. You can, for example, import images into Exchange and save the results as a PDF, and you can import pages or entire PDFs into other PDFs and save them as a new PDF. In addition, you can use the Scan and Capture plug-in to create new PDFs, as discussed in Chapter 8.

Editing in Acrobat terminology does not mean the same as it does in other applications, such as word processing and page layout programs, where you have nearly unlimited layout and editing capabilities. You use Exchange's limited editing tools for touchups, rather than for full-blown editing and rearranging of documents.

Most of your document elements — text, overall layout, graphics, and so on — should be taken care of before you convert the document to PDF. With that in mind, this chapter shows you how to use Exchange's limited text, page, and graphics touchup features. You also look at setting security options and creating notes. Security lets you protect the document against editing by other Adobe Acrobat users. *Notes* are little pop-up messages you can leave to users or to other people in your workgroup who may be involved in the PDF creation process.

Editing Text in Exchange

In Exchange, text blocks consist of only one line, instead of the blocks that flow from line to line in word processing and layout programs. You can't type and expect the text to automatically wrap when the line fills up. Although you can change text in PDFs, your options are limited.

Suppose that the original line reads "Eat at Joe's." You can't comfortably change the line to "Come to Joe's place for the best hamburgers you ever ate: fat, juicy, and cholesterol laden" without making drastic changes to the text size. I'll take this opportunity to again drive home the point that Exchange's editing tools are actually touchup tools, not composing tools.

Figure 7-1 shows an example of a text block in Exchange. The editable area is inside the rectangle in the last line. Each line of text contains its own rectangular area. To display the area of a line that can be edited, you simply click the TouchUp tool (the button with the *T* on it), and then click on the line you want to edit. Now that the line is selected within the rectangle, you can edit that text in the following ways:

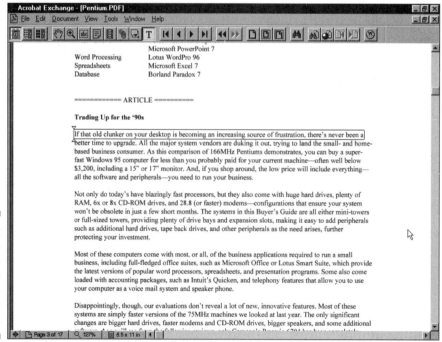

Figure 7-1:
The line in the rectangle is the editable area for this text block.

- ✔ Change words and characters
- ✔ Change typefaces, type attributes, and type size
- ✔ Adjust the character width and height
- ✔ Adjust the position of the line

Changing words and characters

After you select a line of text, as described in the preceding section, editing characters and words in Exchange is similar to doing so in most other programs. You simply click the I-beam in the text (with the TouchUp tool selected), and then start typing, or press Backspace to delete letters before the cursor, or press Delete to delete characters after the cursor. (There's no Backspace on a Mac.) You can also select all or part of the text block by dragging, and then typing to replace the highlighted text.

That's all there is to it. But keep in mind that you can only make corrections that keep the text line about the same length as the original text. If you add a little too much (or a little too little) text, you can use a few tricks to make it fit. I'll show you those tricks in a moment.

If you want to replace a single word in the selected line, you can easily select it by double-clicking the word — as in most other programs. Other shortcuts you may be familiar with, such as triple-clicking to select a sentence or quadruple-clicking to select a paragraph, do not work in Exchange.

Changing typefaces, type attributes, and type sizes

Making hypertext stand out from the rest of the text is the most common reason to change type. (You can find out how to do it in Chapter 6.) You can also change type to make it fit better on a line. Or you may want to change the appearance of headings — especially when the Acrobat font substitution doesn't give you the desired result.

To change type in a line:

1. **Drag the text cursor over the desired text.**

2. **Choose Edit⇨Text Attributes.**

   The Text Attributes dialog box appears. From here you can change the

   - Typeface
   - Type attributes

- Type color
- Type size
- Type width and character and line spacing
- Text block's position, or left and right indentation

Changing the typeface

When changing the font, or *typeface,* of selected text, you simply click on the list box in the Font tab of the Text Attributes dialog box (see Figure 7-2), and then select the new typeface. You need to remember a few things, though.

Typeface

Figure 7-2:
The Text
Attributes
dialog box.

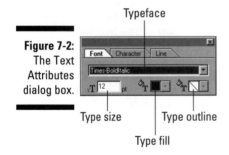

Type size   Type outline

Type fill

Keep in mind that the only fonts that are available are those you embed in your PDF during conversion with either Distiller or PDFWriter and those already present in the Acrobat font database. If you use other fonts, Acrobat will use its substitution table to replace the font with the nearest available facsimile.

To use attributes, such as bold or italic, you select the specific font for the attribute you want. If you're using the Times font and you want bold, you don't simply choose Bold. Instead, you choose Times, Bold from the font list. You can't go back and change the type to bold with a shortcut key combination or by clicking on a Bold button.

Changing the type size

You change the type size by typing a new point-size value in the first field below the typeface list. You can choose any size you like, but keep in mind that if you make the type size too big or too small, it won't fit well on the text line. You usually change the type size to make headlines, subheads, or captions look better or make them easier to find when your user scans the page.

Changing the type color

You use the Font tab of the Type Attributes dialog box also to change the type color. You have two options for changing the selected type color. You can change the type body (or fill) of the character or the outline of the character.

The middle drop-down box in the Font tab changes the type fill. You can choose eight predefined colors, or create your own color from the Choose a Fill Color dialog box shown in Figure 7-3. If none of the colors on that palette will do, you can define your own colors from the Define Custom Color dialog box. You can define colors by choosing a color swatch, or you can click on the Define Custom Color dialog box to create your own colors.

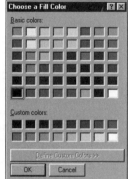

Figure 7-3:
Use this dialog box to choose a fill color for your text.

You change the text outline in much the same way you change the fill. From the second drop-down box, select one of the eight colors or select Other to display the Choose an Outline Color dialog box. From here, you can either choose a color or create a custom color and add it to the palette. You may use outline text to spruce up headlines and the like or to offset hypertext.

Changing character width and character and line spacing

Like PageMaker and some other programs, Acrobat lets you change the width of the characters in a selected block of text. You can also change character and word spacing (called *tracking*), line spacing (called *leading*), and pair kerning. These options are controlled from the Character tab of the Text Attributes dialog box, shown in Figure 7-4.

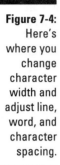

Figure 7-4:
Here's
where you
change
character
width and
adjust line,
word, and
character
spacing.

Character width

Letter tracking

Word tracking

Line spacing

Changing the character width

With the character width option, you can make characters wider or narrower. You may use this feature to create an aesthetic effect, as shown with the heading in Figure 7-5. Another reason to change the character width is to make slight adjustments so that text fits better on a line.

Figure 7-5:
To spruce
up the
heading, the
character
width
has been
changed to
200 percent
of its
original
size.

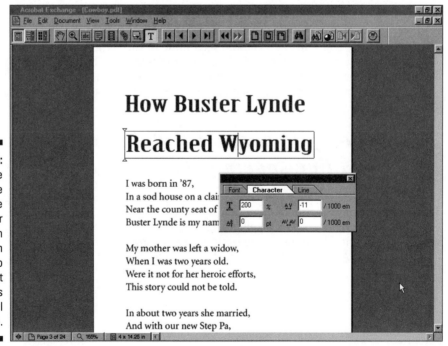

Character width settings are controlled from the first field in the Character tab of the Text Attributes dialog box. The value entered is a percentage. To make text wider, enter a value above 100. To make text half again its original size, for example, enter 150. To make text narrower, enter a value less than 100. To make text half its original size, for example, enter 50.

Changing character and word tracking

One way you can adjust text so that it looks better and is easier to read is by setting the distance between characters and words. Be careful, however, when using this option. Too much adjustment one way or the other can make your text look funny, as shown in Figure 7-6.

You adjust letter tracking in the Text Attributes dialog box using the second box on the right. In the box below it, you can change word tracking. Each type of spacing is measured in ems. An *em* is the widest character in the font set, the letter *m*. When you set your tracking values, you set a percentage of the *m* in the font set — 100/ems, 200/ems, and so on. Exchange allows you to set em spacing up to 1/1,000 of an em. Now that's precise!

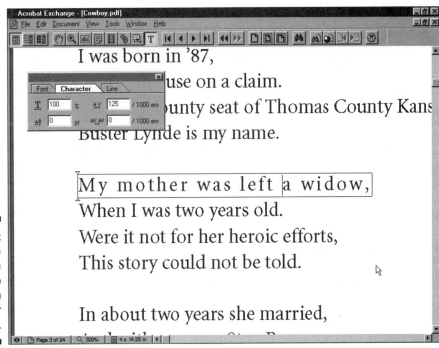

Figure 7-6:
An example of a line with too much character tracking.

Line spacing

In typesetting, line spacing is called *leading*. The term comes from the days when type was set on lead plates. Adjusting the leading consisted of adding or removing lead between the lines.

The leading, or line spacing, option is the box on the bottom left of the Text Attributes dialog box. (Refer back to Figure 7-4.) Like fonts, leading is set in points. You can adjust the leading of a selected line down (using negative values) or up.

Indents and outdents

You can indent a line or outdent a line. (The latter causes the line to hang over the rest of the text in a paragraph on the left side.) You make these changes with the Line tab in the Text Attributes dialog box, as shown in Figure 7-7.

Figure 7-7:
Use this portion of Text Attributes to move a line of text left or right.

You can use the boxes at the bottom of the dialog box in conjunction with the Left Aligned, Center Aligned, Right Aligned, and Justified buttons to move the text. I find it much easier, however, to simply drag the text into place — use the small triangles attached to the box around the text.

Working with Graphics in Exchange

The title of this section should actually be, "How Not to Work with Graphics in Exchange." The simple truth is that Exchange does not provide much in the way of editing graphics. For example, you can't select and move graphics as you can in most other programs, nor can you resize them, extract them from the PDF, edit them in an image editor, or place them back into the PDF.

Well, what can you do? Answer: two things. You can select a graphic and copy it to the Clipboard for pasting into another document, and you can import images into PDFs as separate pages or a new PDF.

Copying graphics to paste into another application

To copy an image or a portion of an image to paste into another application, do the following:

1. **Choose Tools⇨Select Graphics (Ctrl+Shift+5 or Cmd+Shift+5 on the Mac).**

   This gives you a crosshair cursor.

2. **Drag the cursor around the image you want to copy.**

3. **To copy the image to the Clipboard, choose Edit⇨Copy (Ctrl+C or Cmd+C on the Mac).**

4. **Open or go to the program containing the document in which you want to paste the image.**

5. **Choose Edit⇨Paste (Ctrl+V or Cmd+V).**

   And that's it.

Importing graphics into PDFs

When you import images into Exchange, you have two options: append the image to the end of the PDF or create an all new PDF. During the import, Exchange resamples the image to PDF format and creates a new page at the end of the existing document. Or, if you choose to create a new document, Exchange creates a page for each image you import.

To import an image into Exchange, simply

1. **Choose File⇨Import⇨Image.**

   The Import Image dialog box appears.

2. **Navigate to and select the image file you want to import.**

3. **Click on Open.**

   Exchange displays the Acrobat Import Image Plug-in dialog box shown in Figure 7-8.

4. **Determine whether you want to import the image into the end of the current document or have Exchange create a new document.**

Figure 7-8:
Use this
dialog
box to
determine
whether
an image
should be
imported
into the
current
document
or a new
document.

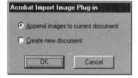

Figure 7-9 shows an example of an image imported into Exchange. Are you wondering what you can use the Import option for? Well, you can use it to create catalogs of images. Or you can use it to import images that don't exist in the original PDF and then create links to them, such as bookmarks or hypertext links. After you import the graphic into the PDF, you can move the page around in the document and place it wherever you'd like, as you see in the next section.

Figure 7-9:
An example
of an image
imported
into
Exchange.

Working with Pages in PDFs

Exchange does not provide immense flexibility when working with page elements, such as graphics and text. You can, however, change your document in many ways by manipulating pages. For example, you can move a page to another location in the document, insert and extract pages, crop pages, and rotate them. More than any other method, this capability to manipulate pages can be used to update and edit your PDFs.

Moving pages in PDFs

Sometimes, you may want to change the order in which pages appear in your PDF. For example, suppose you import a graphic and want it to fall behind a specific page. You can easily move pages from Thumbnail and Page view. Simply click on the page number below the thumbnail for the page that you want to move, and then drag the page to its new position, as shown in Figure 7-10.

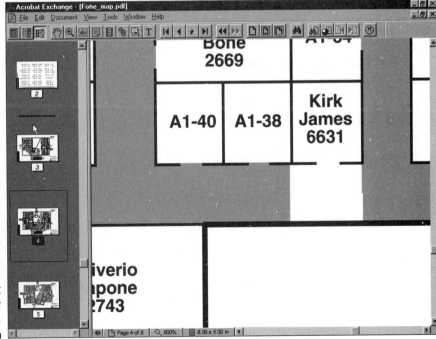

Figure 7-10:
To move a page, simply select the thumbnail and drag it to its new position.

You can move several pages at once by clicking on the page number of the first page to select it, and then Shift+clicking on subsequent pages to select them. After they're all selected, drag the page number of one of the thumbnails to the new position. When you release the mouse, all selected pages will move. Easy, huh?

Inserting pages in PDFs

You can insert pages from other PDFs with the Insert Pages command on the Document window. This option enables you to bring another PDF file — the entire file — in the current PDF:

1. Choose Document⇨Insert Pages (Ctrl+Shift+I).

The Select File to Insert dialog box appears. This dialog is similar to the Open dialog box you use to open files.

2. Navigate to the folder containing the PDF you want to insert.

3. Select the file, and click Select.

The Insert dialog box appears, as shown in Figure 7-11.

Figure 7-11:
Use this dialog box to tell Exchange where to insert the new PDF pages.

4. Decide where to put the pages from the PDF you are inserting:

a. Use the Before or After option to place the pages before or after (respectively) the current page.

b. Use the First or Last option to place the pages at the beginning or end (respectively) of the current document.

c. Use the Page option to designate which page you want the new pages to go before or after.

For example, to put new pages before page 6, select Before, select Page, and type **6** in the Page field.

5. Click OK to return to the document.

What if you want to insert only a portion of a PDF? You can do so in several ways, but the easiest is to drag and drop from thumbnail view. Simply open both documents side-by-side, and then turn on thumbnails for both documents. Then click on the number below the page you want to insert in the target document. (Use the Shift+Click method to select several pages.) Now, drag the page to its new position in the thumbnail window in the document where you want it inserted. You can tell where the new page will be inserted by the appearance of a black bar in the thumbnail window.

When pages are inserted, the existing links and bookmarks in the target document are maintained and notes from both documents are combined. Links and bookmarks from the inserted pages, however, are not transferred.

Extracting and deleting pages

Extracting and deleting may seem like the same thing; they're not. When you extract pages, you create a new file from selected pages in a PDF. When you delete pages, you remove them from the PDF, obliterating them. So be sure what you want to do before invoking either of these options.

Extracting pages

You may want to extract a few pages from a PDF for several reasons. Perhaps you want to create a new, smaller PDF containing only certain pages. Or you may want to extract pages to insert them into another PDF. In any case, to extract pages from the current PDF, do the following:

1. Choose Document⬦Extract Pages (Ctrl+Shift+E).

The Extract Pages dialog box appears, as shown in Figure 7-12.

Figure 7-12:
Use this
dialog
box to
designate a
page range
to be
extracted.

2. Designate a range of pages to extract in the From and To fields.

Notice, too, that you can also choose to have the pages deleted after they are extracted.

3. Click OK.

The pages are extracted and opened as a separate document in Exchange.

Unfortunately, Exchange does not let you select random pages for extracting. So, if you want to create a new PDF from noncontinuous pages in a PDF, you'll have to extract each range separately, and then use Insert Pages to combine them. After you have them all in one file, you can move them around as needed. Note that bookmarks and thumbnails are not extracted along with the page. You have to go back and create them, as described in Chapter 6.

Deleting pages

When you delete pages, you remove the pages from the PDF — poof. To delete pages:

1. Choose Document⇨Delete Pages (Ctrl+Shift+D).

The Delete dialog box appears.

2. Designate a range of pages to delete in the From and To fields.

3. Click OK.

The only way to get the pages back is to exit the file without saving it and then reopen it again. Remember, after you save the file, the pages are gone for good!

Deleting pages does not remove corresponding bookmarks. You need to go back and remove them. Otherwise, you have bookmarks leading to nowhere — they won't do anything when you click on them. In fact, that's a good way to find them. If you click a bookmark and it does nothing, you referenced a page you deleted. Get rid of it!

Replacing pages in PDFs

Of all the Pages commands on the Document menu, the Replace Pages command is the one I use most often. It is ideal for updating PDFs. For example, suppose that you've created a PDF from a lengthy Word document. After a month or so, the file requires updating. Rather than generating an all-new PDF, going back and recreating all the links and bookmarks, you can create a PDF from only the pages you updated, and then use Replace Page to replace the old pages with the new ones. (Keep in mind, though, that you'll have to create new bookmarks and links on the new pages.)

To replace pages with pages from another PDF:

1. Choose Document⇨Replace Pages (Ctrl+Shift+R).

The Select File with New Pages dialog box appears.

2. Use the dialog box to find the PDF containing the pages you want.

3. Select the file and choose OK.

The Replace Pages dialog box appears, as shown in Figure 7-13.

Figure 7-13:
Use this
dialog box
to select a
range of
pages you
want to
replace and
a range of
pages you
want to
replace
them with.

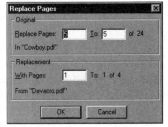

4. In the Replace Pages box and its corresponding To box, type the pages you want to replace.

5. In the With Pages box, type the last page of the document that you want to use for the replacement.

For example, if your document contains 10 pages, you enter 4 to import the first 4 pages. To import 6 of 10 replacement pages, you would enter 6.

When pages are replaced, the existing links and bookmarks in the target document are maintained and notes from both documents are combined. Links and bookmarks from the replacement pages, however, are not transferred.

You can replace pages also by dragging thumbnails from one document to another. Simply use Window⇨Tile to display both documents. Then in thumbnail view, drag the page from the thumbnail view of one document to the thumbnail view of another. (Use the Shift+click method to select more than one page.) Place the cursor on the page number of the thumbnail for the page you want to replace. When the page number becomes inverted (dark box with a light-colored number), release the mouse cursor. The page is replaced with the new page. This method is handy for replacing noncontiguous pages.

Setting the page action

Previous chapters have discussed actions, mostly page views. Page actions tell Acrobat what to do when a specific page is displayed. For now, you only need to know that you can trigger an event, such as starting a sound file or a movie, when a certain page is displayed. You look more closely at this process in the chapters that correspond to specific actions. (Chapter 11, for example, discusses sound.)

Cropping pages

When you convert pages to PDF, the pages are usually the size you want. Sometimes, though, you want to make changes to the size or the position of the page. For example, when you print slides to a PostScript file in PowerPoint, the page may be framed incorrectly. Or you may want to remove a margin of unwanted white space or other portions of a page. This is where the Crop Page command comes in.

To crop a page, several pages, or all the pages in your document:

1. Choose Document⇨Crop Pages.

The Crop Pages dialog box appears, as shown in Figure 7-14. From here you control the amount of cropping and which pages to crop.

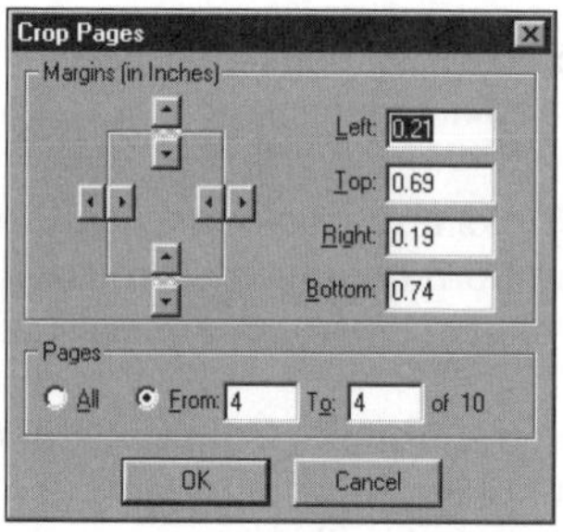

Figure 7-14:
Use this
dialog box
to crop
pages.

2. Crop pages by clicking on the arrows, which represent all four sides of the page.

You can also enter values in the boxes on the right. I prefer the first method because I'm never sure exactly how much cropping is needed.

As you click on the arrows, a small hairline moves from the edge of the paper in the direction you're clicking. (I'd provide a screen shot, but the line is so fine that you won't be able to see it.)

3. **To crop all four sides, click on arrows on each side, until the cropping lines are in the positions you want.**

4. **In the Pages section, designate the pages to which you want to apply the cropping.**

5. **Click OK.**

Exchange crops each page you designated.

Cropping a page wipes out the thumbnail. You can get a new one by choosing Document⇨Create All Thumbnails.

Making Your PDFs Secure

If only we lived in a world where everybody could be trusted. In many situations, you want to protect your PDFs against tampering. If you don't, anybody with a copy of Exchange can make changes to your creations.

Security options are controlled from the Security dialog box, which you display by choosing File⇨Save As⇨Security. (See Figure 7-15.)

Figure 7-15:
Use this dialog box to control who can mess with your PDF.

| Security |
| Specify Password To |
| Open the Document: |
| Change Security Options: |
| Do Not Allow |
| ☐ Printing |
| ☐ Changing the Document |
| ☐ Selecting Text and Graphics |
| ☐ Adding or Changing Notes and Form Fields |
| OK   Cancel |

You can apply security to several aspects of your PDF, as follows. You can

✔ Require a password to open the document

✔ Require a password to change security options

✔ Disallow changes to the document text and structure

> ✔ Disallow printing of the document
> ✔ Disallow the selecting of text and graphics for copying to the Clipboard
> ✔ Disallow the changing of notes and form fields

Each of these options is discussed in the following sections.

Setting password options

Exchange lets you set two types of passwords for your PDFs: a password for opening the document in Reader and Exchange, and a password for turning security options on and off.

Securing a document from prying eyes

To keep the wrong people from reading your document, simply do the following from the Security dialog box:

1. In the Open the Document box, type a password.

Exchange displays a dialog box asking you to confirm the password.

2. Type the password again the same way you typed it the first time.

3. Click OK.

The Save As dialog box appears.

4. Type a file name.

5. Click Save.

The next time folks try to access the file, they are greeted with a dialog box requesting a password. If they don't type the correct character string, they won't get the document open. Period. The same applies to you, so write down the password somewhere.

Securing a document against changing and copying

Many times, you don't want to give other people the opportunity to change or copy elements of your PDFs. To control who can change a document, and what aspects can be changed, do the following in the Security dialog box:

1. In the Change Security Options box, type a password.

This password supercedes the Open the Document password. If you want to change the Open the Document password, you must first type the Change Security Options password.

2. In the Do Not Allow section, click the options that you want to disallow.

3. Click OK.

Exchange asks you to confirm the password.

4. Type the password exactly as you did the first time.

5. Click OK.

The Save As dialog box appears.

6. Type the name of the document.

7. Click Save.

Depending on which options you chose, various aspects of the Exchange interface appear dimmed, which indicates that they are unavailable. For example, if you turned on Do Not Allow Changing the Document, all editing options (such as the TouchUp tool, Insert Pages, Replace Pages, and Create Bookmarks) are unavailable to you and other Exchange users. Only those who know the password can turn the editing options back on again. Remember the password!

Changing security options

Okay. You've ratcheted down the security on your PDF. Now, a month or so later, you need to make some changes. Or maybe you want to print the PDF. What do you do? You reverse the procedure you followed to set the security options:

1. Choose File⇨Save As⇨Security.

2. Click on the check boxes for the options you want to turn back on.

Exchange prompts you for the Change Security Options password.

3. Type the password.

4. Click OK.

5. Click OK again.

The Security dialog box closes.

6. Click Save to save the document.

You can now make changes or print the document again, depending on the security options you cleared.

I'm compelled to remind you one more time to *remember the password*. You can lose a lot of work otherwise.

Forms aren't discussed until Chapter 10, but there's something to note about forms now. If you choose the last option in the Security dialog box — Adding or Changing Notes and Form Fields — users can't change form fields but can fill them in. The Changing the Document option prohibits users from both filling in a form field as well making any other changes to the form field. So, when a PDF contains forms that users fill in, you need to leave Changing the Document turned off.

Checking a document's security

If you don't remember which security options you set in PDF, or if you want to check the settings of someone else's PDF, choose File⇨Document Info⇨Security. The Document Security dialog box appears, indicating what you (or someone else) can or can't do in the PDF in its current state.

Adding Author and Other General Info

In a work group, network, and other PDF distribution environments, it's often a good idea to declare in your PDFs the author, subject, title, and keyword search terms — otherwise known as General Info. This makes the work identifiable to others as well as easier to find on a hard disk crammed with PDFs, such as a file server drive.

To set General Info:

1. **Choose File⇨Document Info⇨General Info.**

   The General Info dialog box appears, as shown in Figure 7-16.

2. **Fill in the four fields (Exchange fills in everything else).**

   The first three are self-explanatory, but you may not be familiar with Keywords. In this field, you type identifying words by which you or a user can search for the document after it has been cataloged. Cataloging PDFs is discussed in Chapter 13. (Note that the other fields here can be searched from a catalog; you can find out more about that in Chapter 14.)

To change General Info on a PDF, the Do Not Allow Changing the Document option in the Security dialog box must be turned off. Security is discussed in the preceding section.

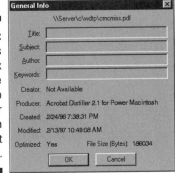

Figure 7-16:
Use this
dialog box
to provide
authorship
and other
information
about
the PDF.

Creating and Editing Notes

Notes are a nifty, useful feature. You can use them, for example, to include
instructions to users. They're also helpful in work groups where PDFs are
created by two or more people. Or your boss or client can use them to
annotate your work, as shown in Figure 7-17.

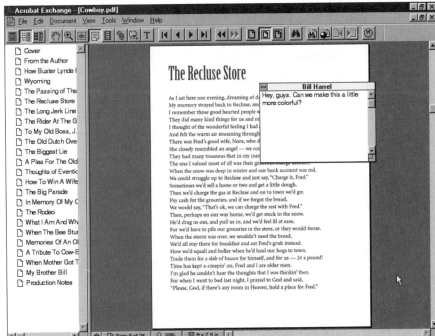

Figure 7-17:
I've left a
note to one
of my staff
about the
content of
this PDF.

Creating a note

Creating a note is easy:

1. **Go to the place in the document where you want to place the note.**
2. **Select the Text Note tool.**

   This tool is the seventh from the left.
3. **Click in the document where you want the note to appear.**
4. **Type the note.**
5. **Click on the small bar in the upper-left corner of the note window.**

   The note is minimized to an icon.

To open the note again, for either editing or viewing, simply double-click on the note icon. To edit the note, click the cursor on the portion of the note you want to edit, and then edit the text as you would any other text.

Changing a note's properties

You can change the appearance of the note icon or the note itself in a variety of ways. For example, to move the note:

1. **Click on the note to select it.**
2. **Drag the note to its new position on the page.**

To delete the note:

1. **Click on the note once to select it.**
2. **Right-click on the note. (On a Mac, press Cmd+I.)**
3. **Choose Clear from the pop-up menu.**

To change the note icon's color:

1. **Click on the note once to select it.**
2. **Choose Properties from the pop-up menu.**

   The Note Properties dialog box appears.
3. **To change the color of the icon, choose a predefined color from the list or choose Custom to display the Color dialog box for a wider range of colors.**

4. **To change the title of the note, type new text in the Label field.**

By default, Exchange titles the note with the PDF author's name.

To change the size of the note box itself:

1. **Double-click on the icon to open it.**

2. **Drag the small box (in the lower-right corner of the note box) down and to the right.**

You can also change the size of the note text and the font from the Note Preferences dialog box.

You get to that dialog box as follows:

1. **Choose File⇨Preferences⇨Notes.**

2. **To change the font, select a font from the Font list.**

3. **To change the type size, either type a new size in the field or choose one from the list.**

4. **Click OK when you've made all your changes.**

And that's that. You now understand the basics of editing PDFs in Acrobat.

Chapter 8

Using the Scan and Capture Plug-Ins

In This Chapter

▶ Scanning documents using Acrobat Scan

▶ Using Acrobat Capture's optical character recognition (OCR)

*P*art of editing PDFs (the subject of Chapter 7) is adding pages to existing PDFs with the Insert Pages and Extract Pages commands in Exchange. Acrobat provides another way to include outside material in PDFs with the Acrobat Scan and Acrobat Capture plug-ins.

Acrobat Scan works as an interface to your desktop scanner, allowing you to scan hard copy documents directly into Exchange. You can then save the scanned images as PDF pages, import them into other PDFs, or use Acrobat Capture to perform OCR on the text in the scanned image and downsample graphics (see Chapter 16).

Capture is basically an OCR application. But unlike most OCR packages, such as Caere's OmniPage, which turns scanned text into editable text for manipulation in a text editor, Capture turns the scanned text into PDF text that you can edit, search, and index.

In this chapter, you first look at scanning pages into Exchange, and then look at using Capture to turn the text on the pages to editable text.

As I write this, Adobe has not yet finished the Scan and Capture plug-ins for the Macintosh, which are supposed to work similarly to the Windows versions. Be sure to check the Adobe Web site (http://www.adobe.com) occasionally for the appearance of the Mac versions of the plug-ins.

Setting Up Your Scanner to Work with Scan

The Scan plug-in works from Exchange. You can interface your scanner with either the ISIS (Image and Scanner Interface Standard) scanner drivers that ship with Acrobat, or you can use the TWAIN (technology without an interesting name) drivers and the interface that came with your scanner, such as Hewlett-Packard's DeskScan. Each type of interface has both advantages and disadvantages.

ISIS scanners

ISIS scanner drivers provide a number of automatic features, such as automatic brightness and contrast controls, not available in most TWAIN scanner interfaces. But unlike most TWAIN interfaces, ISIS scanner software will not let you preview a page to select a portion of it before scanning. When you use ISIS scanner software, the settings remain in effect, page after page, until you change them.

The advantage of this approach is that, in most cases, the interface software makes the appropriate contrast and brightness adjustments for each page. In addition, you can process pages simultaneously, without pausing to make adjustments for each page. The disadvantages are that you can't select regions of a page for scanning, and you can't get a page preview.

Twain scanning interfaces

Most TWAIN scanner software lets you preview the page, as shown in Figure 8-1, allowing you to make adjustments to improve the quality of the scan. This software also allows you to select a portion of the preview to scan, without forcing you to scan the entire page, as the ISIS interface does. You can also select the scanning mode (such as color, grayscale, or black and white) and the resolution of the image in dots per inch (dpi).

TWAIN scanner software usually requires you to set up each scan, or page, because the default settings are restored each time you scan. This makes the process of scanning multiple pages more time-consuming and tedious — unless you are using a multiple-sheet feeder that the TWAIN software supports, such as the Hewlett-Packard's 20- or 50-sheet feeders with DeskScan. If you use TWAIN software with Acrobat Scan, the double-sided scanning option (in which you scan one side of the page and then turn it over and scan the other) is not available.

Figure 8-1:
I'm using
Hewlett-
Packard's
DeskScan
to select a
region of
the page
and make
adjust-
ments —
a feature
unavailable
with the
ISIS
scanner
interface.

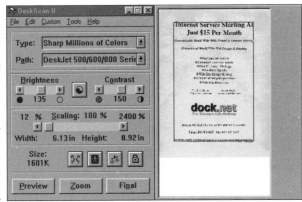

In the following scanning procedure, I use the ISIS scanner interface, which is the easiest scanner to use with Acrobat. Besides, the TWAIN scanner interfaces are so diverse that I couldn't cover them all here. If you want to use the interface that came with the scanner, refer to the scanner's documentation.

If you have additional questions about Scan after reading this section, check out the *Scan Online Guide.* From Exchange, choose Help⇔Scan Online Guide.

Choosing a scanner

The first time you attempt a scan in Exchange, the Scan plug-in displays the Acrobat Adobe Scan dialog box shown in Figure 8-2. Before you can go any farther, you must choose the type of scanner you use.

Figure 8-2:
Use this
dialog box
to begin the
process of
choosing a
scanner.

Adobe Acrobat Scan

Scanner
<No device selected>   Select...   Configure...

Document Type
● Single-Sided Page   ○ Double-Sided Page
○ Single-Sided Stack   ○ Double-Sided Stack

Scan   Cancel

To choose a scanner to work with the Scan plug-in, follow these steps:

1. **In Exchange, choose File⇨Scan.**

2. **Click the Select button.**

   The Select Scanner dialog box appears, as shown in Figure 8-3. During the Acrobat Installation, I chose my scanner from the list of supported scanners, so Acrobat is showing me only the scanners supported by the driver I selected.

Figure 8-3:
Use this
dialog box
to choose
your
scanner.

If your scanner is not displayed in the list, use the Acrobat installation CD-ROM disc to install it. Simply go through the install procedure, selecting only the Scan plug-in to reinstall. After the list of scanners is displayed, select your scanner from the list.

3. **Select your scanner from the list.**

4. **Click Select.**

   This returns you to the Adobe Acrobat Scan dialog box. You are now ready to configure your scanner to work with Acrobat.

Configuring your scanner

In most cases (when using the ISIS interface), the default scanner settings work fine, especially if you are scanning documents for OCR with Capture. Occasionally, though, you may want to change the default settings — especially if after scanning you don't get the desired results. You change scanner settings from the Scanner Settings dialog box shown in Figure 8-4. You get here by clicking the Configure button in the Acrobat Scan Plug-in dialog box, and then clicking Settings in the ISIS Plug-in dialog box.

Take a look at the various options in the Scanner Settings dialog box:

Mode: Use this list to choose the type of document you're scanning, such as black-and-white or color. When scanning predominately for OCR, you would use black-and-white. If you want to scan a page and have it look in Acrobat exactly as it does in hard copy, choose a setting based on the document.

Figure 8-4:
Use this
dialog box
to make
adjustments
to the
scanner
interface.

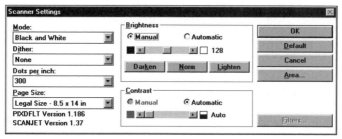

Dither: Dithering is a method of breaking images into dots to simulate colors. It's used primarily when you're scanning a document that contains more colors than the mode you're scanning in (such as scanning a full-color image in black-and-white). Most often, you would leave this setting at None.

Dots Per Inch: This setting pertains to the resolution of the image. When scanning documents for OCR purposes, you should use a setting of 300 dpi.

Paper Size: This setting refers to the page size you are scanning. Most people scan either letter- or legal-sized paper. Acrobat also supports several magazine and European paper sizes.

Brightness and Contrast: These settings are important primarily in scanning images. If an image scans too dark, for instance, turn up the brightness. If it lacks detail because of a low range between light and dark areas, turn up the contrast. For OCR scanning, you can set both of these settings to Automatic.

Area: Clicking the Area button displays the Set Scanning Area dialog box, which allows you to adjust the scanning area. Setting the X and Y positions sets the scanning area measured from the upper-left corner of the page. Setting the Width and Length determines the actual scanning area.

Scanning your documents

Scanning into Exchange with the Scan plug-in is quite easy. All you need to do is tell the plug-in whether you're scanning a single page or a stack of pages, and whether the page or pages are double-sided. You have four options in the Document Type section of the Adobe Acrobat Scan dialog box, as follows:

Single-Sided Page: Use this setting for scanning one page. This setting scans the page and then displays it in Exchange.

Double-Sided Page: Use this setting to scan one page with two sides (which is actually two pages, right?). When you use this setting, the program scans the first side, and then pauses, allowing you to turn the page over to scan the other side.

Single-Sided Stack: This setting is for use with an automatic sheet-feeder. Use this option to scan one page after another automatically. When the scanning is finished, the pages are displayed in Exchange.

Double-Sided Stack: This setting is used for sheet-feeders, too. The difference between it and Single-Sided Stack is that after all the sheets are scanned on one side, Scan pauses to allow you to turn them over; then the other sides are scanned.

You can scan pages into any PDF by scanning with the PDF open and current in Exchange. The pages are added to the end of the document. You can then use the techniques described in Chapter 6 for rearranging the pages.

After you make your document type selection, click Scan. Adobe Acrobat Scan then scans the page or pages according to the settings you've chosen. When the scanning is finished, the scanned pages are added to the current PDF. If you scanned with no PDF open, a new PDF is created to hold the scans. Figure 8-5 shows a page I scanned using this method.

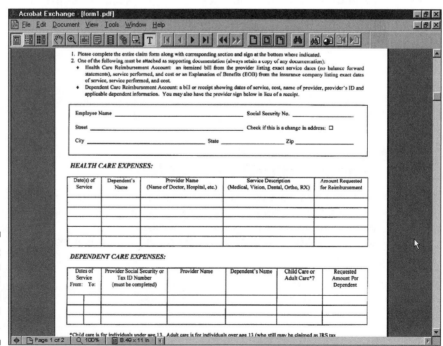

Figure 8-5:
A form
scanned
with
the Scan
plug-in.

At this point, Exchange treats the scanned document as a graphic, similar to those you import with the Import command (as discussed in Chapter 6). The text on this page is not yet editable. You can make it editable in the next section with the Capture plug-in.

Turning Graphics into Text with Capture

If you thought the scanning part was easy, wait until you see what a no-brainer capturing text is. Basically, the Capture plug-in takes any graphic containing text and turns the text into PDF-editable text. You would use Capture most often with the Scan plug-in to convert scanned documents to editable text. For example, you may want to scan a document and then use Capture to start the process of turning the form into a PDF form.

To use Capture, you usually choose Document⇨Capture Pages and let 'er rip. But you can also make some minor changes to how Capture works in the Capture Preferences dialog box.

Another reason to use Capture to convert scanned images is that the process can significantly reduce the size of the scanned graphics by down-sampling. Downsampling is discussed in Chapter 16. Capture's built-in resampling is discussed in the following section on Capture preferences.

Changing the Capture preferences

You change Capture's preferences from the Adobe Capture Plug-in Preferences dialog box, shown in Figure 8-6. To display this dialog box, choose File⇨Preferences⇨Capture. You can also choose Document⇨Capture Pages to display the Acrobat Capture Plug-in dialog box, and then click the Preferences button.

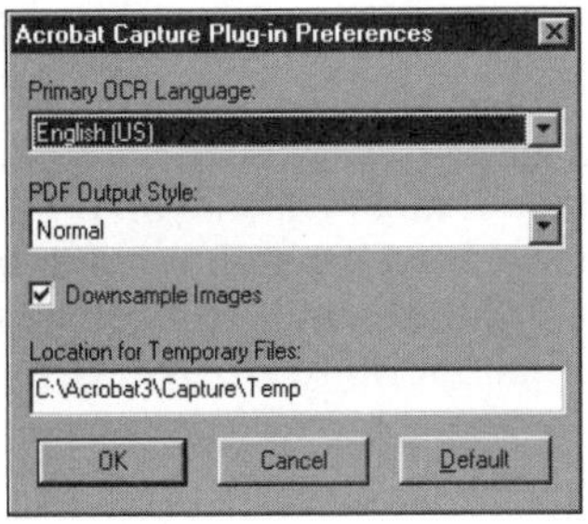

Figure 8-6:
Use this
dialog box
to change
the Capture
plug-in
preferences.

Acrobat Capture Plug-in Preferences

Primary OCR Language:
English (US)

PDF Output Style:
Normal

☑ Downsample Images

Location for Temporary Files:
C:\Acrobat3\Capture\Temp

OK   Cancel   Default

As you can see, you don't have a lot of options for the Preferences settings. You can choose a language, a PDF output style, a directory for capture to work in, or decide whether to downsample images while Capture performs its magic. The Primary OCR Language option speaks for itself. The rest of this section looks at the other three options.

PDF Output Style option

The PDF Output Style option has two settings. The first setting, Normal, simply converts the scanned image or imported graphic to a standard PDF with editable text and images downsampled.

The other setting, Original Image with Hidden Text, combines features of a PDF Image Only page (a scanned or imported image page) and PDF Normal pages. Original Image with Hidden Text pages contains a complete bitmap image of the original scanned or imported document, but with editable text "hidden" behind the image. This gives you the benefits of searchable text (as discussed in Chapters 13 and 14), while ensuring that a document looks identical to the original. Use this setting when you need to keep the original scanned image of a document (for example, for legal or archival purposes).

Downsample Images option

Capture has its own downsample settings, based on the type of images it encounters during the capture process. (Downsampling is discussed in detail in Chapter 16.) The Capture downsample settings are as follows:

- ✔ Color and grayscale images downsample to 150 dpi. Images with original settings less than 225 dpi are not downsampled.

- ✔ Black-and-white images downsample to 200 dpi. Images with original settings less than 300 dpi are not downsampled.

- ✔ When you select both the Original Image with Hidden Text and the Downsample Images options, color and grayscale page images are downsampled below 200 dpi. As a result, the captured pages cannot be processed again in Capture. You have to scan them again.

Location for Temporary Files option

The last option, Location for Temporary Files, designates where Capture creates temporary files while processing. In most cases, you don't need to change this, unless the default directory is on a drive that contains very little disk space. If you get an error from Capture while processing that it has run out of disk space, you can change this option to a drive with more space. If you have only one hard disk, you may have to delete some files.

Capturing pages

To capture scanned or imported pages, you simply start the plug-in, choose which pages you want captured, and go. Here's how:

1. **With the document containing the pages you want to capture open, choose Document⇨Capture Pages.**

   The Acrobat Capture Plug-in dialog box appears, as shown in Figure 8-7.

Figure 8-7: Use this dialog box to start the capture process.

2. **Choose the page or page ranges you want to capture.**

   You can choose a page range by using a hyphen (such as *2-4*) or several page ranges with hyphens and commas (such as *2-4, 7-10, 12-14*). To choose specific pages, use commas (such as *2, 5, 7, 9, 12*).

3. **Click OK.**

Capture goes to work. Depending on the complexity and number of pages, capturing can take some time. When the process is complete, the captured document replaces the scanned image (unless you choose the Original Image with Hidden Text option discussed previously in this chapter). Now it's time to make corrections.

Correcting words that Capture can't recognize

Capture is pretty good at OCR, — under ideal conditions, that is. Your scanned page must be set straight in the scanner. Text should not be placed over colorful backgrounds or patterns that can interfere with the recognition. And the text should be in a font that Capture has available to it with the PDFWriter driver, as discussed in Chapter 4.

If Capture misses some words or characters, you can use the Show Capture Suspects and Find First Suspect commands to help you locate and correct unrecognized text.

The Show Capture Suspects command (choose Edit⇨Show All Suspects) draws red rectangles around all the areas on a page that Capture could not recognize, as shown in Figure 8-8.

You can then go from suspect to suspect correcting each occurrence by following these steps:

1. **Choose Edit⇨Show All Suspects.**

2. **Go to the first suspect and double-click on it.**

   Capture shows you what it thinks the word or characters are by displaying the suspect in the Capture Suspect dialog box, shown in Figure 8-9.

3. **Accept or reject the suggestions from Capture.**

   If you choose Accept, the graphic is converted to text. If you choose Next, Capture leaves the suspect as-is and continues to mark it as suspect. In some cases, Capture can't make an educated guess about a suspect. It leaves these suspects marked for you to correct manually.

4. **Go through the remaining suspects by accepting or rejecting suggestions by Capture.**

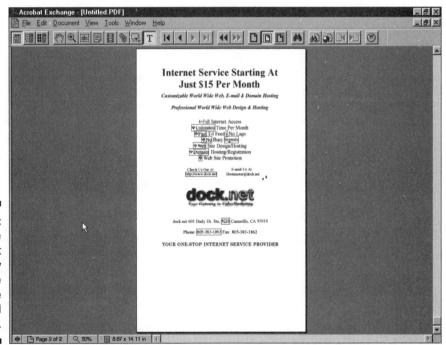

Figure 8-8:
Capture
could not
readily
recognize
these
marked
suspects.

Figure 8-9:
When it can, Capture makes an educated guess about the text it thinks a suspect contains.

To correct a suspect manually:

1. Click on the suspect with the Text touch-up tool (the tool on the toolbar with the *T*).

Capture displays what the scanner saw. You can use this as a guide for correcting the suspect. If you can't tell from the Capture suspect what the text should be, refer to the hard copy you scanned.

2. Type what the text should be.

3. Click Accept to accept the change.

Find First Suspect works similarly to Show Capture Suspects, except that it does not display all the suspects on the page at once. Instead, it goes to the first suspect on the page, marks it, and opens the Capture Suspect dialog box. After you accept, reject, or correct the suspect, Capture moves on to the next suspect, and the next, and so on, until it reaches the last suspect.

That's it! You've finished your crash course in scanning and capturing documents with Acrobat. I told you it was easy.

One last word on Capture. After you have captured a document, you can't run Capture again without first rescanning the document. If you aren't happy with the results of a scan and capture session for some reason, you need to scan the document again.

Chapter 9

Creating Interactive Tables of Contents and Indexes

● ●

In This Chapter

▶ Using non-Acrobat-savvy applications

▶ Using Acrobat-savvy applications

● ●

*1*f you've gone through the past eight chapters, you've discovered a lot about generating PDFs, creating hyperlinks, and editing PDFs. Before moving on to more advanced Acrobat features, take a breath and apply some of what's been discussed to an actual PDF document.

One of the benefits of PDFs versus paper documents is the capability to hyperlink information, making it easier to find. We were taught in school to find information in multipage works through reference lists, such as tables of contents and indexes. You can make your PDFs easier to use by providing the same vehicles. However, your table of contents and indexes will be more useful than the conventional ones because your users need to only click on the entry in the list to jump to the referenced section.

This chapter approaches creating interactive lists from two perspectives: non-Acrobat-savvy applications and Acrobat-savvy applications. The ex-amples use two common applications, Microsoft Word and Adobe PageMaker. If you use a different word processor or page layout program (such as Adobe FrameMaker or QuarkXPress), you use similar procedures but the commands and processes vary slightly. After you get your document into Exchange, however, the procedures are the same.

In conventional document-speak, an *index* is a list, or reference, at the back of a book where you find the pages on which specific topics are discussed. Acrobat uses the term *index* to refer to lists generated during the PDF cataloging process. In this chapter, I use *index* in the conventional sense. In Chapter 13, you look at indexing in the context of creating searchable catalogs.

Creating an Interactive List from a Word Processor Document

With word processors such as Word and WordPerfect, you can generate tables of contents, indexes, and other lists automatically. In other words, after you complete the document, you generate the table of contents and index entries without having to go from page to page noting the location of each heading, subheading, and table of contents entry. If you've used this feature before, you know what a time-saver it can be.

Setting up the file in your word processor

In Word, for example, you generate tables of contents and indexes with the Index and Tables command on the Insert menu, which displays the dialog box shown in Figure 9-1. From here, you define your index entries and set up formatting for your lists. Tables of contents entries are defined in paragraph style sheets. (Note that although the dialog boxes and commands are slightly different for other word processors, the procedures are similar.)

Figure 9-1:
An example
of the table
of contents
and index
feature in
a word
processor.

Figures 9-2 and 9-3 show a table of contents and an index, respectively, generated in Word. Unfortunately, this is the extent of the help you get in creating your PDF index. Non-Acrobat-savvy applications cannot maintain the links between the list and the actual pages during a PDF conversion. The good news is that when you convert the document to PDF, the pagination is maintained. Therefore, you won't have to go back through the document and re-reference or reindex. Whew!

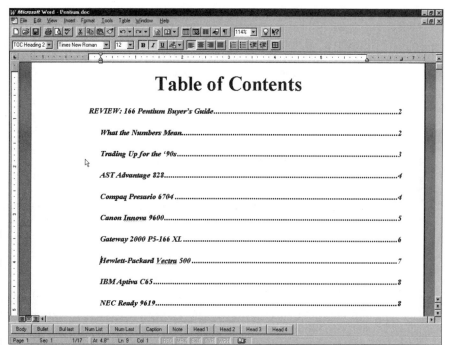

Figure 9-2:
A table of
contents
generated
in a word
processor.

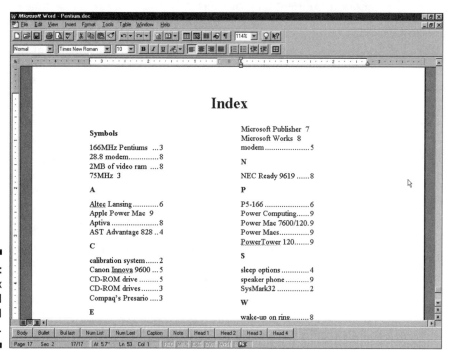

Figure 9-3:
An index
generated
in a word
processor.

After you generate and format your lists, you're ready to convert the document to a PDF. Because word processor documents do not typically contain a lot of high-quality graphics, you can safely use PDFWriter, instead of going through the hassle of printing to a PostScript file and then using Distiller to convert documents. (If you don't understand the difference between PDFWriter and Distiller, check out Chapter 4.) In Word for Windows and some other popular word processors, you can convert your documents to PDFs by using the Create Adobe PDF command on the File menu, which was installed when you installed Acrobat.

In Chapter 6, where I show you how to create hyperlinks, I suggest that you change the hypertext links to a different font and make them a different color so that your users can differentiate the links from other text in your document. If you know in advance what text will be hot, as is the case with a table of contents and an index, you can change the appearance of the text in your word processor before converting the document to a PDF.

Creating the links in Exchange

As mentioned, links from your lists to the pages they reference in the body of the document are not maintained during the conversion process. Therefore, you need to open the new PDF in Exchange and manually create the hyperlinks for each table of contents and index entry. If your document is large and contains a lot of references, this process can be time-consuming.

However, this procedure is a much simpler and less time-consuming process because you created the list before converting the document to PDF. The page numbers for each link are right in front of you — you don't have to search out each occurrence corresponding to the reference and create links manually.

Here's an easy way to create links between your lists and the places in the documents they refer to. (If you don't understand the linking process, check out Chapter 6.)

1. **Select the Link tool.**

   It's the tool with the chain on it.

2. **Using the Link tool, drag a box around the text you want to make hot.**

   When you release the mouse, the Create Link dialog box shown in Figure 9-4 appears. (If you are not familiar with this dialog box, see Chapter 6.)

3. **In the lower-left portion of the screen, click on the button reading Page *x* of *x*.**

   The Go To Page dialog box appears.

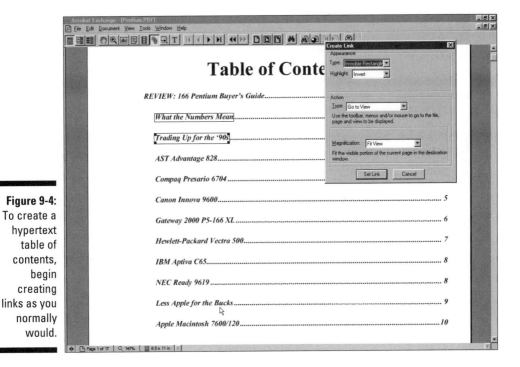

Figure 9-4:
To create a hypertext table of contents, begin creating links as you normally would.

4. Type the number of the page for the current entry.

5. Click OK.

At this point, you can either zoom in on the portion of the page that most pertains to the table of contents or index reference, or you can simply leave the page in the current view. The former process involves a few more steps. But it also makes the document easier to use by zeroing in on specific information corresponding to the link.

Creating an Interactive List from a Page Layout Program

The advantage of using a page layout program over a word processor for creating PDFs is that several of them — PageMaker, FrameMaker, and QuarkXPress (with an XTension) — can maintain the links between reference lists and the places in the text they refer to. This automatically creates your hyperlinks for you, saving you from having to define them one-by-one in Exchange.

In addition, you can create lists across several documents. In PageMaker, for example, you can generate tables of contents and indexes across several chapters in a book, even though the chapters are separate PageMaker files. When you convert the document to a PDF, these links are maintained, saving you time and the tedium of manually hyperlinking long lists.

When creating a book, the table of contents, preface, and other front matter are typically numbered with roman numerals (i, ii, iii, and so on) instead of sequentially with the rest of the book. In addition, some books start page numbering over in each section (A-1, B-1, and so on). Acrobat does not support these kinds of page numbering. Page numbers start at 1 and go until the end of the document. When you convert all the files in a book to PDFs, they are combined into one file with contiguous pagination. You should renumber your publication, if necessary, before converting.

Setting up the document in your page layout application

When preparing a document in PageMaker and similar applications for conversion to a PDF, you first lay out your document as you normally would. Table of contents entries are defined in paragraph styles with the Include in table of contents option shown in Figure 9-5. Index entries are defined with the Index Entry command, which displays the dialog box shown in Figure 9-6.

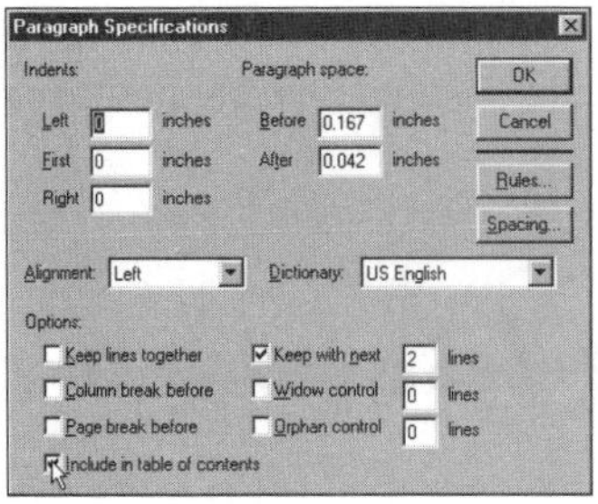

Figure 9-5:
Use this dialog box (or one like it) in a page layout program to define table of contents entries in paragraph styles.

When you finish laying out the document and defining all your lists, use the Create TOC and Create Index commands on the Utilities menu to generate your lists. Place and format them as you normally do. Then you're ready to convert the document to PDF.

Figure 9-6:
Use this
dialog box
(or one like
it) to define
entries.

In PageMaker, the Adobe PDF command is under File⇨Export. (It may be in
a different place in your layout application, and the ensuing dialog box may
also look somewhat different.) This displays the Export Adobe PDF dialog
box shown. For this exercise, you're interested in only the PDF options of
this dialog box. Clicking on the PDF Options button displays the dialog box
shown in Figure 9-7.

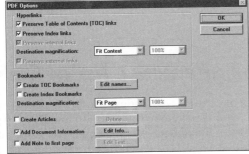

Figure 9-7:
This is
where
you tell
PageMaker
to create
hyperlinks
from the
index
and TOC
definitions.

To tell PageMaker to automatically create links from the index and table of
contents definitions, make sure the Preserve Table of Contents (TOC) links
option and the Preserve Index links option are selected. If the document
doesn't contain any of either type of link, these options appear dimmed.

Notice in the next section of the PDF Options dialog box, Bookmarks, that
you can create bookmarks from your table of contents and index definitions.
This is a quick and easy way to create bookmarks automatically. But I'd
think twice about making bookmarks from your index, especially if it's large.
You wind up with a huge, difficult-to-use bookmark list. (If you aren't sure
what bookmarks are or how to create them, check out Chapter 6.)

You can change the view of the destination of the table of contents and index links from the Destination magnification list. Most of the views in the list are self-explanatory. (Check out Chapter 6 for an explanation of views.) The one that may be unfamiliar is Fit Context. You use this option when you want to center the linked destination on the Exchange or Reader desktop.

After you select the proper options, follow these steps:

1. **Click OK.**

   You're asked where you want to save the PDF file.

2. **Navigate to the folder where you want to save the file, and name it.**

3. **Click OK again.**

   PageMaker prints the file to a PostScript file, and then opens Distiller to convert it to a PDF.

4. **Open Exchange, and open the new PDF.**

You can have the PDF automatically displayed in either Reader or Exchange at the end of the conversion. From the Export Adobe PDF dialog box, select the View PDF Using option, and then select the target application from the list.

Setting up the interactive list in Exchange

When converting tables of contents and indexes from PageMaker and other PDF-savvy applications, you usually don't need to do much else to the lists and the destination views in Exchange — especially if you selected the proper view in PDF Options when setting up the conversion. I like to use Fit Context (a Destination magnification choice when converting the file) to zoom in on the portion of the page that contains the destination link.

You may want to go in and check each link to make sure that it displays the optimal view. Perhaps you want a better magnification level, or you want to tweak the page centering using the methods discussed in Chapter 6. Even if you have to adjust a few destination views now and then, you can't beat using a PDF-savvy application for automatically creating your tables of contents and index links.

Chapter 10

Creating Forms

- -

- -

We all use (and curse) forms in one form or another — government forms, forms to buy things, forms to get credit, even forms to get married. If you work for a company, you probably have a whole set of forms to contend with — forms to take a vacation, forms to evaluate subordinates, forms to request a lunch break. It never ends. And now, we are deluged with a bunch of forms on the Internet.

Smart companies have implemented ways for employees to fill out and submit forms electronically. Acrobat can help your company (or your clients) better manage the massive forms headache by providing an easier way to fill out, print, submit, and archive forms.

In this chapter, you check out the basics of creating forms in Acrobat. Then you look at the application of forms from two perspectives: forms that users fill and print, and forms that add interactivity to PDFs.

Acrobat supports two additional types of forms: forms for the submission and retrieval of data over the Internet, and forms for the submission and retrieval of data over company intranets and networks. These two types of forms are covered in Chapters 15 and 17, respectively.

The Anatomy of PDF Forms

If you have any HTML (World Wide Web page) authoring under your belt, this introduction to PDF forms will be familiar. Designing forms in Acrobat is similar, although PDF forms are more versatile. For example, you can export and retrieve form data on a network (not the Internet) without a lot of elaborate programming. PDF forms also support more functions than HTML forms — but I'm getting ahead of myself.

Here's an oversimplified list of the three types of PDF forms:

- ✔ Forms your users fill out and print
- ✔ Forms your users fill out and submit electronically
- ✔ Forms that perform actions in a PDF

In this section, you take a brief look at all three.

Forms to be filled out and printed in Reader

The most common application for PDF forms is to have your users open them in Reader, fill them out, and print them. You can use this option for all types of applications, such as mail-in purchase orders, employment applications, and requisitions. All you do is design the form, distribute it on disk, over a network, or over the Internet. Keep in mind that if you distribute the form files on disk (or CD-ROM), you can also freely distribute Acrobat Reader so that your users can access, fill out, and print the forms.

The limitation of this application is that Reader users cannot save the filled out forms. To do so, they also need to have Exchange, which you cannot distribute without infringing on (actually, shattering) the Adobe copyright and licensing agreement.

Forms to be filled out and submitted electronically

You probably see electronic forms all over the Internet. You fill in text fields, click on radio buttons, check boxes, select from menus and lists, and then click on a Submit button to send the form flying to its destination.

You can create this same type of form in Acrobat Exchange. Form data can be processed in HTML *or* PDF format and sent to a Web URL, e-mailed, or saved in Acrobat's FDF format. Much of this may be unfamiliar to you now, but these topics and various formats are covered in Chapters 15 and 17.

Forms that add interactivity to your PDFs

An *action* is what happens when you click on a hyperlink or bookmark. Acrobat supports several types of actions — everything from jumping to a destination page and view to launching a movie or sound file. (See Chapter 6 for more on actions.) In addition, you can create forms that allow users to make choices about what action the PDF should take, such as going to a destination, executing a command, or starting a movie.

The benefit of using forms, rather than standard text or graphic hyperlinks, is that you can provide the user with a list of choices, such as three or four destinations or one of several multimedia events. This gives your PDFs a polished look and makes using the document a more pleasurable and satisfying experience.

Creating PDF Forms

Creating a form is a three-step process. You begin by creating the shell for the form. The basic layout, including the form's title, instructions, labels, and so on, are laid out in a creator application, such as a word processor or a page layout application. Then you convert the document to a PDF with either PDFWriter or Distiller, as described in Chapter 4. After the document is converted, you open the PDF in Exchange and add your form elements.

You can also use the Scan and Capture plug-ins to scan an existing form and convert it to a PDF, as described in Chapter 8. This process gives you the basic form layout. Then all you need to do is add the form elements.

Creating form elements

Like HTML forms, Acrobat form elements (also know as *objects*) come in six flavors: text fields, radio buttons, list boxes, combo boxes, check boxes, and buttons, as shown in Figure 10-1.

Unlike HTML, which allows you to design forms containing generic elements that all look the same, PDF form elements can be customized in appearance so that they have borders, colored backgrounds, and various shapes. In addition, PDF form elements can trigger more sophisticated actions than standard HTML form elements.

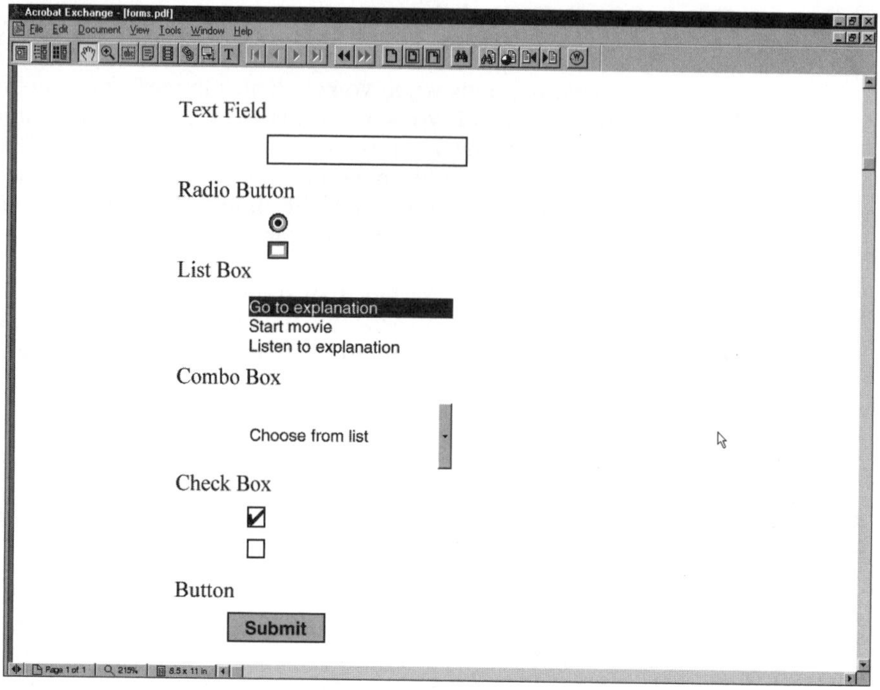

Acrobat Exchange - [forms.pdf]

File Edit Document View Tools Window Help

Text Field

Radio Button

List Box

Go to explanation
Start movie
Listen to explanation

Combo Box

Choose from list

Check Box

Button

Submit

Page 1 of 1   215%   8.5 x 11 in

Figure 10-1:
Examples of
six form
elements
(or objects)
in Acrobat.

To create a form object in a PDF, you simply do the following:

1. Select the Form tool.

It's between the Link and TouchUp tools on the toolbar.

2. Go to the place in the PDF where you want to place the element and drag out a rectangle.

This is similar to creating links with the Link tool.

3. Release the mouse button.

The Field Properties dialog box shown in Figure 10-2 appears. From here, you set up the form element by choosing the type of element, naming the object, setting appearance options, and setting actions.

4. In the Type box, choose the type of object.

The contents of the tabs in the Field Properties dialog box changes depending on the type of element you choose. Therefore, the first thing you should do when defining a form element is to choose the type of object it will be.

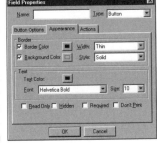

Figure 10-2:
Use this
dialog box
to define
the form
element.

5. **Go through the various tabs of the Field Properties dialog box, defining the object's options, appearance, and actions.**

(If you aren't sure what actions are, check out Chapter 6.) The following sections describe the contents of each of the tabs for each element.

6. **Click OK.**

The object is defined. Because the Form tool is selected, however, all you see is the object's bounding box and the name of the object.

7. **Select another tool, such as the TouchUp tool or the Hand tool.**

This way, you can see how the object will appear to your users.

The Hand tool is the required tool for filling in a form field, selecting a form entry, or pushing a form button. This is also the tool your users would click in Reader to use the form.

Let's take a look at the six different objects and how you can use them.

Defining text fields

Text fields are where your users type the text. For example, you may have fields for Name, Address, Phone, and so on. When a user hovers the Hand tool cursor over a text field, the cursor changes to a text I-beam, which means the user can click in the field to fill it in.

Acrobat lets you use text fields in all types of forms — forms designed for printing, electronic submissions, and interactivity. Other types of objects, such as buttons and radio buttons, are better suited for interactivity, though. It makes little sense to have your users type data in a field to launch an event when you can have them click on buttons.

The Text Options tab of the Field Properties dialog box, shown in Figure 10-3, allows you to set the following properties for your text field.

Figure 10-3:
Use this
portion of
the Field
Properties
dialog box
to set the
initial
values for
your text
field.

Name: Each form object must have a name. You should give each form object a different name. Otherwise, when the form is submitted or printed, all fields will return the same value.

Default: The text that appears in the field if the user doesn't type anything else. You can use it to place the most common answer in the field, such as a number (Annual Salary: $20,000,000), or to leave a note to the users telling them what kind of data goes in the field (Type Your Name Here). When the user clicks the Hand tool on the field, the default text is selected. All the user does is type the new data.

Alignment: Determines whether the text in the field is left-aligned, centered, or right-aligned in the field.

Multi-line: Allows the user to type more than one line of text in the field.

Limit of characters: Limits the amount of text that a user can type in the field.

Password: Determines whether the field is a password field. You can use this security option with an action, such as opening another PDF or launching a movie, to restrict access to material or to restrict access to the form itself.

The options in the Appearance portion of the Field Properties dialog box, shown in Figure 10-4, allow you to customize how your object will look. You can control border type, background color, the fill text font, size, and color, and several other options as follows.

Border Color and Width: Selects a border color and the width of the text field.

Figure 10-4:
Use this
portion of
the Field
properties
dialog box
to set the
appearance
of the Text
field object.

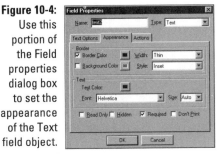

Background Color and Style: Selects the field background and border style (such as solid, dashed, inset, or beveled) for your text field. The Style options allow you to create border shadows, make the borders appear as 3-D buttons or inset fields.

Text: Options in this section change the color, font, and size of the text that the user types into the field. This is pretty straightforward, except for two things. If you select Auto for the text size, the text fits the size of the field. And if you want text to be bold or italic, you have to choose the font for that attribute, such as Helvetica, Bold.

Read Only: Does not allow the user to change the contents of the field. You use this option primarily if you want to use a text field as a custom action button or if you want the field to always return the same value in an electronic submission. (Electronic submission forms are discussed in Chapters 15 and 17.)

Hidden: Used only in forms destined for electronic submission. A hidden form object does not appear to the user.

Required: Used only for electronic submissions. If a required field is not filled out, the form cannot be submitted.

Don't Print: Ensures that the form object and the text typed into it won't print.

Actions are discussed in several places in this book, especially in Chapter 6. Setting actions for form objects is similar to setting actions for other types of hyperlinks and bookmarks, except that you control what happens on four separate mouse movements: Mouse Up, Mouse Down, Mouse Enter, and Mouse Exit, as shown in Figure 10-5.

Mouse Up and Mouse Down refer to mouse clicks, when you release the mouse and when you press it, respectively. Mouse Enter and Mouse Exit refer to when you move the mouse over a form object. For example, when

the cursor moves over a field (Mouse Enter), you can have a sound play
(Sound action). Or when the cursor leaves a field (Mouse Exit), you can
have the field disappear (Show/Hide Field action).

To set an action for a form object, you first select the mouse movement, and
then click the Add button to select an action. Again, actions are discussed
where they are pertinent to the topic. As with other types of hyperlinks, you
can use form object actions to navigate through PDFs, such as go to a
specific view, play a movie, play a sound, or execute menu commands.

You should take note of three actions specific to forms: Show/Hide Field,
Reset Form, and Submit Form. Show/Hide Field does just what it says; it
shows and hides the field according to the mouse movement you set. You
can even define an object to hide and show other form objects, which is a
great way to customize a form based on the choices the user makes. Reset
Form returns the form to its default values. For example, suppose that all
form fields were blank before the user began filling out the form. If the user
clicks an object containing the Reset Form action, the fields would all be
empty again. If the fields contained default text or settings, the text and
settings would return to the fields. Submit Form, which requires some programming, submits the form to the World Wide Web.

To edit a text field, or any form object for that matter:

1. **Select the Form tool.**

2. **Use the Form tool to double-click on the object's rectangle.**

   The Field Properties dialog box appears

3. **Change the settings.**

To delete an object:

1. Select the Form tool.

The tool turns red.

2. Use the Form tool to select the object.

3. Press Delete.

Defining radio buttons

Anyone who's used a computer more than a few days is familiar with radio buttons. They're common to many dialog boxes. In dialog boxes and HTML forms, they are always round circles that you fill in by clicking on them. In PDFs, however, they can be round, square, beveled, inset, different colors, and more.

Like other PDF form objects, radio buttons can be used in all types of forms. They work best for choosing values of either on or off. In other words, selected is on and not selected is off. You can also use radio buttons (or check boxes) when users can make more than one selection in a list. Another option is to use radio buttons as action buttons.

When naming radio buttons, you should use different, meaningful names. When the forms are submitted electronically, the name of the field is submitted, rather than the corresponding text beside the button. I like to give them the same names as the text beside them. I just use the Text Selection tool to copy the text (Ctrl+C in Windows or Cmd+C on a Mac), and then paste it into the Name field (Ctrl+V in Windows or Cmd+V on a Mac) in the Field Properties dialog box.

You can assign more than one mouse behavior to a field, and more than one action to a mouse behavior. For example, you can have the object play a sound when the user clicks it, and then go to a view when the user releases the mouse button. You can also stack actions to create a sequence of events, such as go to a view, launch a movie, and then (after the movie) provide a sound issuing instructions on how to use the options on the current page. You see how to do this in the chapters on sound and movies, 11 and 12, respectively.

Creating radio buttons is similar to creating text fields:

1. Select the Form tool.

2. Draw the object rectangle.

3. Use Field Properties to define the object, as described in the preceding section on creating text fields.

Keep in mind that radio buttons are usually small — about the same height as the text they correspond to and about two characters wide.

Figure 10-6 shows the Field Properties dialog box for radio buttons. Most of the options in the Appearance and Actions tabs are the same as they are for text fields, except you can't change the font and type size because radio buttons don't contain text.

Figure 10-6:
The Field Properties dialog box configured to work with radio buttons.

Besides typing the name of the button, you can set three items in the Radio Button Options tab: Radio Style, Export Value, and Default is checked.

Radio Style: Lets you choose the shape of the button. The six options to choose from include Square and Check.

Export Value: Used for forms that will be submitted electronically over the Internet or a network (as discussed in Chapters 15 and 17). Whatever value you type here (on or off) is the value returned when the form is submitted, unless the user changes it. Unless the form will be submitted for automatic inclusion in a database, you should leave this field blank.

Default is checked: Tells Acrobat to check this option unless the user unchecks it.

Defining list boxes

A list box allows a user to choose one option from a list of choices. When the form is printed, the user's choice prints highlighted. When the form is submitted electronically, the user's choice is submitted. You can use list boxes in all types of forms, but they work best in forms designed for printing or electronic submission, and don't make a lot of sense for interactive forms. You should use them when you want to confine your users to making only one choice from a list.

You create list boxes similarly to text fields and radio buttons:

1. Select the Form tool.

2. Drag out the box to contain your list.

Your list box can display all the choices in the list, or the box can scroll, as shown in Figure 10-7. The scroll buttons don't appear unless the box is selected, so you may want to include some text that tells the user how the list works. I prefer using boxes that show all the choices in the list, when space permits.

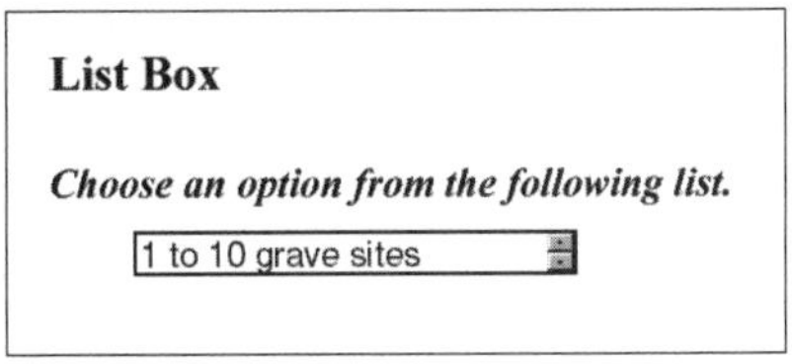

Figure 10-7:
An example
of a list box
with scroll
buttons.

List Box

Choose an option from the following list.

| 1 to 10 grave sites |

3. When you've finished drawing your list box, release the mouse button.

Exchange displays the Field Properties dialog box.

4. In the Type list, select List Box.

This configures the dialog box for working with list boxes, displaying the dialog box shown in Figure 10-8. The Options tabs for List Box and Text Box elements are different. The Appearance and Actions tabs, however, are the same, so I won't repeat the description here.

Figure 10-8:
Use this
Field
Properties
tab to add
items to
your list.

5. To create the entries in your list, follow these steps:

a. In the Name field, give the list box a name.

b. In the Item field, type the first entry for your list, and then click Add.

    c. **In the Item field, type the next entry, and click Add again.**

    d. **Continue entering items until the list is complete.**

6. **If you want the items sorted alphanumerically, select the Sort Items check box.**

7. **Click OK.**

8. **Drag on the corner or side boxes to reshape the list box rectangle so that your items fit neatly inside.**

To see whether your text fits in the rectangle, you must select the Hand tool.

You can remove items from the list by selecting them and clicking Delete. The default item in the list is the one that is highlighted when you close the Field Properties dialog box, or the default item is the last item selected by the user.

I like to put a thin border around my lists to make it more obvious that they are list boxes. A thin black border with a gray bevel looks cool. You can set these options from the Appearance tab of the Field Properties dialog box.

Defining combo boxes

A combo box by any other name is a drop-down menu. When you click on the arrow to the right of the box, a menu of choices drops down (as opposed to pops up). You can use this form object for any type of form, but it makes sense only in forms designed for electronic submission. When printed, the options on the drop-down menu can't be seen, unless you make the box big enough to see them all, which defeats the purpose — no need for a drop-down menu, right?

Combo boxes are great space-savers. You should use them, though, only when your users can make a single choice from the list. They don't work for multiple selections.

You create combo boxes as you would other types of form objects:

1. **Select the Form tool.**

2. **Draw a rectangle to hold the first item in the menu.**

3. **After you finish drawing your combo box, release the mouse button.**

   Exchange displays the Field Properties dialog box.

4. **Define the combo box.**

   The selections on the Combo Box Options tab and the other tabs of the Field Properties dialog box are identical to those discussed in the previous section about list boxes, with one exception. By selecting the

Editable option in the Combo Box Options tab, you give your users the option of editing the text for each menu item. This means that they can actually change the selection that is submitted with the form.

If you make the combo entries editable, you should instruct the user in a brief note before the object that they can edit their entries. Otherwise, most users would not know this.

The default entry is the one that's selected in the list of entries in Combo Box Options when you close the Field Properties dialog box. When using combo boxes, I like to make the default entry an instruction to the user, such as "Choose from this list," or "Make your selection." This lets the user know that more than one item is available.

Defining check boxes

Check boxes are almost identical to radio buttons (discussed previously in this section). Check box fields, however, require different names.

Suppose you have a group of five check boxes. If you try to give a check box the same name as another in the form, Exchange will not let you close the Field Properties dialog box. Why? When the form is submitted electronically, the name of the field is submitted, rather than the text corresponding to the check box. Therefore, give your fields meaningful names or, better yet, the same names as the corresponding text.

Defining buttons

Acrobat lets you create all kinds of buttons, and you can customize them in just about any way you see fit, as shown in Figure 10-9. (The first two buttons are standard buttons defined using the options in Field Properties. The last two are icons imported into the document as buttons.) You can use the Field Properties options to create simple buttons, or you can import images to use as button icons. Although you can define buttons in all your forms, they make sense only with forms designed for electronic submission and for creating interactivity. Buttons serve no purpose I can think of for a form designed to be filled out and printed.

You create buttons similarly to other form objects:

1. **Select the Form tool.**

2. **Draw a rectangle to hold the button.**

3. **When you've finished drawing your button, release the mouse button.**

    Exchange displays the Field Properties dialog box.

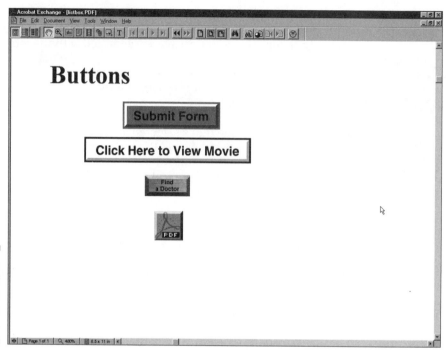

Figure 10-9:
Examples of
buttons
created in
Exchange.

4. Define the button's appearance and action.

The primary differences between buttons and other fields are that you
have much wider control over the button's appearance and buttons
should always be associated with some sort of action.

Figure 10-10 shows the Button Options tab of the Field Properties dialog box.
From here, you control the overall appearance of the button itself, such as
whether the button face displays text (such as *Submit Form*), or an icon, or
text and an icon. From the Appearance tab, you can further control a
button's appearance, such as outline color, background color, font, type
size, and type color.

Following are the selections on the Button Options tab that are different
from those associated with other form objects.

Highlight: Selects the overall look of the button, whether it is a beveled, 3-D
pushbutton (Push); a flat, solidly outlined button (Outline); or an indented
button (Inset). You would use the None option to create a flat, text-only
button or when using an icon for a button.

Figure 10-10:
Use this
section of
the Field
Properties
dialog
box to
define the
appearance
of your
buttons.

Layout: Chooses whether a button contains text, an icon, or both. When using text and an icon, the various options on the Layout list control placement of the text in relation to the icon.

Appearance when UP: Controls the appearance of the button in its up, or un-pushed, position. Use the text field to type the text that you want to appear on the button. If you select any Icon options under Highlight, click on the Icon button to retrieve the image you want to use as an icon. For a description of how to use icons on buttons, see the sidebar "How to make fancy buttons with icons," later in this chapter.

Appearance when PUSHED: Controls what appears on the button face when the button is pushed, or clicked (in the down position). For example, you can type *Submitted* in the text field. When your users click the button, the button changes from *Submit Form* to *Submitted*. You can also get cute by placing messages such as *Congratulations!, Whew! You're Finished,* or *You Blew It Now.* You can use icons for this option, so that users get a different icon when they click the button than the one displayed when the button is up. For a description of how to use icons on buttons, see the sidebar "How to make fancy buttons with icons."

How to make fancy buttons with icons

You can use almost any computer graphic for a button icon. Think twice, however, about using large photographs or other intricate images, unless you want some big buttons. You'll have better luck using small, simple images, like those on the Acrobat Reader and Exchange button bars.

To use an image as a button, you must first convert it to a PDF file with the File menu's Import command in Exchange, as described in Chapter 7. You can import all the icons you want to use into one file, and then save the file. Then use the Field Properties dialog box to import the icon. To place an icon on a button, follow these steps:

1. **Select the Form tool, and Draw a rectangle to hold your button.**

2. **When you're finished drawing, release the mouse button, and the Field Properties dialog box appears.**

3. **Click the Button Options tab, and in the Type list, select Button.**

4. **In the Highlight list, select None.**

   This gives you blank button, allowing you to place the icon without any bevels or insets. If you want to place on icon on a beveled button, you can set the highlight to Bevel.

5. **Make sure that the Border, Width, Style, and Background Color options in the Appearance section of the dialog box are turned off (or set to None), unless you want to include any of these options on your button.**

   You can place an icon on a background color, but you'll have to experiment to get the right combination.

6. **In the Layout list, select Icon Only.**

   If you want to create a button containing an icon and text, select one of the several other icon and text options, such as Icon Top, Text Bottom.

7. **In the Appearance when UP section, click on the Icon button.**

8. **Browse to the folder where you saved your icon PDF file, select the icon PDF file, and click Open.**

   The Select Appearance dialog box appears.

9. **If you imported more than one icon into the selected PDF, use the scroll bars and buttons next to the Sample display to go to the icon you want to use for the current button.**

   If only one image is in the file, scroll bars do not appear.

10. **Click OK.**

    The icon now displays in Field Properties, as shown in the figure.

11. **If you want to include a different icon for the pushed, or down, state of the button, click on the Icon button in the Appearance when PUSHED section, and repeat Steps 8–10 to select that icon.**

12. **In the Actions tab, set the Actions that you want for the button. Click OK.**

    The Field Properties dialog box closes.

13. **Resize and position the button as desired.**

    You're finished.

In Chapter 7, I said that you can't add graphics to your PDF pages. You may have figured out by now that there's an exception — you can add images in form fields. This provides a limited way to import graphics onto existing PDF pages; you can use it in a pinch when you need to slip in a small image.

Creating Forms for Filling Out and Printing

Practically all the forms you design for filling out and printing from Reader originate in a creator application (such as Word or PageMaker) or in forms software (such as Caere's OmniForm). You should lay out in the creator application as much of your document as possible, including the other graphics elements. Remember that Exchange lets you perform only minor touchups to your documents. You can't add anything else to your pages, except form objects. In fact, additional pages must be imported from other PDF files.

First, lay out the form's shell in a creator application

While designing your form in the creator application, leave spaces for the form objects, as I did in the Word document in Figure 10-11. In addition to instructions and labels, you should also include any boxes or tables. It's easier to create these objects in other applications (rather than in Exchange), and you can use the gridlines for guides when drawing your form fields.

When creating forms designed for printing, keep in mind that many of your users will not be printing in color. These users get a grayscale version of colored forms. Shy away from the temptation of creating forms with colored text and colored backgrounds, which can be difficult or impossible to read when printed on black-and-white printers. You can, however, safely use reverse type (white type on a black background), as shown in Figure 10-11. You can usually use white type on any colored background, as long as it's not too light a shade, and still get type that is easy to read. This design tip pertains also to the text fields, combo boxes, and other fields you create in Exchange.

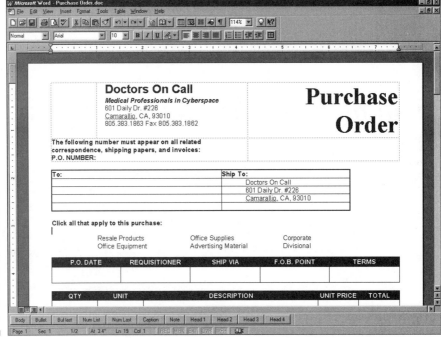

Figure 10-11:
A word processor document form destined to become a PDF.

Second, complete the form in Exchange

After you convert the form shell you created in the creator application to PDF and open it in Exchange, simply create the various fields as described earlier in this chapter. The type of fields you use depends on the type of information your form requests. In Figure 10-12, I used a combination of text fields and check boxes. In each field, I also included text telling the user what to type — the user simply selects the existing text and replaces it.

This is an easy form to use. Each field contains hints. The user clicks on the text with the Hand tool to select the current text, and then begins typing to replace it. To select from a list, the user clicks in the check boxes.

Notice in Figure 10-12 that I used the Courier typeface for the form fields. This font gives the form the appearance of having been filled out using a typewriter, differentiating the form data from the form itself.

In the SHIP VIA field, the user has only four shipping options. Instead of leaving it to chance that the user would know these options, I provided a list. When the user clicks on the SHIP VIA field, scroll buttons appear for scrolling through the list. But only the option the user chooses will print. You can be as creative as you want, as long as you don't confuse the user or the person who receives the printed form.

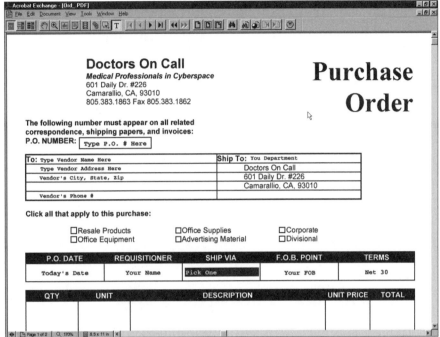

Figure 10-12:
A form
designed
for printing.
To use this
form, the
user clicks
in a field
and starts
typing.

Before leaving this discussion of printed forms, I want to make sure that I haven't left you with the conclusion that Acrobat forms have to be one kind or another. Your forms can perform double or even triple duty. You can use the same form for printable, electronic submission, and for interactivity. For example, I like to provide interactivity and fill-ins on the same form by including buttons to PDF pages that provide help for the user on the various fields in the form.

Using Forms to Add Interactivity to Your PDFs

Basically, when it comes to interactivity using form objects, we're talking buttons — buttons to navigate, buttons to invoke events, and so on. If you've been reading this book chapter by chapter, you already know a bunch about interactivity. I talked a lot about interactive hyperlinks as bookmarks, thumbnails, text, and graphics links in Chapter 6. This discussion of creating hyperactive links with form objects is merely an extension of that discussion.

If you have no idea what I'm talking about here, head on over to Chapter 6 and read it before going on with this section. Also, if your book just happened to fall open to this section, and you haven't read the rest of this chapter, especially the section on creating form elements in Exchange, go back a few pages and check out that stuff first.

You can use any of the form objects to create hot buttons in PDFs, but button objects work best and make the most sense. As you saw earlier in this chapter, you can either define your form buttons by using the various options in the Field Properties dialog box, you can import icons and use them as buttons, or you can use a combination of both.

Because I haven't yet described the juicy advanced stuff, such as movies (Chapter 12), sounds (Chapter 11), and electronic form submission (Chapters 15 and 17), this section looks at using buttons for document navigation.

Buttons are good for navigation links because they can communicate with the user, they make it easy to give the user a list of choices, and they can be used to stack several actions, invoking several events with a single button click.

Buttons make more sense

Buttons are better for navigational hot links because they speak loudly to the user. You see a button; you push it. Hyperlink text and hot graphics work well for seasoned computer users, but buttons are more meaningful to people. Period.

Buttons make it easier to provide choices

Buttons are more obvious than the hyperlink options discussed in Chapter 6. In addition, because they are form objects, you can add them to a PDF instead of having to plan for them when you lay out the document in the creator application.

Buttons containing icons provide you, the designer, with a wealth of design options. You can use arrows to prompt the user to move backward and forward in the document. You can use icons to return the user to the main menu, or to jump them to the Web or from one URL to another. The possibilities are limited only by your imagination.

Buttons can perform multiple actions

Until now, I've talked about using hyperlinks to move from one place in the document to the other. And I've teased you about multimedia events and other sophisticated events. As mentioned previously in the chapter, you can assign multiple mouse behaviors to a form object, and then add multiple actions to the mouse behavior. For example, you can have a sound play (a fanfare, perhaps) before a certain page appears.

Sound and movies are discussed in Chapters 11 and 12, respectively. Before you go on to those exciting topics, let me show you how to assign multiple events to a button:

1. **While defining your form object, go to the Actions tab of the Field Properties dialog box.**

   You can also go to the Actions tab after you define your form object by double-clicking on it with the Form tool.

2. **Select the mouse behavior for which you want to assign the actions.**

   Usually, you would choose Mouse Up, which is when you release the mouse button after clicking. Remember, you can assign more than one mouse behavior to a form object.

3. **Click Add.**

   The Add an Action dialog box appears.

4. **Select an action.**

   Depending on the action you choose, the Add an Action dialog box configures itself to help you set the action. If you choose Go to View, it gives you a list of views. If you choose Sound, the Add an Action dialog box provides Select Sound button. Click it to browse your system (or the network) for the desired sound file.

5. **Define the action.**

6. **Click Set Action.**

   You are returned to the Field Properties dialog box. A green light appears beside the mouse behavior you selected and the action shows up in the list, as shown in Figure 10-13.

7. **To add another action to the current mouse behavior: Click Add, select and configure the next action, and click Set Action.**

8. **To select another mouse action and assign actions to it, repeat Steps 2 to 7.**

9. **Click OK in the Field Properties dialog box.**

10. **To test your series of actions, select the Hand tool and click on the button.**

You can rearrange your series of actions by selecting the action you want to move in the Field Properties dialog box, and then using the Up and Down buttons to change its position in the list.

Figure 10-13:
An example
of a mouse
behavior
and a
corres-
ponding
action.

To change an action, select it and click Edit. To remove an action from the list, select the action and click Delete.

Well, you now have the basics about forms — and then some. Later, I tell you a lot more about using and creating forms.

Part III
Bringing PDFs to Life

"SOFTWARE SUPPORT SAYS WHATEVER WE DO, DON'T ANYONE START TO RUN."

In this part . . .

*N*ow that you know the basics of creating and enhancing PDFs, use the information in this part to bring your PDFs to life — by adding sound, movies, and searchable indexes. In addition to finding out how to include multimedia files in your PDFs, you also get a crash course in multimedia file formats and how to optimize them for fast playback. In addition, discover how indexes make your PDFs easier to use by providing users with the ability to search libraries of PDFs.

Chapter 11

Making Your PDFs Alive with Sound

• •

In This Chapter

▶ Finding out about sound technology

▶ Getting sound files

▶ Placing sound in your PDFs

• •

*I*n previous chapters, I describe basic PDF stuff: creating them, editing them, and making them interactive. Now it's time to get down to the exciting stuff, turning your PDFs into multimedia extravaganzas. This chapter describes how to make your PDFs alive with music, sound effects, and narratives.

Placing sound in PDFs is simple, as you'll see in a moment. You have several options for how and when a sound file plays, and setting these options is also easy. Digital sound technology (the sound played on computers), however, is not so simple. Before rushing headlong into the discussion of enhancing your PDFs with sound, you should get a basic understanding of how sound works on a computer.

Getting to Know Computer Sound Technology

Here's the part of computer books most people hate — the technical stuff. It's also the part where we computer nerds get to show off.

Before delving into this discussion of digital sound on a computer, I should say that if you're apprehensive, don't be. In most cases, using sound in PDFs is straightforward, especially if you use sounds prerecorded and sampled specifically for use on computers, such as CD-ROM clip media collections.

Sound technology *can* get a bit confusing when you try to record or capture sound (from music CDs, videotape, camcorders, and the like). It's a bit beyond the scope of this book to cover sound technology in such depth, but I provide the basics. If you plan to capture sound from other types of devices, you really should get a good book on multimedia technology, such as *Multimedia and CD-ROMS For Dummies,* 2nd Edition, by Andy Rathbone (published by IDG Books Worldwide, Inc.).

With that said, you'll look at sound technology from the following perspectives:

- Computer sound hardware
- The sound file formats supported by Acrobat
- Sound quality and file size

Computer sound hardware

To play sounds, your computer must have the appropriate sound board and speakers installed. Macintosh computers come sound-ready. If you want the sound to play with reasonable quality, however, you should attach a pair of stereo speakers to the sound port. Otherwise, you get only the tiny, weak, and hollow sound that squeaks out of the built-in Macintosh speaker.

You can buy speakers that work with both Mac and Windows machines at most computer stores. You can choose from ultra cheap ones to full-fledged surround sound stereo speakers that can make your computer emanate sound comparable to your home entertainment center. How much sound you need depends on the types of sounds you plan to use and the quality you need. (The higher the wattage rating on the speakers, the better the sound.) Keep in mind that you can use a top-of-the-line computer stereo system to create multimedia files that blow you away, but your users won't get anything close to the effect you do unless they have comparable sound systems.

Most Windows machines come sound-ready, too, but some don't — especially workstations for use in a company or corporate environment. And lots of computers that were sold before multimedia became the rage are still in use. If your computer is not ready to play sound, you need a sound card and speakers (and so will your PDF users). The good news is that you can get a good Windows sound system, such as a Creative Labs SoundBlaster Pro, for about a hundred bucks.

So how much sound system do you need? Well, what do you use your computer for? From an Acrobat perspective, the electronic documents you create will probably be designed to play on many types of computers. Most of your users will not have sophisticated sound systems. Although Acrobat *is* capable of creating multimedia titles, these types of documents are not its primary function. Full-fledged multimedia authoring programs, such as Macromedia Director, are better suited to creating games and other full-blown titles that require great sound systems for maximum effect. If you plan to use your sound system primarily for creating and playing back sound-enhanced PDFs, save your money and purchase a middle-of-the-road sound system. If you're into playing Doom, Ascend, and other multimedia extravaganzas, go all out.

Sound formats and Acrobat

Unlike other types of computer applications, sound files do not come in a lot of formats, which makes compatibility not a big issue. In addition, Acrobat supports only a few formats, most of which are cross-platform.

On the Macintosh, you can use

- QuickTime movie files
- System 7 sound files
- AIFF (Audio Interchange File Format) sound files
- Sound Mover (FSSD) files
- Microsoft Video for Windows WAV files

Acrobat automatically converts System 7 sound files and Sound Mover (FSSD) files to QuickTime movies.

With Windows, you can use

- AIF (Audio Interchange Format)
- Microsoft Video for Windows WAV files

If the sound file you want to use is not in one of these formats, you need a sound-editing application, such as Sound Fonic SoundForge, to convert the files to a supported format. The good news is that the conversion is straightforward. You simply save the file in another format, without any loss of data or quality.

Wait! Before you run out and buy a sound editor, check out the applications that came with your computer or sound card. Most provide competent sound-editing applications for making simple edits and converting sounds between various formats. SoundBlaster Pro, for example, comes with several nifty utilities for editing sound files and capturing sounds from music CDs.

How Acrobat uses sound files

When you import a sound into an Acrobat file, in most cases Exchange does not import the file directly into the PDF, as it does with text and graphics. Instead, a *pointer* is established so that the PDF remembers the location and name of the sound file. When a user invokes the sound, the file is loaded and played.

Acrobat is not unique in this approach to using multimedia files. Most multimedia applications treat sound and movie files this way. It keeps the size of the document, in this case the PDF, manageable. When you distribute the PDF, however, you must also distribute the sound file. And you must maintain the original file and folder structure.

Sound complicated? Well it can be if you don't do a little planning. Most multimedia authors approach this problem in one of two ways. If your PDF points to only a few multimedia files, simply copy them into the directory containing the PDF *before adding the sound to the PDF.* Then after you copy the PDF to a disk, a CD-ROM, or a network drive, make sure you copy the multimedia files with it.

For more complicated documents that contain pointers to several multimedia files (and even other PDFs), you can create a subordinate folder structure. For example, you can place your PDFs in a folder one level higher than the other supporting files, and then place the multimedia files in their own folders within the folder containing the PDFs. If you have lots of movies and lots of sounds, you may want to create separate folders for each type of file.

Confused? Check out Figure 11-1. I created the directory structure so that the PDF resides in a folder by itself, and the multimedia files are in subfolders. When I move the PDF to another disk, I copy the top folder in the structure; the subfolders come with it automatically, maintaining the folder structure.

If you are preparing PDFs to be distributed over a network, you'll probably use a different file structure. Most networks have separate folders for different types of files. The easiest way to maintain pointers on a network is to work on files saved on the network itself, rather than on your workstation. That way, the pointers are never changed. Chapter 17 takes an in-depth look at using PDFs on a network.

When working in Windows 95 or on a Mac, you may be tempted to use the convenient long file name conventions. Transferring long file names from platform to platform, however, is not foolproof (unless everyone is connected to the same network or over the Internet). For example, when Macs open files with long file names created on a Windows machine, the names are *truncated,* or chopped, to the DOS file name convention: 8 characters for the file name (and 3 characters for the extension). This can play havoc

Figure 11-1:
By saving your PDFs in top-level folders and supporting files in sub-folders, you prepare the document for distribution without disturbing file structures and pointers.

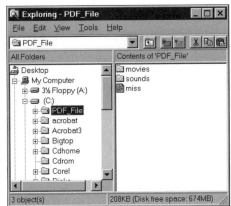

with your pointers. So, if your PDFs will be used on cross-platform (or Windows 3.x) machines, you should use DOS naming conventions. (Mac/OS System 7.6 users will be happy to know that this file naming problem is resolved between Macs and Windows 95 and NT.)

There is one exception to all this pointer business. When you use an action (discussed later in this chapter) to access a sound file, the sound is embedded in the PDF file (becoming part of the PDF file) in a cross-platform format that will play in Windows and on the Macintosh. On the Macintosh, you can embed QuickTime movies, System 7 sound files, AIFF sound files, Sound Mover (FSSD) files, and WAV files. With Windows, you can embed AIF and WAV files.

Balancing sound file size and quality

Most sound boards can produce 16-bit, 44.1 kHz audio — the same level of digital audio you get from a compact disc player. The 16-bit rating indicates how much data the board can store in each sound sampling. 8-bit sound is okay for voice, but you need 16-bit for the higher fidelity audio required for music. The 44.1 kHz rating refers to the number of times (44,100) per second that the sound board can process incoming or outgoing sound. Combined, these two measurements are known as the sound files *sample rate*. The higher the sample rate, the bigger the sound file.

Much of multimedia authoring, especially with Acrobat, doesn't require sound with the same quality as music CDs. 16-bit, 44.1 kHz sound creates huge sound files that work well for music and game special effects. Because these high-quality digital sound files are so big, they can hamper the overall speed and responsiveness of your PDF.

So, creating sounds for inclusion in your PDFs involves finding a balance between quality and file size. If you plan to only import sound effects and music from sound clip collections (of which there are many), don't worry about finding this balance. The vendor has already *resampled* the sound files for you so that they run optimally on most computers. If you plan on capturing your own sounds from a music CD or with a microphone (as discussed in the next section), you need to be mindful of sample rate and the size of your sound files.

Sound files are resampled in sound editing packages. (Several packages are available.) The settings at which you save your sound files are important. In Figure 11-2, I'm resampling a sound file in Creative Labs Studio Wave. I can change the Hz and the bits. A good rule is to resample voice-only files to 8-bit, 1,105 Hz. Resample music and sound effects to 16-bit, 1,105 Hz. If the sound quality degrades too much, though, try 22,050 Hz. Keep in mind that each step up in bit and Hz settings can greatly increase your file size.

Figure 11-2:
A dialog box from a sound editing program used to resample sound files.

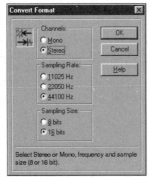

Most barbers or hair stylists would rather err on the side of cutting your hair too long than too short. You can always cut more off, but you can never put more hair back on. The same is true of sound files. Computers are pretty good at reducing data — such as reducing a 16-bit sound file down to 8 bits. But they aren't good at adding information to sound files, which is almost like creating something from nothing or guessing. So, when recording or capturing sound on your computer (discussed in the next section), record the sound at a high sample rate and reduce it to the desired rate, rather than trying to go the other way. This is also true of video and graphics files.

Anatomy of a sound file

Digital sound files, also known as wave (.WAV) files, are the most readily available type of audio clip media. Wave files are compatible with most sound cards on the market. The wealth of .WAV samples available means that you can find anything from "burp" to a piano concerto.

Wave files do have a few drawbacks: file storage requirements and variable sound quality. Consider yourself warned. A 30- to 60-second .WAV file can easily consume from 2 to 10 megabytes of disk space. Exactly how much disk space depends on three factors: sampling frequency, bit parameter, and stereo versus mono.

Sampling frequency: Digital audio is typically recorded at 44.1 kHz, 22.05 kHz, or 11.025 kHz. The higher the recording frequency, the better the sound quality. The highest frequency, 44.1 kHz, is the quality produced by your stereo's compact disc player. You should use it only when you need high-quality stereo sound, such as music. Voices and sound effects usually don't require the highest sample frequency.

You can save disk space by changing the sampling frequency. As you'll see in a later section on sound editing software, any sound editor worth its salt will let you resample the frequency.

Bit parameter: Audio clip media is generally available as both 8-bit and 16-bit samples. The higher the bit rate, the closer the sample is to approximating the original sound source. You have the best luck if you stick with 16-bit samples. The bit rate, like the sampling frequency, can be changed with sound editing software. You gain little or nothing, however, by trying to resample a file upward. Sound editors change the frequency sample and bit rates by removing data. They cannot improve quality by replacing data.

Stereo versus mono: Stereo audio samples demand as much as twice the disk space than a mono audio clip. Again, the question is what quality of audio clip do you need?

Obtaining Sound Files

You can find sound files to include in your PDFs in a variety of places. This section is a brief introduction to the most common places where designers get their sounds. These venues are: from clip media collections, by recording voice with a microphone, from CD-audio, and by separating sound tracks from digital video.

Clip media

Clip media consists of any ready-to-use audio, video, or animation clips, as well as royalty-free graphics images. In other words, you don't have to create it yourself — someone else already did if for you.

You can get clip media from a variety of sources, namely CD-ROM collections, floppy disk clip art collections, the Internet, on-line services such as CompuServe and America Online, and bulletin board services. Also, most image editing, video editing, and multimedia authoring programs come with collections of clip media. CorelDRAW!, for example, ships with about 18,000 drawings, photographs, sound files, and animation files.

Sounds recorded with a microphone

Whether you use Windows or a Mac, your computer is most likely equipped to record voice annotations from a microphone. In fact, most Mac systems and many Windows machines come with microphones. You can use Windows Sound Recorder or set up your sound recordings using the Monitors and Sound Control Panel on your Mac. You can also mix music and sound effects on both platforms with relative ease and without purchasing any new software.

The quality of the voice recording is greatly affected by the quality of the microphone. Unfortunately, the microphones that come with most computers are not up to the task of making quality voice recordings. So, if you plan on recording voice annotations for your PDFs, hop down to the local Radio Shack and buy yourself a good microphone. (Ask them to let you test it first on one of their computers.)

CD-audio

CD-audio is just what it sounds like, capturing snippets of music from a CD. Both Windows and Mac machines come with software for recording sound from a CD-ROM drive to your hard disk. In Windows, you can use Sound Recorder and CD Player. On a Mac, you can use Apple CD Player. You have better luck, however, with a third-party sound recording utility that lets you control recording sample rates and frequencies, such as WaveStudio from Creative Labs.

Before you capture and distribute sounds in your PDFs, check out the copyright laws. Most music CDs are copyrighted to either the publishing company, the artist, or both. Get permission, or run the risk of getting into big trouble.

Sound tracks separated from digital movie files

Editing digital video is way beyond the scope of this book, but I wanted you to at least know about this valuable resource. To capture video on a computer, you need additional hardware and some kind of record and playback device, such as a camcorder or a VCR. After the video is digitized (saved on your hard disk), you can use a video editor, such as Adobe Premiere, to lift the sound track out of the video, as I'm doing in Figure 11-3.

Enhancing Your PDFs with Sound

Adding sounds to PDFs is very easy. During the following discussion, keep in mind that Acrobat treats sounds and movies similarly. In fact, you point to sounds with the Movie Annotation tool. (The one that looks like a filmstrip.)

Figure 11-3: In this example I'm taking the sound track from a digital video for placement in a PDF.

Sound track in this video

You can add sounds to your PDFs as either annotations or actions. Annotations are invoked when you click in the rectangular box you create when adding the movie with the Movie Annotation tool. Actions are set with the Link tool, the Form tool, a bookmark property, or a set page action. (If you don't know what any of these objects are, see Chapter 10 for a discussion of form objects, and Chapter 6 for a discussion of the others.)

Embedding sounds with the Movie Annotation tool

Using the Movie Annotation tool is a lot like using the Link tool and Form tool. The typical procedure is demonstrated in the following:

1. **Select the Movie Annotation tool.**

2. **Drag a box where you want the user to click to invoke the sound.**

3. **Release the mouse button.**

   The Open dialog box appears.

4. **Select the sound.**

5. **Click Open.**

   The Movie Properties dialog box appears, as shown in Figure 11-4.

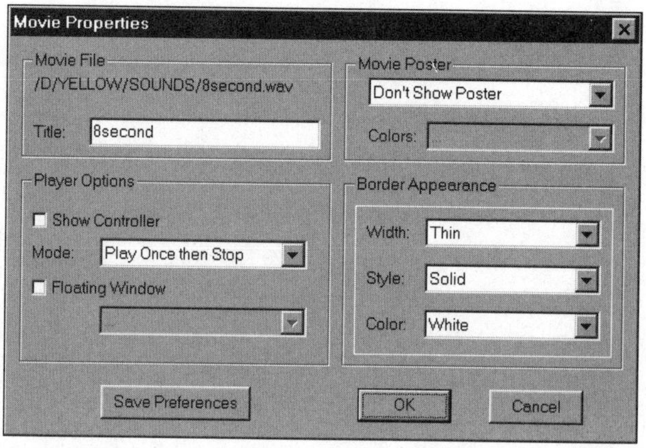

Figure 11-4:
Use the
Movie
Properties
dialog
box to
define the
properties
of the
sound.

6. **From Player Options, choose whether to show the controller, whether the movie should play once or loop, and whether the sound should play in a floating window.**

7. **Choose the border appearance for the sound link rectangle.**

Using the rectangle created with the Movie Annotation tool is not an efficient way to identify your sounds for users. The only change you can make to the appearance of the rectangle is to define its width and color. The user is presented with only an empty box. A much better way to create a visible sound file link is to drag the Movie Annotation tool around an identifying object, such as an icon or text that identifies the placement of the sound. In Figure 11-5, for example, I created a graphics button, and then dragged the Movie Annotation tool around it.

Most of the options in the Movie Properties dialog box pertain more to movies than to sounds. Some, however, are pertinent to both. Let's take a look at the options in this dialog box that help you control the behavior of sounds.

Title: Here's an easy one. The Title field simply shows the name of the sound file. You can change the sound file (either get a different sound or the sound's properties) by double-clicking the Movie Annotation tool on the Movie Annotation rectangle or on the rectangle you drew when placing a sound.

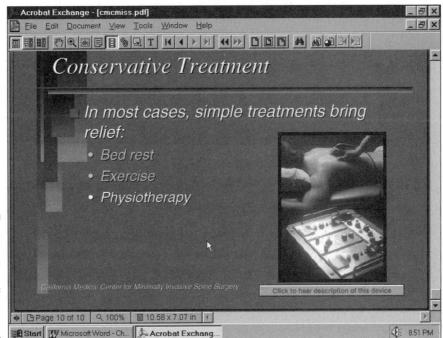

Figure 11-5:
The graphic identifies the existence of a sound file to the user.

Show Controller: The controller is a small bar at the bottom of the Movie Annotation rectangle that lets the user control when the sound plays. To play the sound, the user simply clicks on the arrow button. When the sound is playing, the arrow changes to a box, which the user can use to stop the sound. To move to different points in the sound file before playing it, the user can use the slider. The slider is more effective with movies, as you'll see in the next chapter.

Mode: The options in the Mode list control how the sound plays. These options follow:

Play Once Then Stop: Does this one really need an explanation? The sound plays and that's that.

Play Once, Stay Open: This one is for use with the Show Controller option. When the sound finishes playing, the controller stays open, allowing the user to play the sound again if desired.

Repeat Play: Another term for this option is *loop.* The sound continues to play until the user clicks somewhere else in the document or goes to another page and view.

Back and Forth: This options pertains only to movies.

Setting sounds to play as actions

Actions are events that occur as the result of user input or another event, such as the display of a page. (To find out more, see Chapters 6 and 10.) You can set a sound as an action. For example, when the user clicks on a button or a form object, a sound could play.

Actions can also be stacked. In other words, one action occurs, and then another, and so on. You can, for example, play one sound file after another. Or you can have a sound play when the user clicks a button, and then have the document go to a destination.

You can define a sound action to several objects:

- Page action
- Bookmark
- Hyperlink
- Form object

The following sections look at how each works.

Playing a sound as a page action

You can assign a sound to a page action in two ways: The sound plays when a page appears or when you leave the page.

To set a sound as a page action, follow these steps:

1. **Go to the page where you want to set the page action.**

2. **Choose Document⇨Set Page Action.**

   The Page Actions dialog box appears, as shown in Figure 11-6. From here, you set the action and when it occurs.

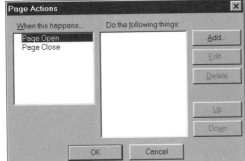

Figure 11-6:
Use this
dialog box
to set a
page
action.

3. **Choose whether you want the sound to play when the page opens (appears) or closes (the user goes to another page).**

   You can define a sound (or sounds) to both Page Open and Page Close, if you want.

4. **Click Add.**

   The Add an Action dialog box appears.

5. **Select the Sound action.**

   The dialog box now has a Select Sound button.

6. **Click the Select Sound button.**

   The Open dialog box appears.

7. **Find and select the sound on your system (or on a network drive).**

8. **Click OK in the Open dialog box.**

   Exchange returns to the Add an Action dialog box.

9. Click Set Action.

The Page Actions dialog box shows your new action and the page behavior it is associated with.

10. Define another action, or click OK to return to the document.

You can open and edit your page actions at any time, as follows:

1. Return to the page for which you are changing the action.

2. Choose Document⇨Set Page Action.

3. To delete a page action, select it in the list and click Delete.

4. To change the order of actions (when several actions are defined for the same page), select an action, and the use the Up and Down buttons to change its position in the list.

5. Click OK to close the dialog box.

Playing a sound from a bookmark

Unlike page actions, actions for bookmarks can't be stacked. A bookmark can do only one thing when the user clicks on it. Usually, the bookmark action is to go to a specific destination. You can, however, define bookmarks to play sounds.

To play a sound from a bookmark follow these steps:

1. Click the icon for the bookmark.

2. Right-click the bookmark. (On a Mac, go to the next step.)

3. Choose Properties from the pop-up menu. (On a Mac, press Cmd+I or choose Edit⇨Properties.)

The Bookmark Properties dialog box appears.

4. In the Type list, select Sound.

This changes the dialog box to work with sounds, as shown in Figure 11-7.

5. Click Select Sound.

The Open dialog box appears.

6. Find and select the sound you want to assign to the bookmark.

7. Click OK in the Open dialog box.

8. Click OK in the Bookmark Properties dialog box.

You return to the document.

Now, when your users click on the bookmark, they hear the sound. (Bookmarks are discussed in Chapter 6.)

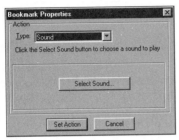

Figure 11-7:
After you select Sound as the action, the dialog box displays a Select Sound button.

Playing a sound from a hyperlink

In Chapter 6, you can find out about creating hyperlinks for navigating through PDFs and setting destinations. You can use hyperlinks also to set actions, such as playing sounds. You can assign only one action to a hyperlink; you can't stack actions as you can with page actions and form objects (discussed next).

To set a sound to play when a user clicks a hyperlink (text or a graphic object), follow these steps:

1. **Select the Link tool (the tool with the chain).**

2. **Draw a rectangle around the text or graphic object that you want to make hot.**

   You should differentiate the hyperlink object in some way, such as with different colored text or an obvious sound icon, so that the user knows to click it to play the sound.

3. **Release the mouse button.**

   The Create Link dialog box appears.

4. **Under the Action section, select Sound from the Type list.**

5. **Click Select Sound.**

   The Open dialog box appears.

6. **Find and select the sound.**

7. **Click Open.**

8. **Click Set Link.**

   The Link Properties dialog box closes, and you are returned to the document.

When your users click the hyperlink, the sound plays. To redefine the hyperlink to play a different sound or invoke a different action, double-click on the link rectangle with the Link tool, as described in Chapter 6.

Playing a sound with a form object

Form objects and setting form actions are discussed in detail in Chapter 10. Rather than going over these topics again here, this section covers form actions only in their relation to sound.

Form objects can be associated with several actions. You can also assign the actions to four separate mouse movements: Mouse Up, Mouse Down, Mouse Enter, and Mouse Exit.

To associate a sound with a form object:

1. **Either draw a new form object with the Form tool, or double-click the Form tool on an existing form object.**

   The Field Properties dialog box appears.

2. **Click the Actions tab.**

3. **In the When This Happens list, select a mouse movement.**

4. **Click the Add button.**

   The Add an Action dialog box appears. This is identical to the dialog box of the same name discussed earlier under in the portion of this section about Page Actions.

5. **In the Type list, select Sound.**

6. **Click Select Sound.**

   The Open dialog box appears.

7. **Find and select the sound.**

8. **Click Open in the Open dialog box.**

   You return to the Add an Action dialog box.

9. **Click Set Action.**

   You return to the Field Properties dialog box and your list of mouse movements and actions.

10. **Define other sounds and mouse behaviors, or click OK to close the dialog box.**

This description of assigning sounds to buttons is short and sweet. If you don't know how to use Field Properties, go back and read Chapter 10. Then this section will make a lot more sense to you.

Chapter 12

Making Your PDFs More Interesting with Digital Movies

· ·

In This Chapter

▶ Finding out about digital video

▶ Discovering how Acrobat uses digital video

▶ Adding movie annotations to your PDFs

· ·

*W*hether you're using Acrobat to convert your documents to a portable file format or to create multimedia titles or presentations, you may want to add movies to your PDFs for a number of reasons. In converted documents, movies can make the document more fun and interesting. For example, you may include a movie showing a procedure discussed in the text or instructions on how to use the PDF. In multimedia titles, you can use movies for all kinds of things, such as process descriptions and demonstrations.

Adding movies to PDFs is relatively easy. Digital video, however, like digital sound technology, is not a simple subject, especially if you will be creating, capturing, and editing your own movies. It is far beyond the scope of this book to teach you how to capture and edit filmstrips. These tasks often require sophisticated hardware and software and a steep learning curve.

This book can, however, give you an overview of digital video technology — a few things to be aware of and to look out for. If you decide to tackle creating digital movies on your computer, find a book on the subject. I wrote one called *Multimedia Authoring Workshop* (published by Sybex).

The following section looks at digital video. Then you find out how to include movie annotations in your PDFs.

Everything You Never Wanted to Know about Digital Video

There are several types of digital video file formats, but Acrobat supports only two: Microsoft Video for Windows and Apple QuickTime. Undoubtedly, the reason Adobe restricts the types of videos you can add to your PDFs is to ensure cross-platform compatibility. This means, however, that movies you have or create in other formats must be converted to one of these two formats.

Most film editing software, such as Adobe Premiere and Corel Lumiere, is expensive ($500 or more). In addition, the hardware for capturing video from analog video devices, such as camcorders, VCRs, and televisions, can also be costly.

Digital video formats

There was a time when the type of video file format you used depended largely on the platform you worked in. Microsoft Video for Windows (AVI) files worked best in Windows, and Apple QuickTime files worked best on Mac systems.

Nowadays, however, QuickTime is a universal, or cross-platform, format. QuickTime is native to Macintosh System 7 software. In addition, when you install Acrobat (or when your users install Reader to view your PDFs) on a Windows machine, QuickTime is also installed.

So, when you create PDFs for cross-platform applications, you should convert all your movies to QuickTime. The following sections take a closer look at digital video file formats.

AVI

AVI (Audio Video Interleaved) is a type of video that alternates bits of audio and video data one after the other to create a complete digital movie clip on Windows machines. The AVI process allows video frames to be stored and played back efficiently at speeds supported by hard disks or CD-ROM drives. AVI is part of the Windows 95 operating system, and you can easily add it to Windows 3.1.

QuickTime

QuickTime movies, which are cross-platform compatible, are a type of video clip media that uses a technology known as *scaleable compression*. Scaleable compression synchronizes audio data with video data using a specialized decompression schedule. (Compression is discussed in the "Anatomy of a digital video clip" sidebar.) QuickTime is part of MacOS, is easily installed in Windows, and is popular on the World Wide Web.

Animation files

Animation files, which are also considered to be a type of video clip media, create motion by displaying still frames in quick succession. They are usually used for cartoons and animated diagrams.

Animation files are typically identified with the .FLI or .FLC extension, a standard developed by Autodesk for use with Autodesk Animator. You may, however, also come across animation files with the .MMM or .DIR extension, which means they were created in Macromedia Director. In addition, other programs, such as Gold Disk Animation Interface, have their own proprietary formats.

So many formats and Acrobat supports only two? The good news is that most of these animation programs have the capability to convert their native formats to QuickTime or AVI. But you almost always need the program itself to make the conversion.

Animation files are a rich source of movies for any type of multimedia project. In addition to cartoons and diagrams, this type of animation is also used in *morphing,* or changing one object into another, usually to depict some sort of process, such as a young face slowly changing into an older one.

3-D modeling clips

Animation clips created by 3-D modeling programs, such as Macromedia Extreme 3D, RayDream, or Corel Dream 3D, are another important resource for movies. Figure 12-1 shows an example of a 3-D model.

This type of animation is great for displaying objects in 3-D space, such as rotating a widget so that the viewer can see it from all sides. They make highly impressive moving medical diagrams and depictions of the inner workings of a machine or other device. Most of today's 3-D modeling programs allow you to save the animation as a QuickTime movie.

Figure 12-1:
A 3-D
model
created in a
modeling
application.

Anatomy of a digital video clip

Here's a tangent into the super-nerdy: digital video technology and terminology. Getting optimal digital video on your computer calls for a balance of file size and quality. The most important variables affecting file size and quality for movies are frame rate, frame size, color depth, compression, and image quality.

Frame rate: Video delivery relies on the perception of motion. When a series of still images is displayed in rapid succession, the human eye perceives them as continuous motion. In the television and film industries, the presentation of a rapid succession of still images is measured in frames per second, or FPS.

Standard television broadcasts are delivered at between 25 and 30 frames per second. The film standard of delivery is about 24 frames per second. Consequently, each still image in a series of images that composes a video segment is termed a *frame*. *Frame rate* is the number of frames per second required to create the illusion of motion to the human eye.

The minimum frame rate for digital video is 15 frames per second. Videos played at less than 15 frames per second produce a noticeable jerkiness in the playback quality of the captured segment.

Frame size: The physical size of the video on your monitor is called its *frame size*. Most computer display systems are set to deliver a screen frame display of about 640 x 480 pixels. Although it is possible to capture and play video at this resolution, most hardware used to replay a video segment can't accommodate a video clip of this size. Attempts to do so result in slow, jerky, low-quality playback and data loss.

A practical frame size for digital video is in the range of 160 x 120 pixels to 320 x 240 pixels. The most common practice is to capture at the large frame size and use your video editing software to resize the frames downward. You won't have much success trying to go from smaller frames to larger frames because computers aren't very good at guessing where to add data.

Color depth: Most video capture equipment can acquire video segments in 8-bit, 16-bit, and 24-bit color (or 256-colors, thousands of colors, and millions of colors, respectively). The rule here is to capture high and reduce. For example, capturing a video segment in 24-bit color provides the best color sample possible, but you often must reduce the segment to 8-bit in the editing process for a manageable file size.

Image quality: Another aspect that affects file size is image quality, which is actually a combination of color depth and compression. As with color depth, it takes a lot of data to reproduce crisp, clear pictures, frame after frame. Creating clips at manageable file sizes and acceptable playback rates is a balancing act. Video editing software allows you to reduce file size by compromising picture quality. With some image editing software, such as Adobe Premiere, you can adjust both compression and color depth in one Image Quality setting.

Compression and decompression: In addition to controlling file size by adjusting frame rate, color depth, and image quality, you can make movie clip files smaller also by using compression and decompression routines built into your video editing software.

Compression and decompression (CODEC) can be understood in terms of the relationship between method and mechanism. *Compression* is a method that facilitates the use of captured digital video segments for desktop video production. *Decompression* refers to the method used to play the clips on the desktop. CODEC is the mechanism used to implement these methods. Each of these concepts is discussed in the following paragraphs.

Compression methods: Working with captured digital video requires the use of compression techniques during the editing process to enhance the quality of the playback image. The two compression methods in common use are the lossless method and the lossy method.

The *lossless method* of compression keeps all the data from the captured video file intact. The image quality of the digital file is high, but the file size is large. This method is called *lossless* because when the file is decompressed, all data in the file is intact.

Typically, lossless data compression can make a file as much as half its original size. A minute of video can take up several megabytes of disk space, however, so 50 percent helps but does not solve the video file size dilemma. The lossless method is preferable when creating video for large storage mediums, such as CD-ROM. But even then, you won't be able to create long clips because you won't have room for the rest of your title.

For most multimedia applications, lossy is the preferable method. The *lossy method* uses compression algorithms to eliminate specific data from the captured video file. The image quality of the resulting digital file may be degraded, but the file size is also reduced.

This is not as bad as it sounds. Many clips contain a lot more data than is necessary to play and display well on a computer display system. For example, 24-bit images contain a lot of unnecessary repeated data and display a lot of subtle color differences people cannot perceive. It does little to image quality to drop this data from the file.

The lossy method is capable of compression rates as high as 100:1. For example, you could compress a 5MB file down to 50K. This is a radical squeeze, though, that degrades the image quality. How much compression a clip can stand depends on the clip and the level of degradation you can live with. If you are new to video editing, you'll probably need to experiment with compression to find the right balance between quality and file size.

Compression can be a complicated subject, but video editing software such as Adobe Premiere attempts to make it easy. The figure shows a dialog box from Adobe Premiere for adjusting the compression and image quality of a digital video.

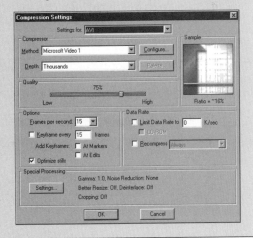

Getting digital videos for your PDFs

As with sound files (discussed in Chapter 11), movies for your PDFs can be obtained in plenty of ways. Some methods, such as using files from clip media collections, are easy and straightforward. Others, such as capturing and editing your own filmstrips, require special equipment and software, as well as technical know-how. Which resources you use depends on the type of clips you need and how much time and money you're willing to spend developing movies for your PDFs.

 A number of movie formats are available, but the most common formats in multimedia video editing are Microsoft Video (AVI) and Apple QuickTime. It's beyond the scope of this book to define and discuss them all. A good rule is to use AVI files for titles designed to play back on Windows machines and QuickTime for Mac systems. Also, because QuickTime can play on both platforms (with some preparation in your video editing software), you should use it when designing titles for playback on both platforms.

Using clip media collections

Digital video collections on CD-ROM, online services (such as AOL and CompuServe), and the Internet are not as prominent as sound clip media collections. I know of two reasons for the scarcity of digital video collections. One, a lot people don't working with digital video on their computers, although this technology is becoming more popular. Two, using a video in a document usually calls for specific content. Unlike stock photography images, which can depict people and other subjects in all kinds of meaningful situations, digital video should be about the subject at hand. The movie should be there for a good reason (other than novelty).

Still, if you want some canned digital videos, search around on the World Wide Web. Be mindful about copyrights, though. A good source for quality movies and animations is CASCOM International (615-242-8900; Fax: 615-256-7890).

Capturing and editing your own clips

By far, the most effective videos for inclusion in your PDFs are those that you (or somebody else in your organization) capture and edit. It is also the most complicated, time-consuming, and expensive way to get clips. Most computers are not equipped to capture video from analog devices (such as camcorders, television, or VCRs). They require special video capture boards, such as Creative Labs' VideoBlaster for Windows. Several boards are available for the Mac, or you can purchase an AV (audio-video) Mac, which comes equipped with the hardware and software for capturing and editing video.

Capture boards can cost a few hundred to a few thousand dollars. For PDF purposes, you can get by with a low-priced board. Note that Macs are much better at capturing and processing digital video than Windows machines. If you'll be buying a computer for this enterprise, check out Apple's line of AV Macs.

In addition to hardware, you'll also need video editing software. Most video capture boards come with rudimentary software for video capturing and resampling. But you need something more powerful, such as Adobe Premiere or Corel Lumiere, to add transitions and create special effects.

How Acrobat Uses Digital Movies

To play movies, your computer must have the appropriate video drivers installed. With Windows, you need Apple's QuickTime 2.0 or later or Microsoft's Video for Windows software. On the Macintosh, you need QuickTime 2.0 or later.

Unlike graphics and text, movie files (and sound files) are not embedded in the PDF. Instead, when you add a movie, Exchange creates a pointer to (that is, remembers) where the movie is saved on your system or network drive. You can add pointers in your PDF documents to movies in the Apple QuickTime format or the Windows AVI format. QuickTime movies can be played back in Windows or on a Macintosh. AVI movies can be played back only in Windows.

As mentioned in Chapter 11, Acrobat is not unique in this approach to using multimedia files. Most multimedia applications, such as multimedia authoring software, treat sound and movie files this way. Movie files are usually huge. Importing them into the PDF would make for humongous, unruly PDF files. The pointer approach, however, causes a different problem. When you distribute the PDF, you must make sure that you also distribute the sound file, so you must maintain the original file and folder structure.

You can solve this problem in two ways. If your PDF points to only a few movie files, simply copy them into the directory containing the PDF *before adding the movie to the PDF*. Then after you copy the PDF to a disk, a CD-ROM, or a network drive, make sure you copy the movie files with it. For more complicated documents that contain pointers to several multimedia files (and even other PDFs), you can create a subordinate folder structure.

You can place your PDFs in a folder one level higher than the other supporting files, and then place the multimedia files in their own folders within the folder containing the PDFs. If you have lots of movies and lots of sounds, you may want to create separate folders for each type of file.

Confused yet? Look back in Chapter 11 at Figure 11-2. I created the directory structure so that the PDF itself resides in a folder by itself, and the multimedia files are in subfolders. When I move the PDF to another disk, I simply copy the top folder in the structure; the subfolders come with it, maintaining the folder structure.

Adding Movies to Your PDFs

If you read the chapter on sound (Chapter 11), you already have a good idea about how to put movies in your PDFs. You use the same tool — the Movie Annotation tool — for both sound and movies. You can also assign movies to actions, such as page actions, form objects, bookmarks, and hyperlinks. In this section, you look at both methods.

Adding a movie with the Movie Annotation tool

To place movies on your pages, you use the Movie Annotation tool (the one that looks like a filmstrip). You can use the tool in one of two ways.

To add a movie to a PDF, follow these steps:

1. **Click the Movie Annotation tool on the spot where you want to place the movie.**

   or:

   Draw a rectangle with the tool over an area on a page where you want users to click to start the movie.

   Use the first method to place the movie in a box for playing directly on the page. Use the second method for creating hot links, such as text or a graphic, that your users click on to launch the movie.

   Either method displays the Open dialog box.

2. **Go to the drive and folder on your system or network drive that contains the movie file.**

3. **Select the movie.**

4. **Click Open.**

   The Movie Properties dialog box appears, as shown in Figure 12-2.

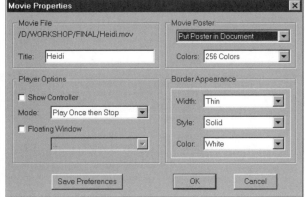

Figure 12-2:
This
dialog box
controls the
appear-
ance and
behavior of
the movie
window.

5. Define the overall appearance and behavior of your movie window.

Refer to the description of the options in the Movie Properties dialog box in the next few paragraphs for information on how to complete this step.

6. Click OK after you're finished.

You return to the PDF page.

Following is a description of the options in the Movie Properties dialog box.

Show Controller: The controller is a small VCR-like panel at the bottom of the window. See Figure 12-3. Users can use it to control how the movie plays. The first button turns the sound on and off. The second is a start and stop toggle button. The slider in the movie lets users go to specific places in the movie. And the last two buttons are rewind and fast forward controls, respectively.

Mode: Use the options in this list to control how the movie plays. Play Once then Stop does just what it says. Play Once, Stay Open is used with Show Controller; when the movie plays through once, the controller remains visible. Repeat Play (loop) plays the movie over and over until the user clicks somewhere else or goes to another page. Back and Forth plays the movie forward and backward repeatedly.

Floating Window: A *floating window* plays the movie in a window separate from the PDF page, as shown in Figure 12-4. This option is used most often when you create a text or graphics hot link for launching the movie, rather than when you place the movie in its own box on the PDF page.

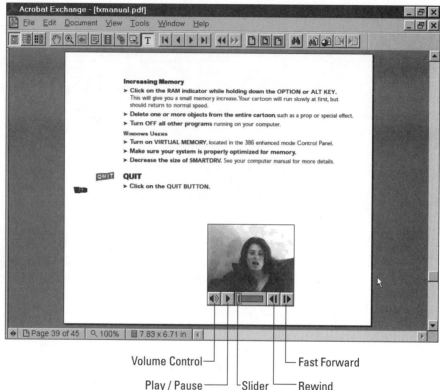

Figure 12-3:
A movie
with a
controller.

Volume Control

Play / Pause — Slider — Rewind

Fast Forward

When you choose the Floating Window option, the list below it becomes available, allowing you to designate a size for the floating window in pixels. In most cases, you'll want to use the default setting, which is the pixel size saved in the movie file itself. Making the movie window smaller or larger than the actual size of the movie usually degrades the movie's quality.

Movie Poster: The *movie poster* is the image that fills the movie rectangle on the page. The poster, which is usually the first frame of the movie, is displayed when the movie is not playing.

There are two lists for this option. The first list defines the contents of the rectangle. You can choose no poster, which leaves a blank rectangle. Use this option when creating hot links from objects other than the movie poster, such as a graphic or text. The other two options fill the rectangle with the first frame of the movie.

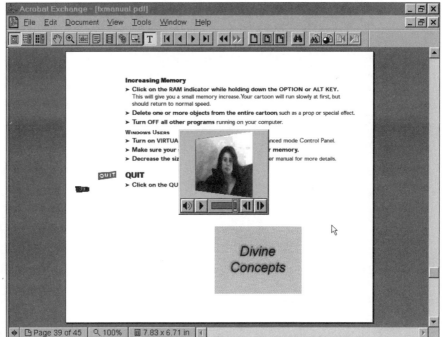

Figure 12-4:
An example
of a movie
playing in a
floating
window.

The second list, Colors, lets you choose the color depth of the poster. Depending on the movie's color palette (the color depth the movie is saved with), you can choose 256 colors, Thousands of Colors, or Millions of Colors. The higher the color depth, the higher the quality of the poster image and the longer it takes to display. Note, though, that it does no good to choose, say, Millions of Colors, if the movie is only 256 colors. You'll still get a 256-color poster.

Border Appearance: As with hypertext links (Chapter 6) and form objects (Chapter 10), you can create borders around your movie annotation rectangles. Use this option to define the color and appearance of the border.

Borders are handy for setting off the movie poster. When you use the Movie Annotation tool to create hot text and graphics links for starting movies, however, you may want to set the Width option (under Border Appearance) to Invisible. Otherwise, you'll get an empty box around the hyperlink, which is not a cool design.

Adding a movie as an action

As with sounds (discussed in Chapter 11), you can add movies to various actions. In fact, setting sounds as actions is similar to setting movies as actions. (If you are unfamiliar with actions, check out Chapters 6, 10, and 11.) The primary difference between using sound files versus movie files as actions is that the movie must already be placed on the PDF page where you want the action to execute.

You can define a movie action to several objects:

- ✔ Page action
- ✔ Bookmark
- ✔ Hyperlink
- ✔ Form object

The following sections take a look at each of these.

Playing a movie as a page action

You can assign a movie to a page action in one of two ways. The movie plays when a page displays, or the movie plays when you leave the page.

To set a movie as a page action, follow these steps:

1. **Go to the page where you want to set the page action.**

2. **Add one or more movies to the page.**

   For more information, see the section "Adding Movies with the Movie Annotation Tool."

3. **Choose Document⇨Set Page Action.**

   The Page Actions dialog box shown in Figure 12-5 appears. From here you set the action and when it occurs.

4. **Choose whether you want the movie to play when the page opens (appears) or closes (the user goes to another page).**

   You can define a movie (or movies) to both Page Open and Page Close, if you want.

5. **Click Add.**

   The Add an Action dialog box appears.

6. **In the Type list, select Movie.**

   The dialog box now has a Select Movie button.

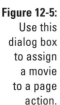
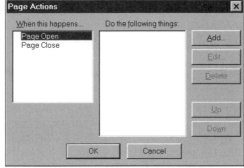

Figure 12-5:
Use this
dialog box
to assign
a movie
to a page
action.

7. **Click the Select Movie button.**

   The Movie Action dialog box shown in Figure 12-6 appears.

Figure 12-6:
Here's
where to
choose a
movie and
set its
action.

8. **In the Select Movie list, select the movie that you want to assign to this page action.**

   If more than one movie is assigned to this page, they are all listed in the Select Movie list.

   If you want the movie to play when a page is displayed but do not want a visible movie rectangle on the page itself, set the Movie Poster to Don't Show Poster and the border width to Invisible when you add the movie to the PDF.

9. **In the Select Operation list, select whether you want the movie to Play, Stop, Pause, or Resume playing as the result of this action.**

   Usually, you want the movie to play.

10. **Click OK.**

    Exchange returns to the Add an Action dialog box.

11. **Click OK.**

    The Page Actions dialog box shows your new action and the page behavior it is associated with.

12. **Define another action (by repeating Step 4 through Step 11), or click OK to return to the document.**

You can open and edit your page actions at any time by returning to the page and selecting Document⇨Set Page Action. To delete a page action, select it in the list and click Delete. When several actions are defined for the same page, you can change the order by selecting an action and then using the Up and Down buttons to change its position in the list.

Playing a movie from a bookmark

Unlike page actions, bookmark actions can't be stacked. You can have them do only one thing when the user clicks on them. Usually, the bookmark action is to go to a specific destination. However, you can define bookmarks to play movies.

To set a movie to play from a bookmark, follow these steps:

1. **Place the movie you want to play on the page where you want it to play, and then go to that page as described earlier in this chapter under "Adding Movies to Your PDFs."**

2. **Click on the icon for the bookmark.**

3. **Right-click on the bookmark, and select Properties from the pop-up menu. (On a Mac, click on the bookmark icon and then press Cmd+I.)**

    The Bookmark Properties dialog box appears.

4. **In the Type list, select Movie.**

    The dialog box changes to work with movies.

5. **Click on Select Movie.**

    The Movie Action dialog box appears.

6. **Select the movie you want to assign to the bookmark, and click OK.**

7. **Click OK in the Movie dialog box.**

8. **Click OK in the Bookmark Properties dialog box.**

    You return to the document.

When your users click on the bookmark, the movie plays. (Bookmarks are discussed in Chapter 6.)

Playing a movie from a hyperlink

Assigning movies to play hyperlinks is similar to creating navigation hyperlinks, as discussed in Chapter 6. Assigning movies to hyperlinks is also quite similar to assigning sounds to hyperlinks, as discussed in Chapter 11.

Remember, though, that you can assign only one action to a hyperlink. You can't stack actions as you can with page actions and form objects.

To set a movie to play when a user clicks a hyperlink (text or graphic object), follow these steps:

1. **Go to the page where you want the movie to play and place the movie.**

   For more information on placing movies, see "Adding Movies with the Movie Annotation Tool," earlier in this chapter.

2. **Select the Link tool.**

3. **Draw a rectangle around the text or graphic object that you want to make hot.**

   (A hyperlink object should be differentiated in some way — for example, use different colored text or an obvious sound icon — so that the user knows to click it to play the sound.)

   The Create Link dialog box appears, as shown in Figure 12-7.

Figure 12-7:
Use this
dialog box
to set
up your
hyperlinks
to play
movies.

4. In the Action section, select Movie in the Type list.

5. Click the Select Movie button.

The Movie Action dialog box appears.

6. Select the movie.

7. Click OK.

The Link Properties dialog box reappears.

8. Click Set Link.

You are returned to the document.

When your users click the hyperlink, the movie plays. To redefine the hyperlink to play a different movie or invoke a different action, double-click on the link rectangle with the Link tool, as described in Chapter 6.

Playing a movie by clicking a form object

Form objects and setting form actions are discussed in detail in Chapter 10, so I won't rehash these topics here. You can associate several actions to form objects, and you can also assign the actions to four separate mouse movements: Mouse Up, Mouse Down, Mouse Enter, and Mouse Exit.

To associate a movie with a form object, follow these steps:

1. Use the Movie Annotation tool to place the movie on the page where you want it to play.

2. Either draw a new form object with the Form tool, or double-click the Form tool on an existing form object.

The Field Properties dialog box appears.

3. Click the Actions tab.

4. In the When this happens list, select a mouse movement.

5. Click the Add button.

This displays the Add an Action dialog box, which is identical to the Add an Action dialog box discussed in "Playing a movie as a page action," at the beginning of this section.

6. In the Type list, select Movie.

The dialog box now has a Select Movie button.

7. Click the Select Movie button.

The Movie Action dialog box appears.

8. **In the Select Movie list, select the movie that you want to assign to this action.**

9. **Click OK.**

You return to the Add an Action dialog box.

10. **Click Set Action.**

You return to the Field Properties dialog box and your list of mouse movements and actions, as shown in Figure 12-8.

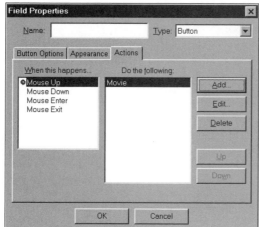

Figure 12-8:
After you define the movie, it appears in the Do the following list.

11. **You can either add other movies (or other actions) and mouse behaviors, as described throughout this chapter, or click OK to close the Field Properties dialog box.**

If you don't know how to use the Field Properties dialog box, check out Chapter 10. Then this section will make a lot more sense to you.

Good. Now you can put together what you discover in this chapter with Chapter 11 to create a multimedia title.

Chapter 13

Indexing with Acrobat Catalog

. . . .

In This Chapter

▶ Finding out about catalogs and indexing

▶ Cataloging and indexing your PDFs

▶ Preparing your PDFs for cataloging

▶ Maintaining your indexes

. . . .

*S*o far, the chapters in this book have been about working in one PDF — creating links and forms and adding multimedia events. In this chapter, you look at working with multiple PDFs with Acrobat Catalog.

When you create a catalog of PDFs, the index generated by the catalog allows Reader and Exchange users to find PDFs by various search criteria, known as *keywords* or *search terms*. The applications for cataloging are many, but the purpose for cataloging, regardless of the application, is to help users find PDFs containing specific information quickly.

As with so many aspects of working with Acrobat, you'll be surprised how easy cataloging your PDFs can be. Isn't it wonderful when programmers turn seemingly difficult tasks into easy ones? Even us computer geeks can appreciate when simplicity really is bliss.

The Importance of Cataloging

No. This section doesn't describe how to use Acrobat to create a product catalog, such as the humongous Sears product listing. The J.C. Penney catalog, however, could certainly be part of an Acrobat catalog.

First, it's time to define some terms. I'm sure you know what the words *catalog* and *index* mean — in the traditional sense. Leave it to computer nerds to take traditional concepts and bend them, forcing them to apply in some abstract way to computer technology. In Acrobat-speak, a *catalog* is a collection of PDFs. Simple enough, right? Well, no. They don't really become a catalog until you index them with Catalog.

An index, then, is what? This is a little more complicated. (If you've worked with database applications, you may know something about indexes.) Basically, an index is nothing more than a file (or a series of related files) containing lists of all the words in all the PDFs in a catalog. Included also in the index lists are the locations of the words in the catalog PDFs as well as the PDFs that contain the indexed words and where the PDFs are located.

The purpose of an index is to match words with the PDFs that contain them. When users search an index for a word or phrase, they are presented with a list of all the PDFs that contain that word. In Figure 13-1, for example, I am searching for the word *employee*. Figure 13-2 shows the results of the search — the PDFs in the catalog that contain the word I searched for.

Figure 13-1:
I'm
searching
indexed
PDFs on my
drive that
contain
the word
employee.

Figure 13-2:
Here are
the files in
the catalog
that contain
the search
word.

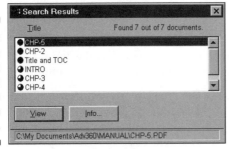

Search uses scores to find PDFs

The Search Results dialog box in Figure 13-2 shows not only the results of the search, but the frequency with which the word or phrase appears in each document. In Figure 13-3, for instance, *employee* shows up frequently in the PDF.

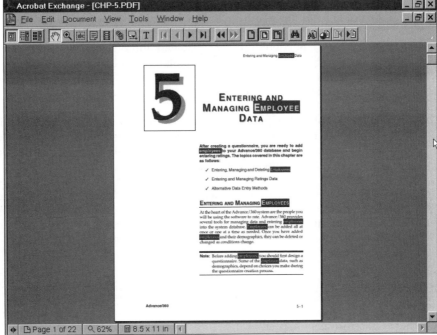

Figure 13-3:
This
document is
at the top of
the list
because
the search
term occurs
frequently.

Acrobat Search (the Reader and Exchange plug-in that provides all this search magic) uses a few different criteria for determining a document's score. As you've seen, the score indicates how frequently the term or phrase occurs in the document. You can also refine searches in various ways. For example, you can search for words that show up only in the Document Info fields, such as Author, Subject, Title, and Keywords. (The Document Info fields, which make up the General Info dialog box, are discussed in Chapter 7.) You can find PDFs by searching for when they were last modified. Searches can also be performed for word stems (such as *seeming* and *seemingly* for *seem*) and even words that have the same or similar meanings, such as *dog* and *pooch*.

I'll show you how to set up these types of searches for your users. In the next chapter, you find out how to execute such searches.

Search one or many catalogs

The power and flexibility of the Acrobat cataloging and indexing capabilities is both impressive and daunting. As a designer or network administrator, you can create one large index of all the PDFs on your system or network, or you can create smaller, topical indexes. And your users can choose to search one index, a few indexes, or all indexes at once.

For example, you can catalog PDFs according to departments, with one catalog for Human Resources, one for Production, one for Marketing, and so on. Users on the network can find relevant documents by department by searching a particular index. They can find occurrences in all documents containing information on a particular subject by searching multiple indexes. They can also find all documents created by the same author, all documents modified after a certain date, and so on.

With Acrobat, the problem is not with providing flexibility. Instead, the challenge is with refining catalogs and indexes in logical categories, and then teaching your users how to access all this information in a way that does not cause information overload.

Here's an idea. Buy multiple copies of *Adobe Acrobat 3 For Dummies* and pass them out to all employees with access to your PDF libraries. Be sure and tell them to read the chapters on using Reader and the next chapter on using Reader or Acrobat to refine and perform searches.

Don't have a company network? Or maybe you're in a huge company with remote offices not connected over the company's wide area network. In these situations, you can distribute your corporate documents in indexed catalogs on CD-ROM. You can find out how to optimize indexes for CD-ROM later in this chapter.

Performing Your First Search

Now that you have a basic understanding of how handy indexes can be, wouldn't you like to see one in action? Acrobat's online documentation, which was included when you installed Acrobat, is a prime example of an efficiently designed index.

By default, Exchange is set up to search the online documentation index:

1. **Choose Tools⇨Search⇨Query.**

   The Adobe Acrobat Search dialog box appears.

2. **Type** catalog.

3. **Click Search.**

   Viola! You just performed your first search.

4. **To view a document in the Search Results dialog box list, simply double-click on its name.**

If you are using Acrobat in a company network environment, you could have several users generating documents all over the place. In these situations, PDFs need to be generated and indexed regularly to make them available to all the users on the network. If you're a control freak (or just don't want a lot of unscreened documents in your catalogs), you can set up a schedule for manually updating your indexes. If you're like most of us, however, you don't have time to ride herd on the network. In these cases, you can have Catalog rebuild indexes automatically, at regularly scheduled intervals. You can use Catalog with the Distiller watched folder option to update and maintain your catalogs automatically, virtually unattended. Chapter 17 shows you how to set up an automatic cataloging system on a network.

Creating Your First Index

One of the things I've enjoyed most about writing this book is being able to repeatedly say how easy procedures are in Acrobat. Creating an index is remarkably easy, especially considering the power of this application.

You can create an index at any time simply by running Catalog and following the steps in this section. You'll have better luck, however, if you read the section "Preparing Your PDFs for Indexing," later in this chapter, especially if you're creating more than one index or indexing several PDFs. The bigger and more sophisticated your PDF library, the more you gain from planning ahead.

Catalog, as shown in Figure 13-4, looks a lot like Distiller. To begin the indexing process (after making sure you've laid out your file and folder structure as discussed in the preceding section), choose Index➪New. (On the Mac, choose File➪New.) In Windows, the New Index Definition dialog box, shown in Figure 13-5, appears. On the Mac, you get the Index Definition dialog box.

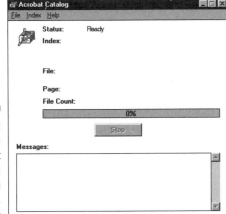

Figure 13-4: The Acrobat Catalog program window.

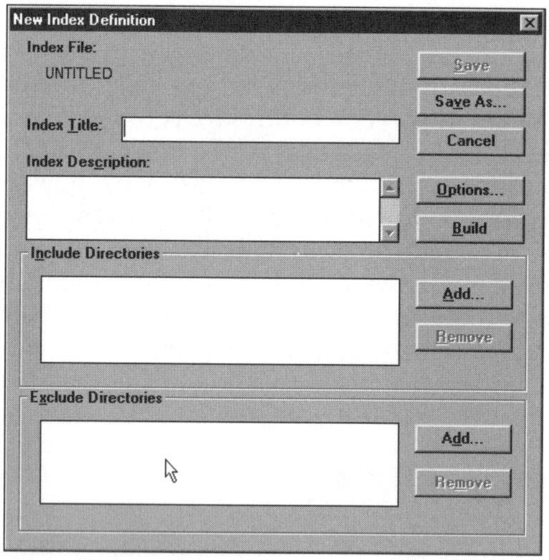

Figure 13-5:
Use this
dialog box
to set
up and
build your
indexes.

Setting up the index is a four-step process, as follows:

1. Name and save the index file.

2. Set the index options.

3. Set which folders to include and exclude.

4. Build the index.

This section looks at each process separately.

Naming the index

You can name the index file whatever you want, but you have better luck
if you use a descriptive name, such as Employee Handbook or Software
Documentation. This name shows up in the list of indexes when you search
in Reader or Exchange.

By default, Catalog gives all index file names the name index.pdx. (All indexes
must have the .pdx extension, which Catalog assigns automatically.) You can
provide a more descriptive file name, such as *legal* or *manuals*. Doing so
makes it easier to identify indexes on systems with multiple indexes.

Setting index options

Index options include searching for word stems, words that sound alike, and words with the same meaning. You can also exclude certain words and numbers (to make the indexes smaller), and optimize a catalog for use on a CD-ROM. These options are controlled from the Options dialog box (click Options in the New Index Definition dialog box), shown in Figure 13-6.

Figure 13-6:
Use this
dialog box
to set
options
for your
indexes,
such as the
type of
word to
search for
and words
to exclude.

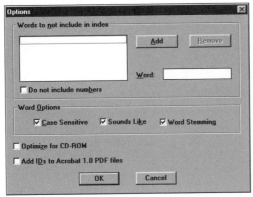

Excluding words and numbers from an index

Frankly, there's only one reason to exclude certain words and numbers from your indexes — to make the indexes smaller. Smaller indexes take up less disk space and don't take as long to search.

Now the question is, which words should you exclude? How about words that people have no reason to search for, such as *the, and, it, to, with, is, are, or,* and so on. By excluding these and other common, meaningless words (at least in terms of searching), you can reduce the size of your indexes 10 to 30 percent, which can be a lot in big indexes. If you use several numbers in your documents, you can save additional space by excluding them.

The drawback to excluding words is that your users can't search for phrases that contain them, such as *the eleventh hour* or *when the time is right.* So, when deciding which words to exclude, think about the content of your documents and how your users may search them.

To exclude words from your indexes, follow these steps:

1. In the New Index Definition dialog box, click Option.

2. **In the Word field of the Words to not include in index section, type the word you want to exclude.**

3. **Click Add.**

   The word is added to the list.

4. **Repeat Steps 2 and 3 for each word you want to exclude.**

5. **If you change your mind about a word, click the Remove button to delete it.**

6. **To exclude numbers, select the Do not include numbers option.**

When you finish excluding words, you're ready to define your search word options, as discussed in the next section. If you don't want to change the word options, you can click OK to return to the New Index dialog box.

Defining word options

Catalog lets you define several ways to let users search your indexes, including searching for case sensitive words, for words that sound like their search words, or even for words with the same meaning. As you can imagine, this makes for some powerful search capabilities. Keep in mind that using any of these options makes your indexes larger. Following is a description of each option.

Case Sensitive: You probably already know this one. If you select this option, your users can designate whether their search terms contain uppercase or lowercase letters. Rather than searching for *president,* for example, they could capitalize the word exactly as it appears in the documents to narrow the search, by typing *President.* The Case Sensitive option makes searches more precise. Not using it makes searching easier and broadens the search. Without a case sensitive index, searching for *president* would find occurrences of *President, president,* and *PRESIDENT.*

Sounds Like: This option helps your users find occurrences of search terms when they're not sure how to spell them. The Sounds Like option uses phonics rather than precise character strings for selecting word search occurrences. This type of search can be helpful, but it usually results in a broad search and a lot of irrelevant documents being returned. For example, when I searched a group of documents for the word *bones,* the list showed documents containing *book, being, Beinz,* and a bunch of other words.

Word Stemming: You may remember word stems, which are similar to root words, from high school English classes. Stemming words are words that stem from other words. For instance, the word *eliminate* can also be part of *eliminated, and eliminates.* This can greatly improve the results of a search by allowing users more flexibility in searching for broader occurrences of a word, rather than forcing them to know (and look for) specific occurrences.

Optimizing PDFs for CD-ROM discs

CD-ROM discs organize and store files differently than hard discs. They are also slower, making for slower searches. Catalog allows you to speed up CD-ROM PDF library searches with the Optimize for CD-ROM option in the Options dialog box.

The Optimize for CD-ROM option arranges index files for the fastest possible access on a CD-ROM disc. For those with 6x, 8x, 10x, and 12x CD-ROM drives, this isn't as big an issue. But if you have a spendthrift boss who won't spring for new equipment, it helps speed up the search. It also helps immensely on a networked CD-ROM drive.

In addition, the Optimize CD-ROM option makes it easier for you to modify Document Info fields or security settings after you have indexed a document. Normally, when a user searches a document that has been modified after it was indexed, a message is displayed asking the user whether he or she wants to use the index anyway. When you select this option, the message and choice are not displayed.

After you've defined all the words to exclude and set the search word options (Thesaurus, Sounds Like, and Word Stemming), you can return to the New Index Definition dialog box and finish the indexing process by clicking OK. If you are creating and indexing a PDF catalog for distribution on CD-ROM, however, be sure to read the sidebar titled "Optimizing PDFs for CD-ROM discs."

Adding and excluding PDFs for indexing

Indexes are created by selecting folders (or *directories,* to use a computer term from the past) containing PDFs, rather than individual PDFs themselves. To add the directories containing the PDFs to be indexed, follow these steps:

1. **In the New Index Definition dialog box, click the Add button that's in the Include Directories section.**

   A standard dialog box for selecting folders (Select Folders) appears.

2. **Go to the folder containing your PDFs.**

3. **Select the folder.**

4. **Click OK.**

   The folder is added to the list, as shown in Figure 13-7.

New Index Definition

Index File:
UNTITLED

Index Title:

Index Description:

Save

Save As...

Cancel

Options...

Build

Include Directories

D:\MANUALS

Add...

Remove

Exclude Directories

Add...

Remove

You can add additional folders by repeating this process, but before doing so you should read the section "Preparing Your PDFs for Indexing," later in this chapter.

To remove a folder from the list of folders to index, select its name in the Include Directories list and then click the Remove button.

The Exclude Directories section is for selecting subfolders of the folders in Include Directories that you don't want to index. To add a subfolder to the Exclude Directories list, you click Add button next to Exclude directories, navigate to the folder containing the subfolder you want to exclude, select the subfolder, and then click OK. Repeat the process for each subfolder you want to exclude.

Building your index

After making all the necessary changes in the New Index Definition dialog box and supporting Option dialog box, it's time to compile your index. To do so, follow these steps:

1. Click Build.

Catalog displays a Save Index As dialog box, allowing you to give the index a file name.

2. Name the file.

The default is index.pdx, which is fine if your system contains only one index. If you have multiple indexes, though, you may want to give them unique file names. Use DOS naming conventions (filename.ext) for catalogs that will be used on multiple platforms.

3. Click OK.

Acrobat begins building your index. When the process is complete, you get a message in the Catalog message window telling you that indexing is complete.

Preparing Your PDFs for Indexing

The title of this section implies that you have to do something special to a PDF before it can be cataloged and indexed. That is not the case. The only *requirement* for indexing a PDF is that it reside in a folder you are cataloging. To set up an efficient indexing and search retrieval application, though, you should do some planning, which often entails a little extra work when preparing your PDFs. This is especially true when multiple users are preparing PDFs for cataloging. The larger the operation, the more crucial the need for implementing controls.

This section provides tips for preparing your PDFs for more efficient indexing. (What I really mean by *tips* is *advice*. For some reason, people can handle tips but often hate advice.)

Keeping those PDFs small

You've heard me say that PDFs are wonderful because they turn large documents into small, portable formats. For example, I converted a 19MB manual into a PDF of about 900K, or close to five percent of the original size. If I were using the same file for indexing, however, I would break it into small chunks, by chapter, for two reasons.

The first reason is that catalogs allow users to search for information by relevance. What service would I provide by returning search results that force the user to sift through a 200-page document? The idea behind indexing is to make information easy to find.

The second and more important reason is that catalogs are faster and more efficient if the indexed documents are short and to the point. Users can use the Find feature in a long PDF to find words and topics. Reserve indexes for pinpointing information across multiple PDFs.

Using and controlling Document Info fields

Document Info fields reside in the General Info dialog box, which is shown in Figure 13-8. You or another PDF author can use these fields to provide detailed information about a PDF, such as the author, the title, the subject, and keywords. Using these fields (and using them systematically) can help you create a highly efficient search and retrieval application.

Figure 13-8:
You can control the efficiency of your indexes by using Document Info fields wisely.

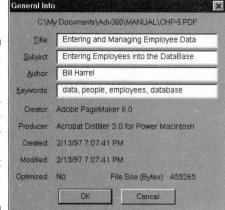

General Info	☒
C:\My Documents\Adv360\MANUAL\CHP-5.PDF	

Title: Entering and Managing Employee Data

Subject: Entering Employees into the DataBase

Author: Bill Harrel

Keywords: data, people, employees, database

Creator: Adobe PageMaker 6.0

Producer: Acrobat Distiller 3.0 for Power Macintosh

Created: 2/13/97 7:07:41 PM

Modified: 2/13/97 7:07:41 PM

Optimized: No   File Size (Bytes): 455265

OK   Cancel

If you are the only person creating PDFs and catalogs, controlling the use of Document Info fields is simply a matter of disciplining yourself to use them and use them systematically. When several users are creating PDFs for cataloging, you have more of a challenge in terms of educating them and riding herd over the process. In either case — whether you're the omnipotent PDF master or the overseer — how these fields are used can make or break the efficiency of your application.

Consistency counts

The key to assuring efficient searches lies in maintaining consistency when filling out the Document Info fields. For example, if finding PDFs by author is one of your search options, make sure the authors use the same naming convention (for example. first name, middle initial, last name, or perhaps last name only). What matters is not the name they use but that they use the same name each time they add a new PDF to the system.

Use the technique described in the preceding paragraph for the Title and Subject fields in Document Info. Titles should be descriptive, for example, *Employee Vacation Policies.* Subjects should contain an explanation of the document content, such as *Applying for a Vacation*. If you use categories for subject fields, use the same term each time. For example, if the subject is *Health Insurance,* don't use *Health Insurance* sometimes and *Employee Coverage* other times.

Your keywords should contain the words that best relate to the content of the document. For a document about sick leave polices, for instance, your keywords might be *sick, illness, leave, benefits,* and so on. Put some thought into what you type in these fields.

If the Acrobat built-in Document Info fields do not provide enough options, you can customize Exchange to support additional Document Info fields. This is a bit tricky, requiring you to edit the Windows acrobat.ini file or make changes in the Catalog Preferences dialog box on your Macintosh. For a detailed description of this process, open the *Catalog Online Guide* in Reader or Exchange (choose Help⇨Catalog Online Guide) and go to page 13.

Fine-tune your file structures

An important consideration when preparing your PDFs for cataloging is the file and folder structure you save them with. This is important for two reasons: Acrobat Search requires a specific structure for finding documents, and you should maintain the portability of your catalogs in case you want to move them to another computer, to another drive, or to removable media.

When you define and build an index, Catalog gives the index definition file a .pdx extension and creates an index support folder with the same name as the PDX file. The support folder contains nine subfolders. Catalog places the PDX file and the support folders in the same folder, as shown in Figure 13-9.

Figure 13-9: An example of the folder structure Catalog creates when you build an index.

(When indexing on a network, you have a few other considerations. Depending on whether you're using a Macintosh server or a Windows server, your choices for folder and file structure are somewhat limited. You can find out more about these limitations in Chapter 17.)

The most logical configuration is to have the index itself — the .pdx file and the support folder containing the nine subfolders — in the folder that contains the indexed document collection subfolders. For example, suppose you have a collection of PDFs in a procedure manuals section. Each manual contains several chapters. You could create a top-level folder named Manuals, and then create subfolders for each manual, as shown here:

Manuals

>   Accounting

>   Benefits

>   Billing

>   Manuals

>   Sick Leave

>   Software

>   Vacations

In this configuration, your Manuals subfolder contains the nine supporting folders. The .pdx file resides in the top-level (Manuals) folder, and the PDFs reside in the lower-level folders. This structure is the easiest for your users to understand and makes it simpler for you to move the catalog to another drive or to a removable medium.

If your network administrator won't let you create this kind of structure, or the configuration is not possible for some other reason, you can use any structure in which the index and the cataloged documents are in a folder structure that can be moved as a single unit. You never know when you may have to move the structure, so keep this in mind as you set up your files.

You can, however, use almost any structure — with one restriction on the Macintosh and three restrictions in Windows. On both platforms, the entire index — both the .pdx file and the support folder containing the nine subfolders — must be in a single folder. In Windows, the indexed PDFs must be saved on a single drive, and the index must reside on the same drive as the indexed documents.

MACINTOSH

What's in a name?

When you're creating PDFs for cross-platform use, be mindful of your file naming conventions. The safest way to assure cross-platform compatibility is to use DOS naming conventions (that is, an 8-character file name and a 3-character extension).

Acrobat Catalog and Acrobat Search use special document conventions and path names to identify indexed documents. DOS file names are not always necessary. However, esoteric conventions caused when names created for one platform are mapped to names usable on another can slow searches and even prevent some documents from showing up in your search.

When using Catalog on a Macintosh to build a cross-platform catalog, you can assure compatibility without using DOS file names by selecting Make Include/Exclude Folders DOS Compatible in the Index Preferences dialog box in Catalog (Edit⇨Preferences⇨Index) before you build your index. If you select this preference, you must use DOS file naming conventions for folder names, but you don't have to use them for the PDFs themselves.

The additional considerations when naming files on a network are discussed in Chapter 17.

Maintaining Your Indexes

As your life and business hums along, new PDFs will be added to your system, and existing PDFs will be changed and updated. This can increase the size of your indexes, making them too big for quick, effective searches. You can rebuild a catalog at any time by following these steps:

1. **Choose Index⇨Build.**

   The Select Index File to Build dialog box appears.

2. **Select the index you want to rebuild.**

3. **Click OK.**

   Catalog does the rest.

To edit an index to change any of the options discussed in this chapter, or to include or exclude folders, do the following:

1. **Choose Index⇨Open.**

   This opens your index in the Edit Index Definition dialog box. This box is identical to the New Index Definition dialog box, except it has the settings you chose for the index when you created it.

2. Make the changes (see the appropriate sections of this chapter for the specific steps), and then click OK.

You can have Catalog maintain your indexes automatically by scheduling automated rebuilds. Because this is typically part of a network operation, it's covered in Chapter 17.

Purging Your Indexes

As you continuously rebuild indexes, entries for deleted documents and for the original versions of changed documents remain in the index but are marked invalid. This increases the size of the index and can affect the speed of searches. Occasionally, you need to purge the index to remove superfluous material.

To purge your indexes, follow these steps:

1. Choose Index⇨Purge.

The Select Index to Purge dialog box appears.

2. Select the index you want to purge.

3. Click OK.

Catalog displays a message telling you how long it will take to purge the index. Big indexes can take quite some time to purge, tying up Catalog and the index itself for other uses.

4. Click OK.

The purge commences, and Catalog gives you a message containing the results of the purge when it is finished.

After a purge begins, you can stop it with the Stop button in Catalog. Stopping a purge prematurely, however, can corrupt the index. You can usually correct this by going back and purging the index again until the purge is complete, or until Catalog finishes the purge and presents you with a message that the purge has finished. But you really shouldn't take any chances by stopping the purge, especially if your indexes aren't backed up.

5. After the purge is finished, rebuild the index to complete the purge process, as follows:

a. Choose Index⇨Build.

b. Select the index.

c. Click OK.

Now you have a nice, fresh, up-to-date index.

To delete an index, you simply delete the .pdx file and the folder containing the nine supporting folders. Good. Now you may want to check out the next chapter on searching indexes, so you can teach your users how to do it.

Chapter 14

Searching Indexed Acrobat Catalogs

• •

• •

*I*n addition to creating Web documents and multimedia titles, Acrobat can create libraries of portable documents for archival and retrieval applications on networks and CD-ROMs. The two most common applications for this type of document library are creating software documentation and creating a resource library on a company network or intranet.

A problem that always arises when storing massive amounts of information in computer documents is finding a way to provide users with a quick and easy way to access the information. In database applications, this problem is solved by allowing users to search for and retrieve information with search criteria, often known as *search terms* or *keyword searches.*

Although Acrobat PDFs are not databases themselves, as a PDF designer or network administrator, you can create full-text databases of groups, or catalogs, of PDFs. (Creating indexes is discussed in Chapter 13.) Users can then use the indexes to find documents containing the specific search terms and phrases.

This chapter is for PDF application designers and users alike. If you are a PDF application designer, you need to know how to perform and refine searches so that you create the most effective indexes for your users. If you are the user of a PDF library, learning search techniques can save you hours of wading through huge groups of documents.

This chapter covers searching indexes from several easy-to-understand angles. If you want to become a Search power user, read the *Search Online Guide.* In Exchange, choose Help⇨Search Online Guide. If you don't have Exchange, but do have Reader with Search, you can open the *Search Online Guide* in Reader. Choose File⇨Open, and then navigate to the Help folder in the Reader folder, whose default location is in the Acrobat folder.

Getting, Installing, and Using Reader with Search

Both Exchange and Reader support searching indexes created with Catalog, but most people use Reader for searching indexes. Reader is smaller and faster than Exchange, it's free, and it can be distributed royalty-free by PDF designers (and anyone else).

Reader is available from many resources, as I discuss in Chapter 2. Most of those resources, however, do not provide the Search plug-in required to perform index searches. (If you have the Acrobat Pro package, the Search plug-in for Exchange is installed when you install the package. And you are provided with an option for installing Search when you install Reader.) Often the easiest way for your users to get Reader with Search is from the Adobe Web site, as follows:

1. **Try to locate the following URL:**

   `http://www.adobe.com/prodindex/acrobat/win95rs.html`

   Adobe changes its Web site often (as do most good Webmasters), so Reader with Search may not be available here.

2. **If you can't find the URL:**

   a. **Stay logged in to the Adobe Web site:** `http://www.adobe.com.`

   b. **Click the Search button.**

   c. **Type** reader AND search **in the field that's provided.**

   You are presented with a list of pages that contain these two search terms.

   d. **Find an entry that refers to Reader with Search.**

   This page should also contain information and links for download-ing the version of Reader that contains the Search plug-in.

3. **Download the file.**

4. **Double-click the file in Windows Explorer or the Macintosh Finder.**

   You are presented with a dialog box asking where you want to save the uncompressed files.

5. **Navigate to the folder where you want to save the file, and then click Save.**

   Be sure to remember where you saved the files.

6. **After the files are uncompressed, double-click Setup and follow the instructions for installing Reader.**

   You're ready to search Acrobat PDF indexes.

Performing a Basic Search

From this point on, whether you use Exchange or Reader for searching Acrobat indexes, the procedures, commands, and dialog boxes are the same.

The procedure for searching for a single word or phrase is a three-part process, as follows:

1. **Select the indexes you want to search.**

2. **Type your search term or phrase.**

3. **View the documents in the Search Results dialog box.**

Seems pretty easy, doesn't it? Take a look at each procedure.

Selecting the indexes to search

Whether you are searching in Exchange or Reader, you begin your search the same way — by telling Acrobat which indexes you want to search in the Index Selection dialog box shown in Figure 14-1.

To choose which indexes to search, follow these steps:

1. **Choose Tools⇔Search⇔Indexes.**

2. **Click Add, and then navigate to the folder that contains the index you want to search.**

Figure 14-1:
Use this
dialog box
to list and
select the
indexes you
want to
include in
the current
search.

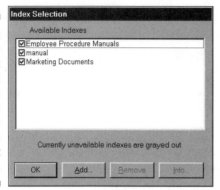

3. **Repeat Step 2 until you select all the indexes you want to search.**

4. **To select an Index, place a check mark in the box beside it.**

5. **When you finish selecting indexes, click OK.**

You are now ready to search for the PDFs you need.

This procedure assumes that you know where the index files are on your system or network. Don't worry if you don't know where they are; finding Acrobat indexes is easy. In Windows 95, choose Start⇨Find. In your Mac's Finder, choose File⇨Find. To search for all the indexes on a drive or a network volume, use the following: ***.pdx.** (On a Mac you would skip the wildcard, *, and simply type **.pdx.**)

You can get information on an index by highlighting it and clicking Info. The Index Information dialog box appears, as shown in Figure 14-2. The amount of information provided here depends on how well the creator of the index filled out the New Index Definition dialog box when creating the index, as I discuss in Chapter 13.

After you find and add the indexes on your system or network drive to the Index Selection list, they remain there, allowing you to select and deselect indexes for searching without having to go through the process of finding and adding them to the list each time you open Reader or Exchange. If an index has been deleted or is going through a purge or build (as I discuss in Chapter 13), the index title appears dimmed, indicating that the index is currently unavailable.

This section shows you how to select indexes through the Indexes command, which connects to the indexes Reader or Exchange uses for a number of functions, including Word Assistant (I discuss this a little later in this chapter). Assistant helps you find words contained in selected indexes before searching for documents. This option can speed up the search for documents, as you see in the section "Refining Your Searches, later in this chapter."

Figure 14-2:
This dialog
box
provides
information
to help you
decide
whether to
include an
index in the
current
search.

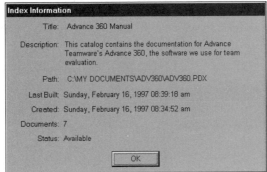

Executing your first search

After you select the indexes you want to search, it's time to begin your first search. In this section, you look at the basics to searching for a word or phrase. In the next two sections, you refine your searches to zero-in on information.

Follow these steps to execute a search:

1. **Click the Search button in the toolbar, or choose Tools⟹Search⟹ Query.**

   (The Search button looks like binoculars in front of a document.) As you can see from Figure 14-3, your search capabilities are extensive.

Figure 14-3:
Use this
dialog box
to define
and
execute
searches
of your
selected
indexes.

2. **In Find Results Containing Text, type the word or phrase you want to search for.**

3. Click Search.

When Search completes the search, it displays the documents containing your search criteria in the Search Results dialog box, as shown in Figure 14-4.

Figure 14-4:
This
document
shows a
list of
documents
that meet
your search
criteria.

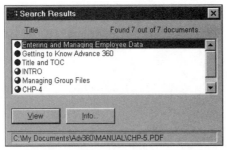

The documents are listed according to their score, or how many times the search word or phrase turns up in the document. The small pie charts to the left of the document name provide a rudimentary indication of the document's score. (A full pie, for example, means the document scored close to 100 percent.)

4. For document information, including the document's actual relevancy score, select the document and click the Info button.

The Document Info screen appears, as shown in Figure 14-5.

Figure 14-5:
This screen
displays
useful
information
about
the PDF,
including
the
document's
score.

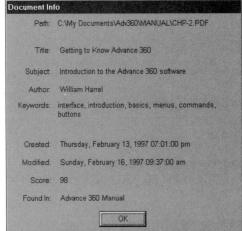

5. To view a specific document, double-click it or select it and click View.

The document opens the same way as any other PDF in Reader or in Exchange.

Notice in Figure 14-4 that some documents in the Search Results window have useful names and others display only file names. This is because the person who created and saved the PDFs containing the file-name-only titles did not take the time to fill out the Document Info fields when generating the PDF. Shame on me — file names like this don't provide a lot of help to the user.

Navigating your search results

If you're reading this book sequentially, you're probably thinking, "Didn't you talk about navigating in other chapters?" You're right; I discuss navigating PDFs in a number of chapters. But now we're interested in a different type of navigation. Rather than using bookmarks and links to find information, we, instead, want to find occurrences of the search terms in the PDFs returned in the Search Results dialog box.

If you search a large index and receive lots of PDFs, finding the specific information will be a chore. (In the next two sections, you see how to refine searches to return fewer documents.) After you use Document Info to determine whether a document has potential, you can open it in Reader or Exchange by double-clicking it. The document will open at the first occurrence of your search term, as shown in Figure 14-6.

The first occurrence of the search term is on page 8. I can jump to the next occurrence in this document by clicking the Next button (the last button on the toolbar), or I can press Ctrl+U (Cmd+U on a Mac). As I move ahead, the Previous button (next to Next) becomes available, or I can press Ctrl+Y (Cmd+Y on a Mac).

Other ways to navigate search terms include Next Document (Ctrl+Shift+U or Cmd+Shift+U) and Previous Document (Ctrl+Shift+Y or Cmd+Shift+U). These commands, also available by choosing Tools➪Search, become available after you open more than one search results document. In addition, you can return to the Search Results list at any time by clicking the Search Results button (fourth button from the right) or by pressing Ctrl+Shift+J (Cmd+Shift+J on a Mac).

Now, you have to admit that this is much, much handier than flipping back and forth in a hard copy text and index!

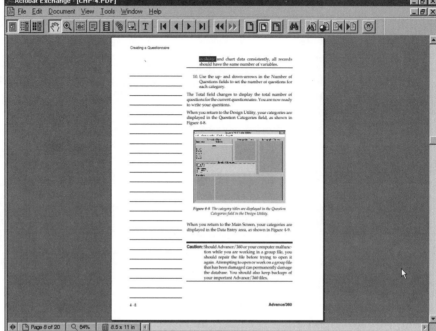

Setting Search Preferences

The procedure in the preceding section is okay when you are searching small catalogs. But many PDF libraries consist of thousands of documents, which could mean search results consisting of 100 or more PDFs. There has to be a better way.

Acrobat provides many options for refining searches. One is to set up Reader or Exchange Search preferences to allow you to define more meaningful searches. Instead of searching for words or terms that occur in the text of the document, you can search for words occurring in Document Info Title, Subject, and Keyword fields. You can also search for documents by author, or by the date that the document was last modified.

You set search preferences from the Acrobat Search Preferences dialog box, shown in Figure 14-7. You can change Query, Results, and Highlight options. Take a look at each and see how each affects your searches and results.

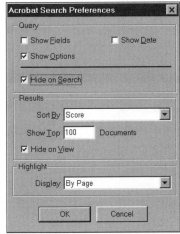

Figure 14-7:
You can
refine your
searches
and
how the
results are
displayed
by changing
settings
in this
dialog box.

Searching by Document Info fields

A well-tuned PDF search and retrieval application is a lot like a well-cared-for Harley-Davidson. Neglect the details and you'll be sorry. Searching indexes by Document Info fields is highly effective, but it requires that the authors of the PDFs insert the proper data into the Document Info fields, as I discuss in Chapter 13. As with any multiuser application, collaboration and coopera-tion are the keys to success. (If you're the only one adding PDFs to the library, you're in control — success is up to you. Such pressure!)

With that said, assume that your PDF library is well-designed and the Document Info fields are used wisely and consistently. Good. To search indexes by Document Info Fields, follow these steps:

1. **Choose File⇨Preferences⇨Search.**

   The Acrobat Search Preferences dialog box is displayed.

2. **Select the Show Fields option, and click OK.**

   When you start a query, your Adobe Acrobat Search dialog box will look like Figure 14-8. Hey! Now you're zeroing in on the information you need.

3. **Click the Search button to begin a search.**

4. **In the With Document Info area, type your search terms or phrases.**

5. **Click Search to begin the search.**

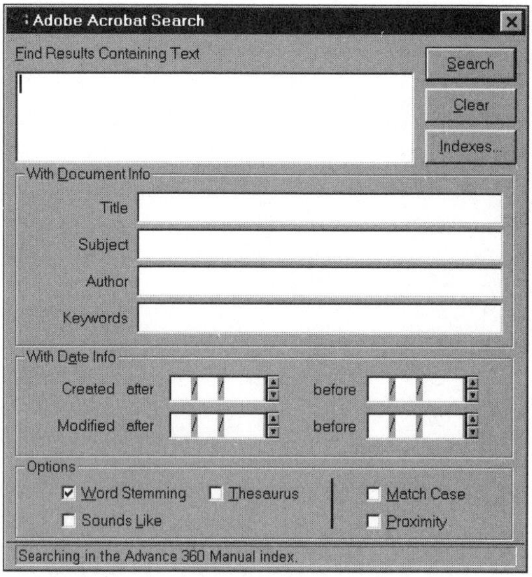

Figure 14-8:
With the
Show Fields
option
selected in
the Acrobat
Search
Preferences
dialog box,
you can
search the
Document
Info fields
for the text
you type
in this
dialog box.

You can further refine your search by searching for documents created
within a range of dates, modified within a range of dates, or both. To do so,
select the Show Date option in the Acrobat Search Preferences dialog box.
Now your Adobe Acrobat Search dialog box looks like Figure 14-9.

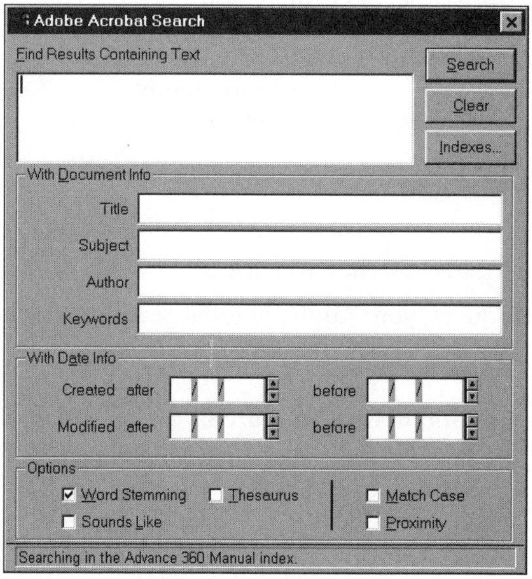

Figure 14-9:
With the
Show Date
option
selected in
the Acrobat
Search
Preferences
dialog box,
you can
refine your
search by
creation
and
modification
dates in this
dialog box.

Are you wondering whether you can use all these options to refine your search? The answer is yes. And that means you can get pretty specific in your search criteria. But, as you see in the "Refining Your Searches" section, you ain't seen nothin' yet.

You might be wondering also about the Show Options check box in the Acrobat Search Preferences dialog box. It simply toggles the display of the options in the Options section of the Adobe Acrobat Search dialog box. You look at those options later in this chapter.

If you want to keep the Adobe Acrobat Search dialog box small and simple, you can type the names of fields in the Find Results Containing Text window instead of turning on the Document Info Fields. For example, to find documents created by an author named Steve Smith, you would type **Author = Steve Smith**. For the Creation Date or Modified Date fields, use *Creation Date = mo/day/year,* and so on.

Changing how results are ordered

I mention relevancy scores previously in the chapter. By default, search results are sorted by scores, or the number of times a word or a phrase appears in a document. You can change how documents are sorted with the Results portion of the Acrobat Search Preferences dialog box, shown in Figure 14-10. The five options are obvious, except Producer, which refers to the creator application. For example, the software manual I use in the examples in this chapter was created in PageMaker for the Macintosh, which would be the Producer.

Figure 14-10:
Use these options to change the order in which search results documents are displayed.

Changing how results are displayed in a document

By default, when you view a document from the Search Results dialog box, Reader or Exchange displays the page on which the search term appears. When you click Next, you are taken to the next page containing the search term. You can tell Acrobat to take you to the next occurrence, rather than the next page, even if it's on the same page. To do so:

1. **Choose File⇨Preferences⇨Search.**

   The Acrobat Search Preferences dialog box appears.

2. **In the Display list (under the Highlight section), select By Word.**

Refining Your Searches

You may be wondering what else you could possibly do to refine a search. (If you're familiar with database applications, you might already know. In that case, you're probably wondering when I'm going to get around to this section.)

In addition to the word, phrase, Document Info fields, creation date, and modification date search variables, you can add the following criteria to your searches:

Stemming words

Sounds like

Thesaurus

Match Case

Wild cards

Booleans

Getting a bit overwhelmed? I would, if I tried to use all these options at once. That's not the way you do it. Instead, you use one option or a combination of a few to find PDFs. In this short course on searching, I'm merely covering the basics; that is, explaining how to use these options. Many of these variables allow you to provide additional variables. If you want to become a power searcher, spend an hour or so reading the 70-page *Search Online Guide*.

Searching for stemming words

Stemming words are words made from other, shorter words, such as the example of *evaluate* I used earlier in this chapter. What variants, or stemming words, can you think of? Without even racking my brain I can come up with *evaluation, evaluating, evaluated, evaluator.* You get the idea. When you select the Stemming Words option in Adobe Acrobat Search, Search will also match any stemming words that occur in the index.

I'll bet you can think of all kinds of combinations and matches. Remember two things, though. For stemming word searches to work, the index must have been created in Catalog with the Stemming Words option turned on (as I discuss in Chapter 13). Stemming words are defined when the index is created in Catalog, and are based on the words in the PDFs, not a built-in dictionary or external database of possibilities. Acrobat does not automatically search for all possible stemming words for a given word; it matches only the stemming words that are present in the index.

You can use Word Assistant to find out which stemming words are in the indexes you're searching — before you search. To use Word Assistant, follow these steps:

1. **Choose Tools➪Search➪Word Assistant.**

2. **In the Word field, type the word you want to find stemming words for.**

3. **In the Assist list, select Stemming.**

4. **Click Lookup.**

In Figure 14-11, I searched for stemming words for the word *evaluate* and came up with these words.

Figure 14-11:
Word
Assistant
can find
which
stemming
words
appear in the
index before
you search.
Cool, huh?

Searching for words that sound alike

The Sounds Like option serves two functions. It allows you to search for words that sound alike and words that you aren't sure how to spell. (For the latter, however, it's more effective to use wild cards, which I discuss a little later in this chapter.)

The Sounds Like option is similar to the Word Stemming option. You select the option in Adobe Acrobat Search, type your search term, and let 'er rip.

What you get, however, is usually a bunch of junk, or words that don't really sound like the search term at all. In Figure 14-12, for example, I used Word Assistant to see which words in my index sounded like *look*. As you can see, some of the resulting words don't sound like *look* at all. Heck, they don't even look like *look*. This option can be helpful, though, if regular word and phrase searches aren't finding the documents you need.

Figure 14-12:
Acrobat
Search
thinks that
these words
in the index
sound like
look.

To use Word Assistant to search for words that sound alike, follow these steps:

1. **Choose Tools⇨Search⇨Word Assistant.**

2. **In the Word field, type your word.**

3. **In the Assist list, select Sounds Like.**

4. **Click Lookup.**

Again, the person who created the index in Catalog must have created it with Sounds Like selected for you to have the ability to search with this criterion. To make this option work more efficiently, you have better luck using it with the Boolean operator *NOT,* as discussed in the "Using Boolean searches" section.

Searching for words that have the same meaning

The Thesaurus option uses the Acrobat built-in thesaurus to match your search words to words with similar or like meanings. Though somewhat more helpful than Sounds Like, this option also provides some rather broad searches because Acrobat has a liberal (or loose) collection of matches in its thesaurus. For example, when I searched for words matching *look,* I got the list shown in Figure 14-13, which continues well beyond the bottom of the window in the dialog box. As you can see, this could return a huge list in the Search Results dialog box.

Figure 14-13:
The words in
Acrobat's
thesaurus
that have the
same or
similar
meaning
as *look.*

To search for words with the same meaning, follow these steps:

    1. Choose Tools⇨Search⇨Word Assistant.

    2. In the Word field, type your word.

    3. In the Assist list, select Thesaurus.

    4. Click Lookup.

Narrowing and broadening searches with Match Case

The Match Case option probably doesn't need a lot of explanation. When you select it, Search finds only exact matches.

For example, you typed *wordperfect* with Match Case not selected, Search would find all occurrences of the word, whether capitalized or not. If Match Case was selected, Search would not find *WordPerfect, Wordperfect,* and so on.

This option is great for finding acronyms, such as CAT for Caterpillar farming equipment rather than every darned occurrence of *cat*. It's also handy for finding proper names that are also words, such as last names (Green, Brown, and so on).

Once again, the index must have been created in Catalog with Match Case selected for this option to work.

Using wild cards

If you use the Windows or Mac Find command much, you may be familiar with wild cards. Wild cards are characters that you use as a substitute for letters. Acrobat supports two wild cards: asterisk (*) and question mark (?). You can use an asterisk in place of one or more characters, and a question mark for one character. Wild cards are great when you don't know how to spell a word, or when you want to find variants of a word.

I find wild cards handy for words in which I can't remember whether the spelling is *tion* or *sion*. In Figure 14-14, for example, I'm searching for the word *evolution,* but I can't remember how the middle of the word is spelled. Or how about words such as *notice?* Do you or do you not drop the *e* when you add the suffix *able?* You don't, for example, in *disagreeable.* Or what about those infernal *ibles* and *ables?*

Figure 14-14: Use wild cards when you don't know how to spell the word you're looking for.

Using Boolean searches

Searching with Boolean operators is common on the World Wide Web. Acrobat supports three Boolean operators: *AND, NOT,* and *OR.* You can use them to widen, narrow, and refine searches to include multiple possibilities. You can use one Boolean or several, as in the example in Figure 14-15. And you can use Booleans in full-text searches or in the Document Info fields, as I discuss previously in this chapter.

Figure 14-15:
This
Boolean
search
finds all
documents
with
evaluate or
appraise
that also
contain
employee.

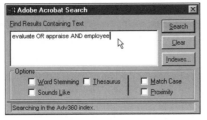

The AND operator

Use the AND operator when you want to narrow your search. This operator tells Search to find documents that contain both (or more, if you use AND more than once) words in your search criteria. You can use AND with the Proximity option in Adobe Acrobat Search to narrow the search even more. This tells Search to return documents with the two AND terms in close proximity (about three pages).

The OR operator

Use OR to broaden your search. This operator tells Search to return all documents that contain both (or more, if you use OR more than once) words on either side of OR. You can set broad searches with this option. Consider the following:

employee OR data OR rating OR evaluate

An equivalent to OR is the comma, as follows:

employee, data, rating, evaluate

The NOT operator

Use the NOT operator to narrow searches by excluding documents containing certain words but not others, such as *employee NOT vacation*. This search returns all documents containing *employee* except those containing *vacation*. And you can stack NOTs to narrow searches further, such as:

employee NOT vacation NOT benefits

An equivalent to NOT is an exclamation point (!), as follows:

employee ! vacation ! benefits

Make sure that you put spaces on either side of the exclamation point.

When is a Boolean not a Boolean?

A Boolean is not a Boolean when it's part of a phrase. If you want to search for the phrase *this or that,* you don't want all the documents containing *this* or all the documents containing *that.* Instead, you want all the documents containing all three words together, in this order. In these cases, put the phrase in quotation marks:

"this or that"

This tells Search to ignore the Boolean.

With all this discussion of searching for phrases, I should mention one caveat. Many people use stopwords when creating indexes in Catalog. Stopwords are words excluded from the index, and are usually prepositions *(to)*, articles *(the),* and the like. These words are excluded to hold down the size of the index, but doing so can play havoc in searching for phrases that contain the stopwords. If you know the author of the index, you can probably get a list of stopwords. If you have Catalog on your system, you can find out the stopwords by opening the index (as I discuss in Chapter 13). In any case, you can get around the absence of certain words by using the other options you've discovered in this chapter, such as the Boolean options with the Proximity option turned on.

Happy searching.

Part IV

Distributing PDFs on the Internet and Other Networks

The 5th Wave   By Rich Tennant

"AND JUST WHAT THE HECK PART OF THE NETWORK DID YOU SAY YOU'RE FROM?"

In this part . . .

Distributing PDFs over networks, such as a
company's local area network or the Internet,
is a highly effective way to make information available
to a wide variety of users. This part covers preparing
PDFs for the Internet and other networks, with lots of
tips to making accessing the information as painless as
possible for your users.

Chapter 15

Publishing Your PDFs on the World Wide Web

. . . .

▶ Understanding the four ways to view PDFs on the Web

▶ Publishing your PDFs on the Web

. . . .

As the Information Age plunges headlong onto the Internet, software companies are clamoring for ways to make their software (and the documents their software packages produce) exploit this exciting and vastly enticing technology. The Acrobat PDFs are poised to take advantage of this technology.

What the Internet and the World Wide Web in particular need is a way to deliver documents to end users in a quick and efficient manner. And, as you've seen if you've read much of this book, PDFs fit the bill. They are compact, quick, and highly portable across platforms. In Acrobat 3, a new Internet technology for delivering documents (called *streaming*) makes PDFs even more adaptable to the Web.

The possibilities for publishing PDFs on the Web are immense. You can use PDFs for everything from simple applications, such as document distribution, to sophisticated database updates and forms submission applications. The latter, however, requires a person strong not only in PDF design but also in CGI scripting, a form of programming that goes far beyond the scope of this book. You can find information about CGI scripts for posting PDF forms at http://www.adobe.com/special/acrobat/moreinfo.

Four Ways Your Users Can View PDFs on the Web

If you haven't read Chapter 3, perhaps you should before checking out this discussion of viewing PDFs on the Web. That way, the information here will be a lot more understandable.

When designing PDFs for the Web, you have four possible viewing scenarios. The option you choose should depend primarily on the type of users (actually, the type of Web browser) you anticipate accessing your PDFs, as well as the type of Internet server the PDFs will reside on.

Now I'm getting highly technical and way beyond the scope of this book. The good news is that Adobe provides a bunch of help on the topics of Web browsers and Internet servers on its Web site (http://www.adobe.com). As you wind your way through this technical stuff, I'll tell you where to get more information on the Web.

The four types of scenarios for viewing PDFs on the World Wide Web are as follows:

✔ Page-at-a-time downloading (also known as byte-serving or streaming)

✔ Non-page-at-a-time inline viewing

✔ Reader as a helper application

✔ Embedded PDFs

The next sections look at each type of viewing in some detail.

Page-at-a-time (byte-serving)

The page-at-a-time scenario is the fastest, most efficient way to present PDFs on the Web. To take advantage of it, the user's browser must support PDF viewing, the PDF file must be optimized (as I discuss in the next chapter), and the Web server must support byte-serving. If all these conditions are met, the PDF file downloads a page at a time. The download begins with the first page and view set in the document's Open Info fields (as I discuss in Chapter 6) and displays in the Web browser window, as shown in Figure 15-1.

Notice in the figure that the Acrobat controls are part of the Netscape Navigator window. This type of document viewing in a browser is known as *inline viewing*. The user can browse the PDF as though the document resided on his or her system or network drive. With this approach, the Internet server sends only the page or pages the user requests.

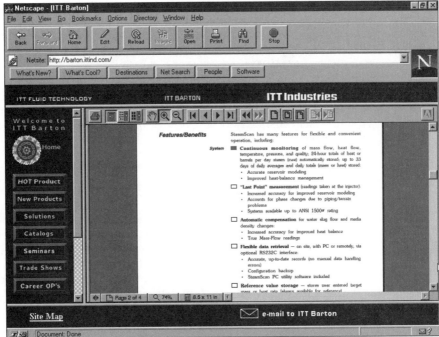

Figure 15-1:
A PDF displayed in Netscape Navigator. This document is navigable in the browser as a PDF present on the user's system.

This page-at-a-time stuff is great for speed, but it does not download and save the entire PDF for you, in case you wanted to read more of it (or print it) later. You can, however, capture the entire file to your hard disk by turning on the Allow Background Downloading of Entire File. To do so, follow these steps:

1. **From your Web browser, choose File⇨Preferences.**

2. **Select General.**

3. **Select the Allow Background Downloading of Entire File option to turn it on.**

4. **Click OK.**

The page-at-a-time process is possible only when users have Acrobat Reader (or Exchange) 3, their browser supports the Acrobat 3 browser plug-in, and the PDF has been optimized in Exchange 3. (You see how to optimize the PDF in Chapter 16.) Also, the server on which the PDF resides must be running an Internet server that supports byte-serving. For a list of current browsers and servers compatible with this byte-serving application, point your Web browser to http://www.adobe.com/special/acrobat/moreinfo.

When you install Reader (or Exchange), the installation application usually finds your browser and installs the proper configuration. If you move or reinstall your browser, however, you may need to install the plug-in again. In these cases, you can install the browser plug-in from the Acrobat installation disks or CD-ROM by copying the plug-in into your browser's Plug-ins folder. In Windows, copy the NPPDF32.dll (Windows 95) or NPPDF16.dll (Windows 3.1) file into your browser's Plug-ins folder. On a Mac, copy the PDFViewer plug-in to your browser's Plug-ins folder. On both platforms, your browser must be Netscape Navigator or Microsoft Internet Explorer compatible.

Non-byte-serving inline viewing

With the non-byte-serving inline viewing option, the PDF still displays as an inline document, as shown in Figure 15-1, but you don't get the benefit of page-at-a-time downloading. Users must wait for the entire file to download before they can start viewing the PDF. In this scenario, the browser supports PDF viewing, but the PDF file is not optimized or the server does not byte-serve files. If this is your situation, remember that the PDFs should be relatively small — users don't like to wait on the Web.

I find that the PDF file size for non-byte-serving applications can be rather large, taking as long as 10 minutes to download (between 2 and 4MB over a 28.8 bps modem). You can get away with this *as long as the user considers the information in the document important enough to wait that long.* Maybe that's not much help. My advice is to keep your PDFs as small as possible. Break large information into small chunks and resample graphics downward, as I discuss in Chapter 16.

An Acrobat viewer as a helper application

In the third scenario, Exchange or Reader is configured as a helper application for the browser. In this case, either the users don't have a browser that supports viewer plug-ins or they are using a version of Reader or Exchange before 3.0. The entire PDF file downloads to the user's machine and the Acrobat viewer launches (or spawns) as a separate application, as shown in Figure 15-2.

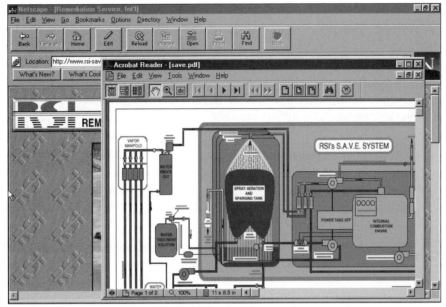

Figure 15-2:
The PDF is displayed in Reader in a separate window. Reader is acting as a helper application.

If you use Microsoft Internet Explorer, there's no need to configure readers and viewers. Internet Explorer uses the Windows registry and OLE to determine how to treat PDFs. Version 3 of Internet Explorer, with its support of ActiveX technology, provides a more sophisticated approach to viewing PDFs, as you see a little later in this chapter. If you are the ultimate authority on your organization's computer system application (or even if they respect your opinion), you might want to have Exchange installed on your network. You get much better results by configuring all your users with Internet Explorer, which Microsoft provides free at `http://www.microsoft.com`.

Installing Reader or Exchange as a helper application in Netscape Navigator

When you install Reader or the Acrobat package, the installation program usually finds Netscape Navigator, determines the version, and installs the viewer in the optimal form for your version of the software. This doesn't always work, though. Or perhaps you installed Netscape Navigator after you installed Acrobat.

In any case, you can install Reader as a helper application at any time by following these steps:

1. **From Netscape Navigator, choose Options⇨General.**

   The Preferences dialog box appears.

2. **Click the Helpers tab.**

   The Helpers sheet shown in the figure appears. You set up your Helper applications from this sheet.

3. **Click Create New Type.**

   The Configure New Mime Type dialog box appears.

4. **In the Mime Type field, type** application.

5. **In the Mime Subtype field, type** pdf.

6. **Click OK.**

7. **Scroll in the list of helpers, and click on application/pdf to select it.**

8. **Click the Browse button.**

   The Click Appropriate Viewer dialog box appears.

9. **Go to the folder where Acrobat Reader (or Exchange) resides, select it, and then click Open.**

10. **In the Helpers section of the Preferences dialog box, type** pdf **in the File Extensions field.**

11. **In the Action section, select Launch Application.**

12. **Click OK.**

Now you're ready to use Reader or Exchange as a helper application. Netscape Navigator and Acrobat will do the rest.

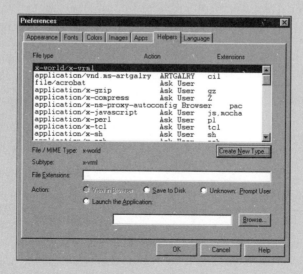

Embedded PDFs

Embedded PDFs are certainly the most impressive PDF-in-browser application. An embedded PDF is also the most difficult to achieve, requiring some basic HTML programming savvy. With this scenario, the PDF shows up as an object on the Web page, as shown in Figure 15-3. To take advantage of this application, the user's browser must support PDF viewing, and PDF documents must be embedded in an HTML page, allowing the PDF file to display in part of the browser window rather than in a full window.

With an ActiveX browser, such as Internet Explorer, that supports navigating through the document in the partial window, users can navigate PDFs in place, right on the page, using either the toolbar or navigational links built into the PDF (as I discuss in Chapter 6). Netscape Navigator-compatible browsers can display the PDF document within an HTML page but require a link to a full-window view (in Reader or Exchange) for navigation. If users attempt to navigate the PDF, they are automatically switched to the viewer application. An exception is a link to a URL (Web location), which you can include in the HTML code for embedding. Clicking on hypertext links in the PDF sends the browser to the new World Wide Web location. (You can find information on this type of linking on page 266 of the *Exchange Online Guide*.)

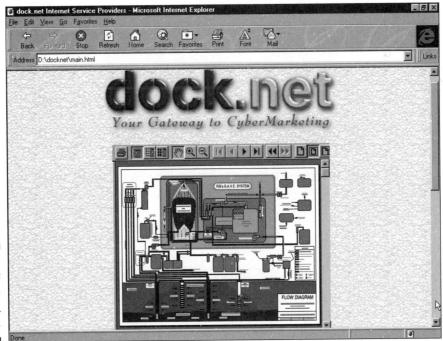

Figure 15-3:
A PDF embedded in an HTML page.

Publishing PDFs on the World Wide Web

As a World Wide Web designer, I realize that for people who don't have an understanding of the Internet, it seems a lot like black magic. The reality is that Hypertext Markup Language (HTML) publishing, which is the type of document displayed in browsers on the Web, has an easy layout procedure, especially now that so many HTML page layout packages are available.

In the preceding section, you found out about the four viewing scenarios for PDFs on the Web. You'll be happy to know that the first three are all achieved in the same way. How they are treated in the browser depends solely on the browser your users use for accessing the Web. The fourth application, embedding the PDF directly on the HTML page, is a bit more difficult, requiring you to add coding directly to the HTML source, or page.

The two methods for making PDFs navigable on a Web page are creating a URL link and embedding. The following sections look at each procedure in detail.

Creating an HTML link to a PDF

If you have experience laying out Web pages, this discussion will make perfect sense to you. If not, you should find out about HTML pages before reading on. Otherwise, you might suffer from techno-overload.

To create a link to a PDF on the Web, you make calls (create codes) to a PDF the same way you make calls to a URL, or location: with the *A HREF* code. To link to IDG Books Worldwide, for example, your code would look like this:

```
<A HREF="http://www.idgbooks.com">Click Here to Go to IDG
Books World Wide</A>
```

All the users see is the bold text, displayed as a hyperlink. The same call to a PDF looks like this:

```
<A HREF="http://www.dock.net/pdfs/userhelp.pdf">Help
Manual</A>
```

All the users see in the Web page is the clickable link, Help Manual. When they click on the link, the PDF begins downloading and, depending on their browser and configuration, is displayed in their browser or in a helper application window.

Creating URL links inside PDFs

In addition to creating links in HTML pages to PDFs, you can create links inside PDFs to Web pages and other PDFs on the Web. You do not achieve this with HTML coding on a Web page. Instead, this magic is performed in Exchange.

To create a link to any Web page or PDF living on the Web, follow these steps:

1. **Open the document in which you want to create a URL link.**

2. **Go to the page containing the text or graphic you want to make hot.**

   I discuss creating links in Chapter 6.

3. **Select the Link tool.**

4. **Drag a link rectangle around the text or graphic you want to make hot.**

   This displays the Create Link dialog box.

5. **Make the desired changes to the link rectangle.**

   I discuss changing link rectangles in Chapter 6.

6. **From the Action Type list, select World Wide Web Link.**

7. **Click the Edit URL button.**

   The Weblink Edit URL dialog box appears.

8. **Type the URL.**

9. **Click OK.**

   The Weblink Edit URL dialog box closes and the Create Link dialog box appears.

10. **Click Set Link.**

   That's it. Now, whenever users click the link, their browser will hop over to the URL you defined in the link. Too easy, huh?

As in PDFs, links can be made from either text or graphics. Believe it or not, we used to do all of this coding by hand, in text documents, as shown in Figure 15-4. Nowadays, these kinds of links are usually set up in an HTML layout program, such as Claris Home Page, Adobe PageMill, or Microsoft Front Page. In Figure 15-5, I'm creating a link to a PDF in Claris Home Page.

Easy enough, right? No? If you're finding this discussion way over your head, check out a good book on HTML, such as *HTML For Dummies,* 2nd Edition, by Steve James and Ed Tittel (published by IDG Books Worldwide, Inc.).

Embedding PDFs in Web pages

To embed PDFs in Web pages, you use the HTML code <EMBED>. In Internet Explorer, you can also use <OBJECT>. The results you get depend on the browser. Netscape Navigator 3, for example, displays the first page of the PDF, without the toolbar and other navigation tools. Internet Explorer, on the other hand, uses the settings you set in the Open Info dialog box when creating the PDF. (I discuss the Open Info dialog box in Chapter 7.) It displays the page, view, and interface settings saved with the PDF.

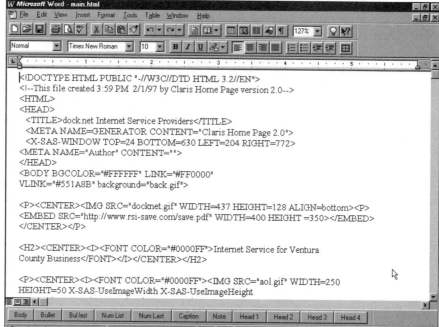

Figure 15-4:
An HTML
source
page. How's
that for
some nerdy
technical
stuff?

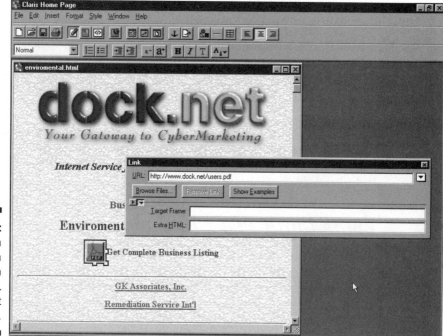

Figure 15-5:
Creating a
link to a
PDF in an
HTML
layout
program.

In addition, you cannot navigate the PDF on the Netscape Navigator page, but you can in Internet Explorer. (When you click an embedded PDF in Netscape, the viewer application — Reader or Exchange — comes to the forefront and allows you to navigate the PDF.)

In the HTML source document, the `<EMBED>` code looks like this:

```
<EMBED SRC="http://www.rsi-save.com/save.pdf" WIDTH=75%
HEIGHT=75%></EMBED>
```

The Height and Width variables allow you to control the size of the PDF in the Web page. In this example, I designate the size using percentages, but you can also use pixels (HEIGHT=300, WIDTH=200). I prefer percentages because the size of the PDF on the page is determined by the size of the browser window. If your users resize the window (or if they are using different monitor resolutions), the embedded PDFs resize accordingly. This method also ensures that Internet Explorer displays the entire toolbar and all the controls.

In addition to adding the codes to the source file with a text editor, you can also embed them in your HTML pages with some Web page layout programs, as shown in Figure 15-6, as long as you know how to use the layout software. This method can be easier than coding the PDF object by hand.

Figure 15-6:
I'm embedding and formatting the PDF on an HTML page in a Web layout application.

The discussion on publishing PDFs on the Web may seem short, sweet, and too simple. But this really is all you need to know to get you PDFs to work on the Internet. You can find supporting information, such as design issues and form application programming, on Adobe's Web site. Try this: While connected to the Internet, from inside Exchange, choose Help⇨Adobe on The Web⇨Tips and Tricks. You find a bunch of valuable stuff on these Web pages.

Chapter 16

Optimizing Your PDFs for the World Wide Web

● ●

In This Chapter

▶ Using Exchange's Optimize feature to prepare PDFs for the Web

▶ Resampling bitmap images for faster downloading

▶ Compressing bitmap graphics for faster downloading and viewing

● ●

*T*he World Wide Web is a marvelous place. The information contained there is nothing short of voluminous (or *vast,* if you prefer). However, a severe limitation of the Web and the Internet in general is bandwidth. *Bandwidth* refers to the speed at which data is transferred from one computer to another, measured in bits per second (bps).

Although all kinds of new, super-fast technologies are on the horizon, right now most people are accessing the Internet over analog (voice) phone lines with relatively slow modems, at about 28,000 bps. (Granted, new and faster modems are being developed and released more quickly than I can type this, but most phone lines in most areas of the United States can handle only 28.8 Kbps. In many other countries, the bps rate is even slower.)

Why is this important? Well, Internet surfers are impatient. They're accustomed to immediate gratification; they want Web pages and supporting documents, such as PDFs, to download and display quickly. Many of them won't wait for slow file downloads. If something takes too long, they cancel it and move on. All your hard work designing and adding those cool links in your PDFs means nothing if users don't take the time to see them.

Unless you know that your users are accessing the Internet over fast connections — such as T1s, frame relays, ISDN, local area networks, intranets, or cable modems — you should assume that most of them are using phone lines and modems. When designing PDFs for the Web, you should keep in mind bandwidth and file downloading limitations. This means designing documents to the lowest common denominator: Make them as small as possible, and don't assume that all your users have browsers that support the latest innovations in Internet file serving technology, such as byteserving, or streaming (as I discuss in Chapter 15).

Optimizing PDFs and reducing file size for quicker downloading and access are the focus of this chapter. First, you look at the most effective technology built into Acrobat 3: optimizing files for byte-serving, which delivers PDFs a page at a time based on user input. Then you look at reducing file size by resampling images and compressing text and graphics.

Optimizing PDFs for Page-at-a-Time Downloading

Byte-serving is the technology for delivering page-at-a-time downloading of PDFs over the World Wide Web. Page-at-a-time means just what it says. When a user clicks a link that initiates a PDF download from an Internet server, the server sends the first page (or the page defined in Open Info, as I describe in Chapter 7), and it is displayed. This provides the user with relatively quick access to the PDF without waiting for the entire file to download.

When the user requests another page (by clicking on a hyperlink or a bookmark), the server sends that page to the browser, and so on. For this scenario to perform properly, a number of conditions must be present. The user must be using a Netscape Navigator 3-compatible browser that supports PDF viewing through a viewer plug-in. The Internet server on which the PDF resides must support byte-serving. (Point your browser to `http://www.adobe.com/special/acrobat/moreinfo` to get a list of Internet servers that currently support byte-serving.) And the PDF must be optimized.

Often, you, the PDF designer, don't have much (or any) control over the first two conditions. You can, however, make sure that your PDFs are optimized. This ensures that every visitor to the sites containing your work get the best possible viewing experience.

Optimizing a single PDF

Optimizing a PDF is another function that Acrobat performs elegantly. Frankly, it can't get much easier than this. To optimize a PDF for page-at-a-time downloading on the Web, follow these steps:

1. **Open the file that you want to optimize in Exchange.**

2. **Choose File⇨Save As.**

    The Save As dialog box appears.

3. **Select the Optimize option.**

4. Click Save.

If this is a new PDF that has not been saved before, or if you're saving it to a new location, Exchange will save the document. If you are saving an existing PDF to its original location, Exchange will ask whether you want to replace the existing file.

5. If Exchange asks about replacing the existing file, click Yes.

That's it. Note, though, that if you edit the file, you must use Save As to optimize it again. Simply choosing Save won't optimize the file; in fact, it removes optimization.

Optimizing several PDFs at one time

If you have a bunch of PDFs you want to prepare for the Web, you can do so with Batch Optimize. Use this option for readying entire libraries of PDFs for byte-serving. Batch Optimize optimizes by folders, rather than by individual files. So, before running a batch optimize, make sure that your PDFs are in the same folder or folder structure. If you're not sure what I mean by folder structure, check out the "Fine-tune your file structures" section in Chapter 13.

After you have all the PDFs you want to optimize in the desired file and folder structure, follow these steps to batch optimize your PDFs:

1. In Exchange, choose File⇨Optimize.

The Select Folder To Optimize dialog box appears, as shown in Figure 16-1.

Figure 16-1:
Use this dialog box to choose the folder containing the PDFs you want to batch optimize.

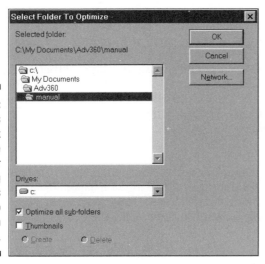

2. **Navigate to the folder you want to optimize.**

3. **If you want to optimize all the PDFs in the subfolders of the folder you're selecting to optimize, make sure that the Optimize all sub-folders option is selected.**

4. **To add or delete Thumbnails for your pages, select the Thumbnails option. Then select Delete to get rid of existing thumbnails or Create to add them.**

   Thumbnails increase file size, especially in PDFs with a lot of pages and graphics. If you don't really need thumbnails, delete them.

5. **Click OK.**

Exchange optimizes all the files in the selected folder and subfolders (if you selected the Optimize all sub-folders option). Depending on how many PDFs you're optimizing, the process can take awhile.

Think twice before optimizing your PDFs. Visitors to your site using versions of Reader later than 3.0 will not be able to access your files.

Controlling Image Size for Fast Downloading

Even if all conditions are right for page-at-a-time viewing, in most situations, not all of your users will be set up to support byte-serving. Thoughtful PDF designers know this and keep their users in mind when designing PDFs. In this section, you look at optimizing bitmap images for faster downloading through resampling (sometimes called downsampling).

Why are we talking only about *bitmap* images? Well, text and line art (vector graphics created in draw programs, such as CorelDRAW! or Adobe Illustrator), are usually pretty small, anyway. Although compressing them doesn't remove tons of data, every little bit helps. To compress them in Acrobat, select the Compress text and line art option at the top of the Job Options dialog box. (To get there, choose Distiller➪Job Options➪Compression.) Compress text and line art except when you're using PDFs in high-end print-on-demand applications.

Downsampling controls are set in Distiller before converting a PostScript print file to PDF. Before a discussion of resampling images, I should point out that, by default, Distiller does a good job of balancing image quality and file size. With a little thought and a few extra steps, however, you might be able to make your images even smaller, making the download even quicker.

Distiller allows you to use two types of file size reduction: *downsampling* and *subsampling*. Both techniques make images smaller by combining pixels. Data that is represented by several pixels in a bitmap image (a paint-type photograph or a scanned image) would then be represented by one larger pixel. Distiller lets you use either downsampling or subsampling to reduce the file size, but keep in mind that either method can result in some loss of detail in your images. By default, Distiller downsamples color and grayscale images to 72 dpi (dots per inch) and monochrome images to 300 dpi. In the following, you look at each type of resampling.

Downsampling and subsampling

Downsampling reduces the resolution of the images in a PDF to the dpi setting you choose. The process works by averaging the pixel color of a sample area and replacing that area with a pixel of the averaged color, or a color that best represents the general color of the area. Between the two Acrobat resampling methods, this one does a better job of maintaining the closest representation of the colors in the original image, but it also results in a larger file size than subsampling.

Subsampling also reduces the resolution of the images in a PDF to the dpi setting you choose. It does so by choosing a pixel in the center of a sample area and then replacing the entire area with that pixel (and its color). This technique can greatly reduce the file size and processing time required to download and display images, but it can also result in color shifts, or changes in color from the original image. You should subsample only when color integrity is not a major consideration. Subsampling works well for images that contain solid, distinguishable colors, such as simple drawings, as opposed to continuous tone grayscale and color photographs.

Resampling your images

Images are resampled in your PDFs in two ways: in Distiller during the conversion process, or individually from an image editing program, such as Photoshop or Corel PHOTO-PAINT. In most cases, the Distiller method works fine. With certain types of images, however, you can gain further control over image quality and file size by first resampling certain types of images in your image editor before converting a document to a PDF.

You can control file size also by limiting the number of fonts in the PDF. When you design documents for retrieval from the Web, use only the fonts that are in the Acrobat basic font set, as I discuss in Chapter 4. This precludes Distiller from having to embed additional fonts in the PDF.

Changing resample settings in Distiller

Chapter 4 takes a close look at Distiller (and PDFWriter), so I won't rehash that entire discussion here. Instead, you look at only the resampling options. These options are set from the Job Options dialog box. From here, you control both downsampling and compression. (I discuss compression later in the chapter.)

To change resample settings, follow these steps:

1. **From Distiller (and before choosing a PostScript file to process), choose Distiller⇨Job Options.**

2. **Click the Compression tab.**

   The Job Options dialog box appears, as shown in Figure 16-2. The resampling settings are the top option in each of the three sections, Color Bitmap Images, Grayscale Bitmap Images, and Monochrome Bitmap Images.

3. **To change a setting from Downsample to Subsample, click the drop-down arrow and then click the down arrow in the list, as shown in Figure 16-3.**

   On a Mac, there is no down arrow. Instead, you get the entire list from a pop-up menu.

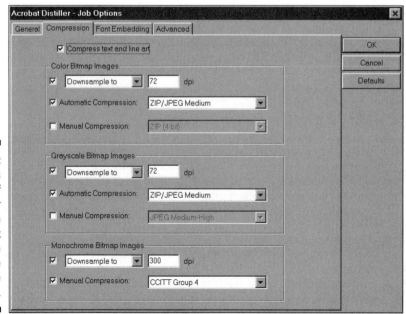

Figure 16-2: Use this portion of the Distiller Job Option dialog box to make image resample settings.

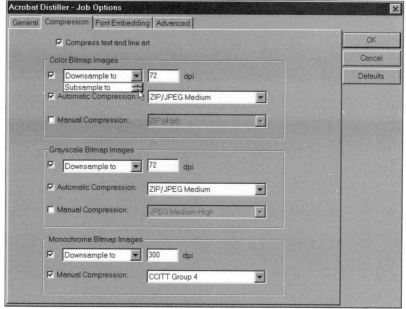

Figure 16-3:
To switch
between
Downsample
to and
Subsample
to, click the
down arrow
in the list.

4. **Set the desired dpi.**

   Note that most computer monitors, except high-resolution graphics monitors, display at 72 dpi. High-resolution monitors can get up to about 95 dpi. Monochrome (black-and-white) images are typically resampled to 300 dpi because they display best on most monitors at this setting. Because monotone images contain only 1 bit per pixel, 300 dpi does not cause large file sizes.

5. **Repeat Steps 3 and 4 for each type of image you want to resample.**

That's it. Now all the images in your new PDF will be resampled using the new settings.

Resampling your images in an image editor

You might want to resample images in an image editor before converting a document to a PDF for two reasons. One, you want more control over how images are resampled. Two, your document contains several types of images (drawings, photographs, and so on), and you don't want them to be treated in the same way. Drawings that contain only a few colors, for example, can be greatly reduced in file size by indexing their colors.

Each image editor handles resampling a little differently. In Photoshop, for example, you reduce an image's resolution with the settings in the Image Size dialog box (Image⇨Image Size), and you reduce colors by choosing

Indexed Color from the Mode menu (Image⇨Mode⇨Indexed Color). From the Indexed Color dialog box, you can set the method for indexing and the number of colors for the image. If an image contains three distinct colors, for example, change the method to Adaptive and set the number of colors to 3.

Confused yet? Photoshop, indexed color, and similar topics are huge technical issues. Unfortunately, I can't tell you much about Photoshop in this book on Acrobat. You can find plenty of help, however, in *Macworld Adobe Photoshop 4 Bible,* by Deke McClellend (published by IDG Books Worldwide, Inc.).

In Corel PHOTO-PAINT, you change an image's resolution from the Resample dialog box (Image⇨Resample). You index colors from the Convert to Paletted Image dialog box.

Many, many Windows users use PHOTO-PAINT to create and edit their graphics. You find a bunch of help for resampling images in PHOTO-PAINT in my book *CorelDRAW 7 SECRETS* (published by IDG Books Worldwide, Inc.).

Before leaving this discussion of indexed color, I show you how resampling images can balance file size and image quality. Figures 16-4 and 16-5 show an image before I resampled it in PHOTO-PAINT (Figure 16-4) and after I changed the resolution from 300 to 72 dpi and reduced the colors from 16.7 million to 50 (Figure 16-5). As you can see, the image looks almost identical, but the file size is reduced by more than two thirds.

Figure 16-4:
An image and its settings before resampling.

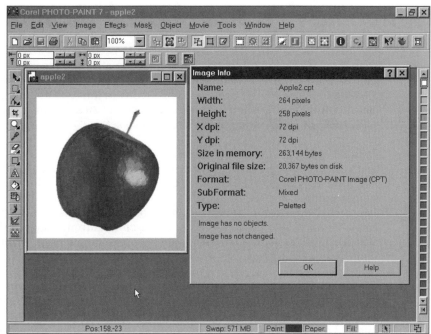

Figure 16-5:
The image
and its
settings
after
resampling.

Granted, this manual resampling can cause a lot of extra work, especially for PDFs containing a lot of images. But it does give you greater control over file size and how your images are displayed.

Remember, too, that if you are resampling images from a document layout program, such as a word processor or a desktop publishing program, you may need to place the images in your creator document again, unless you have linked them with OLE or are using the creator program's auto-linking and updating feature. PageMaker, for example, allows you to create dynamic links between layouts and the images contained in them.

After you've gone to all the work of resampling all your images manually, you don't want to take the chance of Distiller ruining them by attempting to apply further resampling. So, make sure that you turn off resampling in the Compression tab of the Distiller's Job Options dialog box before distilling the document file. If you resampled colored bitmaps before converting the file, turn off the options in Color Bitmap Images. For grayscale images, turn off the options in Grayscale Bitmap Images.

A third method for controlling resampling not discussed in this chapter (primarily because it's too technical) is by direct editing of the PostScript print file before using Distiller to convert it. You can try this if you want, but it's far beyond anything I'm inclined to mess with. You find instructions for adding parameters to PostScript files in the *Distiller Parameters Guide*. (From Distiller, choose Help⇨Distiller Parameters Guide.)

Controlling File Size through Compression

By default, when you turn on Automatic Compression for each image type, Distiller does a good job of balancing image quality and file size. If you choose the Automatic Compression option in the Job Options dialog box, Distiller looks at your images during the conversion to PDF, determines the best compression method for your color and grayscale bitmap images (JPEG, ZIP, or LZW), and applies the optimal setting.

Distiller applies JPEG compression to images with smooth color changes, such as scanned photographs or composites created in image-editing applications. ZIP (Reader 3.0 compatibility) or LZW (Reader 2.1 compatibility) compression is applied to images with sharp color changes, such as screen captures of application windows (like those used in this book). The Automatic Compression option does not affect monochrome images or line art, which you set separately in the Monochrome Bitmap Images section of the Job Options dialog box.

Sometimes, however, automatic settings in Distiller do not reduce file sizes enough. In these situations, you can further reduce the size of your PDFs by making changes to the compression settings in the Job Options dialog box. Here's how:

1. **From Distiller (and before choosing a PostScript file to convert), choose Distiller⇨Job Options.**

2. **Click the Compression tab.**

3. **For color and grayscale images, you have two options: Automatic Compression and Manual Compression:**

   a. **If you select a setting in the Automatic Compression list, Distiller determines which type of compression to use — ZIP or JPEG — based on each image.**

   You can, however, control the image size somewhat by choosing an image quality setting, such as High or Medium High.

   b. **If you select Manual Compression, you should then choose a compression method from the list, either ZIP or JPEG (or LZW, if you are creating an Acrobat 2.1 compatible PDF).**

   For a discussion of compression types, see the "Determining a compression method" sidebar.

4. **Click OK.**

If you make so many changes in the Job Options dialog box that you can't remember how to get back to the Distiller defaults, simply click Defaults.

Determining a compression method

Acrobat uses three types of compression methods for color and grayscale images: Zip, LZW (for Reader 2.1 compatibility), and JPEG. ZIP and LZW are lossless compression methods. JPEG is a lossy compression method.

The *lossless* compression methods keep all the data in the image file intact. (This method is called *lossless* because when the file is decompressed, all the data in the file is still there — nothing is lost.) The image quality remains high, but the file size is also large.

Typically, lossless data compression can reduce a file by as much as half its original size. A good-sized full-color image can easily eat up several megabytes of disk space, however, so 50 percent helps but does not entirely solve the file size problem — particularly when downloading images from the Internet. Lossless is preferable when creating PDFs for large storage mediums, such as a CD-ROM, especially when your documents contain a lot of huge full-color image files.

The *lossy* compression method uses compression algorithms to eliminate specific data from the image file. The image quality of the resulting digital file may be degraded, but the file size is also greatly reduced.

This is not as bad as it sounds. Many images contain a lot more data than is necessary to display well on a computer monitor. For example, 24-bit images contain a lot of unnecessary repeated data and display a lot of subtle color differences that people can't really see. It does little to the image quality to drop this data from the file.

Unlike lossless data compression, lossy data compression is capable of compression rates as high as 100:1. For example, you could compress a 2MB file down to 20K. This, however, is a radical reduction and would degrade image quality significantly. How much compression an image can stand depends on the image and the level of degradation you can live with.

By default, Acrobat uses JPEG for resampling color and grayscale images, which works pretty well. If you want to control how each image looks in your PDFs rather than defer to the built-in routines in Distiller, however, you can use the JPEG resampling built into your image editor. Simply save the image as a JPEG file from your image editor. With this method, you can set certain images to high quality with minimal compression and others to a lower quality with more compression. A lot of work, perhaps, but the real issue is how much of a perfectionist are you? Or better yet, what kind of exacting controls do you need?

All Acrobat monochrome compression routines are lossless (in other words, nothing is lost when the file is decompressed). Choosing the default CCITT Group 4 compression ensures compatibility for all versions of Reader. You gain little by choosing another method. If you choose Zip, your monochrome images won't be compatible with versions of Reader before 3.0.

Chapter 17

Setting Up a PDF Application on Your Company's Network

. . . .

In This Chapter

▶ Incorporating the Acrobat automated features into your network library

▶ Making your PDF library secure

▶ Exporting and retrieving form data

. . . .

*M*ost companies generate a substantial amount of documents, adding new ones and changing old ones depending on work flow and policy changes. When a company relies on hard copy documents, such as forms or manuals, copying and printing costs can skyrocket. In addition, there's the nightmare of trying to locate and destroy older versions of revised documents.

An alternative is to keep an electronic portable document library on your company's local area network (LAN) or wide area network (WAN). With the proper implementation, a pool of PDFs can be easily accessed, searched, updated, and maintained, while ensuring that information is always current and secure from prying eyes.

I can't give you a crash course in setting up a computer network and file structure, but I can provide some basics for setting up an Acrobat library for your company. Some concepts discussed in this chapter assume a basic network savvy — or at least access to the company network administrator to help you understand them.

Laying Out an Automated PDF Library

I describe some basic file and folder structuring in Chapter 13 in the "Fine-tune your file structures" section. Basically, the same kind of structure works well for networked PDF libraries, with some variation by application. The complexity of your file and folder structure depends primarily on the size of the application and the number and types of users on the network.

It would be easy to create a folder on the network drive called *PDFs* or *documents*. But that's hardly planning ahead, especially if you anticipate any growth. Keep in mind, too, that users on your network must be informed of the library structure and how to use it.

The three basic kinds of network users of a PDF library are people who create company documents and PDFs, people who access company documents and PDFs, and people who create and access company documents and PDFs. We could create three new categories of Acrobat people, then: Create-Only, Access-Only, and Create-Access. But that's already been accomplished with basic network terminology: Write-Only, Read-Only, and Read-Write. So I use these standard terms in this chapter.

When beginning your PDF library, you should designate a place on the network drive to hold your documents. Usually, this will consist of parent folders and supporting subfolders. The parent folders would contain indexes, as I discuss in Chapter 13, and subfolders for different topics and for supporting files, such as sounds and movies. (As I discuss in Chapters 11 and 12, these files are accessed through pointers, and not kept in the PDFs themselves.)

Your users will have the best luck keeping track of their movies and sounds if they first copy the files to the designated folder on the network drive, and then import them into their PDFs, That way, the pointers to the files will stay valid.

A typical structure, then, might look like Figure 17-1. In this top-down example, files are arranged according to topic, and it's easy to add new topics as they arise. This structure makes indexing and creating new PDFs easier for everyone involved in maintaining the library. It makes it easy, also, to keep secure documents in their own folders, allowing you to assign permissions by user type on the network, as I describe later in this chapter.

Figure 17-1: Use this kind of file structure to hold your PDF libraries.

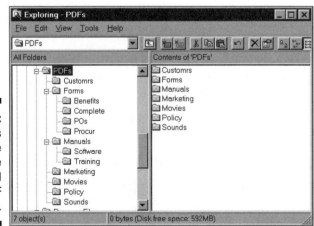

Updating and Maintaining a PDF Library

As the keeper of the company electronic document library, you are responsible for seeing that all PDFs get into the correct folders and that they are indexed properly. Basically, you have two choices for achieving this: Teach your users how to use Exchange and where and how to save PDFs, or create and maintain the files yourself, either using the Acrobat automatic features or manually. Frankly, unless you are on a huge network that generates volumes of documents on an ongoing basis, the second method is a lot easier to control. (If you choose the first method, run out and buy this book for everybody involved.)

In either case, Acrobat provides two important tools to help you: watched folders and automatic index updating. In this section, you look at each one. First, though, check out what maintaining the library manually entails.

Maintaining a PDF library manually

When maintaining libraries manually, you have the most control. You decide which files wind up as PDFs and where they go on the network drive. You also convert them to PDFs and do all the indexing manually. Basically, this means users on the network send you all the files to be converted to PDFs (by copying them to a central location on the network, e-mail, or copying them to a folder on your computer) either as original creator documents or as PostScript files. You would then convert them to PDFs (see Chapter 4), copy them to the proper folders on the network, and update the indexes (see Chapter 13).

If your network users don't send you PostScript files, you need to keep on your hard disk all the programs used by people to generate the files (or install them as the need arises). In a big organization that uses many programs, this could constitute several applications, such as word processors, desktop publishers, presentation programs, graphics editors, and even CAD and accounting packages.

If you go the other route and have users generate PDFs, each user will need a copy of Exchange if they enhance or change the PDFs. This could be costly because Adobe requires a separate license for each user, and each user must learn to use Exchange. Another alternative is to have them all use PDF-Writer, as I discuss in Chapter 4. Unless the users are using PageMaker or another PDF-savvy program, however, PDF Writer will not allow them to create hyperlinks and other types of PDF navigational and multimedia actions. You have to do that for them. But simple, short PDFs often don't require hyperlinks, especially if the PDFs have proper indexing.

Using watched folders

Watched folders work like this:

1. You tell Distiller which folders to watch for new PostScript files.

2. Users generate PostScript files from their documents and copy them to the watched folders.

3. Periodically, Distiller converts the new PostScript files to PDFs and moves them to an Out folder.

Sound simple? In concept, it is. And you, the PDF administrator, have a lot of control over how watched folders work by choosing whether the PDF updating and maintaining process will be semi-automated or fully automated. It's your call — depending on the amount of control your application requires.

With watched folders, you can create either one central place on the network for automatic PDF conversion, or several watched folders based on the types of documents generated. With the first scenario, you would move the newly converted PDFs to the appropriate folders. With the second scenario, your users would copy PostScript files to the appropriate folders and Distiller would do the rest, basically maintaining the library for you. Remember, if you choose a fully automated process, users must be instructed on which watched folders to use and when. Otherwise, you could wind up with a hodgepodge of PDFs all over the network.

Creating watched folders

For Distiller to use watched folders on a network drive, it (or you, if that's the way your network works) must have permission to read, write, and delete files on the machine on which the watched folders reside. I'm not familiar with all types of networks, so you need to get with your network administrator to make sure that your network is set up properly for this operation. On a Windows NT network, the user (in this case, you) must have read and write permission for the folders containing watched folders. This would allow Distiller to perform its magic from your computer when you're logged on to the network.

Another alternative is to install Distiller on the network server where the PDFs will reside. But this entails leaving the server workstation running, which many administrators don't like to do for several reasons — among them, security concerns.

The other users on the network sending PostScript files to the watched folders also need the proper permissions. When all these conditions are met, you are ready to set up your watched folders.

When you create a watched folder, Distiller creates two folders in the watched folder: In and Out. Again, you must have already decided which type of application you'll use: either one central watched folder that you will manage, or several watched folders that Distiller will manage automatically. Distiller can watch up to 100 folders. So, as you can imagine, you can set up a large and complicated automated process.

In sophisticated scenarios, where you have lots of PDFs, you can control who copies what kinds of documents to which folders by designating your file structure by department. You can then use indexing to make the documents easy to find. One way to ensure that the wrong documents don't wind up in your watched folders is to have the network administrator restrict write privileges for the different categories of PDF folders. (For example, only accounting employees can copy files to the Accounting watched folder.)

You have many ways to control who puts what files where. Network server software can create an intricate web of permissions based on users and groups of users. On a peer-to-peer Windows or AppleTalk network, though, you don't have a lot of options for controlling shared files. Usually, a folder or file is either shared or not shared.

To create a watched folder, follow these steps:

1. **From Distiller, choose Distiller⇨Watched Folders.**

   The Watched Folders Options dialog box appears. From here, you set up your watched folders.

2. **Set how often you want your watched folders checked for new PostScript files.**

   By default, Distiller checks watched folders every 10 seconds, which I think is overkill. Every hour or every few hours is sufficient. Remember that Distiller must be running before it can check anything.

   To ensure that Distiller runs all the time, create a shortcut (in Windows) or an alias (on a Mac) and copy it into the system's Startup Items folder. In Windows, you right-click on the Distiller program icon and choose Create Shortcut. On a Mac, you select the icon and then choose File⇨ Make Alias. Another way to ensure that Distiller runs all the time — without interfering with your work on your local machine — is to install it on the network server or the machine that contains your PDF library.

3. **Click Add Folder.**

   The Add Folder dialog box appears.

4. **Select the folder you want to make watched, and click OK.**

   The folder is added to the Watched Folders List, as shown in Figure 17-2.

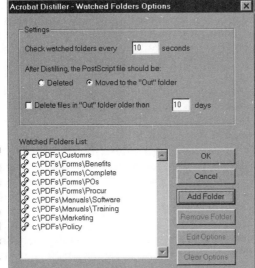

Figure 17-2:
In this
example, I
set up
several
folders as
watched.

Unlike indexed folders, you have to create watched folders for *each*
folder you want watched, *including subfolders.* For example, suppose
you have several subfolders under a parent folder called Manuals. If
you want all the subfolders watched, you must select each one and add
it to the Watched Folders List. Usually, in this scenario, the parent
folder does not contain any documents (except, perhaps, an index), so
you would not set it up as watched. In addition, when your users copy
PostScript files to a watched folder, they should copy them into the In
folder inside the watched folder, not into the watched folder itself.

5. Select an option under "After Distilling, the PostScript file should be."

After converting the PostScript file to a PDF, the file can be deleted or
moved to the Out folder. In a truly automated system, the file would be
deleted, saving you from having to go back and clean out the garbage to
save drive space.

You can also choose to have PDFs in the Out folder deleted after a
designated period. In a library in which you are moving PDFs out of the
watched folders manually, this option performs some housekeeping for
you by getting rid of unwanted files. In an automated system in which
PDFs are generated and added to the system automatically, you should
turn this setting off. An exception would be if your library PDFs expire
after a certain time.

6. Click OK.

Setting watched folder options

As I discuss in several chapters, primarily Chapters 4 and 16, you can set a number of Distiller options, such as version compatibility, graphics compression, and font embedding. You can also set these options individually for each watched folder from the Watched Folder Options dialog box. Simply select a watched folder in the Watched Folder List, and click Edit Options. This displays the Job Options dialog box. (I discuss this dialog box in detail in Chapters 4 and 16.)

You might want to set different options for different folders for several reasons. Perhaps some of your PDFs are optimized for the Web, and others are designed for print-on-demand. You would often want different font embedding and compression options for these two very different applications.

When you set job options that are different from the Acrobat defaults, the icon next to the watched folder in the Watched Folders List changes. In Windows, the eyes icon changes to a delta symbol, as shown in Figure 17-3. On a Mac, both the eyes icon and the delta icon are displayed.

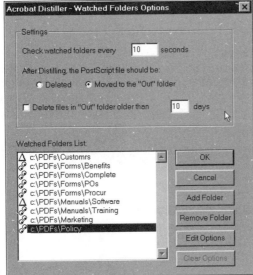

Figure 17-3: The delta symbol beside a watched folder indicates that the job options for that folder have been changed.

Indexing your library automatically

Part of creating an automated PDF library maintenance application is scheduling periodic index updating, or rebuilding. As you and other users add PDFs to the system or revise existing ones, the PDFs need to be added to the index so that users can find them efficiently.

This section discusses only automatic index updating. If you are not familiar with indexing in Acrobat, check out Chapter 13.

Like indexing itself, automatic index updating (or *scheduling,* as Adobe calls it) is controlled from Acrobat Catalog. To set up automatic indexing, follow these steps:

1. **From Catalog, choose Index⇨Schedule.**

   The Schedule Builds dialog box appears.

2. **Click Add.**

   The Select Index File to Add to Schedule dialog box appears.

3. **Navigate to the drive, folder, and PDX file you want to add to the schedule.**

4. **Select the PDX file you want to add to the schedule, and click OK.**

5. **Continue adding indexes to the schedule until you've added all that you want to rebuild automatically.**

   After you finish, you'll have one index or a list of indexes similar to Figure 17-4.

6. **Set the method for scheduled rebuilding.**

   The three options are *Continuously, Once,* and *Every. Continuously* rebuilds the indexes over and over, nonstop, until you click Stop. *Once* starts the rebuild immediately and stops when all the indexes in the list are rebuilt. *Every* schedules periodic rebuilds based on the settings you make in the corresponding fields.

Figure 17-4: After you finish adding indexes, your list will look something like this one.

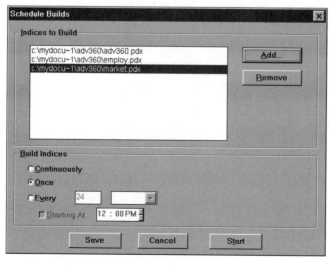

7. **If you selected the *Every* option, set the time period and when the rebuild should begin.**

   You can set your rebuilds to commence by minutes, hours, or days, starting at any time you want.

8. **Click Save to save a scheduled *Every* update, or click Start to begin a *Continuously* or *Once* rebuild.**

When you create new indexes, you can have Catalog add them to your rebuild schedule automatically. You do this when you build the index, as I discuss in Chapter 13. All you do is select the Add Index to Schedule option in the Save Index File dialog box, shown in Figure 17-5.

Figure 17-5:
As you create new indexes and add them to the system, you can automatically add them to the rebuild schedule from this dialog box.

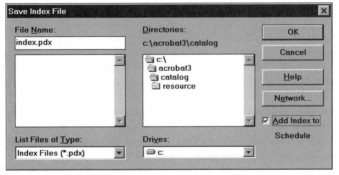

Catalog rebuilds indexes incrementally, adding to the indexes rather than completely starting over. This method increases the size of the index each time it's rebuilt, but allows users to continue searching even though the index is being rebuilt. As the index grows, it takes longer to search. You should purge your indexes periodically, as I discuss in Chapter 13.

Catalog must be running for scheduling to work. If you want to make sure that Catalog runs all the time, you can create a shortcut (in Windows) or an alias (on a Mac) and copy it into the system's Startup Items folder. In Windows, you right-click on the Catalog program icon and choose Create Shortcut. On a Mac, you select the icon and then choose File⇨Make Alias. Another way to ensure that Catalog runs all the time — without interfering with your work on your local machine — is to install it on the network server or the machine containing your PDF library.

Setting Up a Secure PDF Library

A secure PDF library is a happy PDF library. Or, at least your superiors are happy if everyone in the organization doesn't have access to sensitive information. Chapter 6 discusses using Acrobat's security options in Exchange to control who can open documents in Reader or Exchange or edit PDFs from Exchange. In most situations, these options work well. When you have a scenario in which different types of documents are meant for certain users, however, you, the PDF master, wind up juggling passwords, trying to remember whom you should supply passwords to and which passwords go to which users.

A method I prefer in these large, unruly situations is to control access from the network's permission options (usually available only when the PDF library is kept on a file server, rather than on a peer-to-peer network).

If you want to use this type of security but you're not the network administrator for your organization, you'll need to contact the person in charge of the network. This procedure entails setting permissions on the network drive to accommodate specific users and exclude others. For example, suppose that you want only certain users to gain access to files in a folder on the network folder called Accounting. You would use the server software's permission and user rights options to tell the server who gets access to what files and who does not.

Users who try to access files for which they don't have proper permissions will get an access denied error. In Windows NT Server (and perhaps others), an event log entry is also generated, informing the network powers that the user tried to access the file unsuccessfully.

These types of controls can also contain read-only controls, allowing some users to view but not change the files. How you work this out is up to you and your network people. Although it requires some planning, it's an effective way to secure portions, or all, of your PDF library.

Setting Up a Form Application on Your Network

The Acrobat form applications are vast, and include the capability to post form data to the World Wide Web or to a network database. Both of these applications, however, require some programming and knowledge of database applications, which I can't supply here. Much of what I describe here, though, can be ported to either of these applications.

In this section, you find out how to export form data and how to allow your users to import data into a PDF form. Why, you may be asking, would you want to do such a thing? By having as much of the form as possible filled out automatically, you ensure that it's filled out correctly.

Instituting this forms submission and retrieval application consists of two steps:

1. **Designing the form in Exchange.**
2. **Filling out the form and saving the form data.**

Designing the form

I discuss designing forms in Exchange in detail in Chapter 10. This section shows you how to design the form a bit differently, so as to implement a forms retrieval and submission application. For the most part, you design the form as you normally do. Where the procedure varies is in some of the actions you set for the form objects. Certain objects will include a mouse action that retrieves form data.

For example, suppose your firm assigns wage scales and benefits to employees using classifications similar to the military's E-1, E-2, E-3, and so on classifications for enlisted personnel. You could tailor the data for a vacation request form to fill in specific fields on the form (such as pay rate and length of vacation time available) based on an employee's classification.

Or perhaps you have a purchase order system that requires specific fields on a form to be filled out differently based on which department is generating the purchase. Having these critical fields filled in automatically can save time (the employee doesn't need to look up codes and classifications), and the finance department is more likely to get an accurate accounting of how the money was spent and how to define the expense.

I'm sure you can think of many other ways to use procedures described here: by office location, by time of the year, specific employee, and by type of benefit applied for.

To create this type of form, you create form objects that retrieve the form data from files saved in the Acrobat Form Data Format (FDF). You can do this with a list of buttons, check boxes, or radio buttons. When the user chooses an option in any type of list, the form data is retrieved into the fields on the form that you predetermine. For example, when the user clicks on one of the options in Figure 17-6, the appropriate data is retrieved into the remainder of the form, or the fields that you filled in beforehand and saved in FDF format.

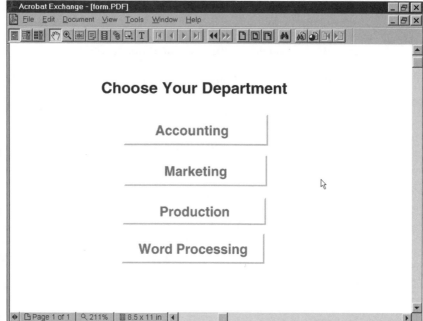

Choose Your Department

Accounting

Marketing

Production

Word Processing

Page 1 of 1   211%   8.5 x 11 in

Figure 17-6:
When the user clicks one of these buttons, the form fields will be filled in automatically.

Remember from Chapter 10 that you should design as much of the form as possible in a creator application, such as your word processor, convert it to a PDF, and then bring it into Exchange and add the form objects. This is especially true if the option choices for automatically filling in form fields are check boxes or radio buttons. You want to create the labels for these objects in the creator application.

To create this list of options, follow these steps:

1. Create your form in a creator application.

2. Convert the document to a PDF.

3. Define your form fields (as I discuss in Chapter 10).

4. Set your form actions for the data retrieval options as follows:

   a. Go to the Action section of the Field Properties dialog box, and select Mouse Down.

   b. Click the Add button.

   c. From the Action list, select Import Form Data.

   d. Click Set Action.

   e. Repeat this process for each option in the list.

Good. Now you are ready to fill out the form and export the data.

Filling out the form and exporting the data

Depending on the number of options you set for each form, you will need to fill out the form a number of times — once for each option. In Figure 17-6, for example, you would fill out the form four times, once for each department, varying the information based on the department data.

Your form will consist of two types of fields, those that are filled in automatically and those that the user fills in. You simply fill in the fields to be returned when the data is retrieved. If your form is a purchase order, for example, your automatic fields might include the fields that the finance department needs to record the data, such as spending limits for the department and the chart of accounts.

After you fill in all the fields you want retrieved with the form, follow these steps to export the data:

1. **Choose File⇨Export⇨Form Data.**

   The Export Form Data dialog box appears. From here, you name and save the file.

2. **Navigate to the folder where your form data files are kept.**

3. **Name the FDF file you want to assign to this option.**

   Give the file a name that you'll remember.

4. **Click Save.**

Now, fill out the form for each of the other options in your Import Form Data list, and export each one with the preceding procedure, remembering to give each file a meaningful name.

All that's left to do is to go back to the options in your Import Form Data list and assign the proper FDF file to the appropriate button, radio button, or check box. To do so, follow these steps:

1. **Select the Form tool.**

2. **Double-click on the first form object in your Import Form Data list.**

   The Field Properties dialog box appears.

3. **Click the Actions tab.**

4. **In the When this Happens list, select Mouse Down.**

5. **In the Do the Following list, double-click Import Form Data.**

   The Edit An Action dialog box appears.

6. **Click the Select File button.**

   The Select File Containing Form Data dialog box appears.

7. **Navigate to the folder containing your form data files, and select the FDF that corresponds to the Import Form Data option you are defining.**

8. **Click Select.**

9. **Click OK in the Field Properties dialog box.**

10. **Repeat Steps 2–9 for each Import Form Data option in your list.**

That's it. When your users click one of the Import Form Data objects, the form data will be retrieved into the form. Your users then need to fill in the rest of the form.

How the form is processed from this point depends on your application. Reader users can only print the form. Or, if your PDFs are part of a CGI scripted World Wide Web application, users can click a Submit button that sends the form to a Web site for processing. Exchange users can print the form, save it as a PDF, or even export the data to a form data file for inclusion in a database application. What happens to the form data depends on what kind of application you have running behind the scenes, separate from Acrobat.

Part V
The Part of Tens

In this part . . .

This part is a collection of useful tips and tricks designed to make working with Acrobat easier. You find ten applications to use when you want to publish and distribute your PDFs as well as ten ways to troubleshoot your PDF applications.

Chapter 18

Ten Applications for Publishing and Distributing PDFs

. . . .

In This Chapter

▶ Interactive PDFs on the World Wide Web

▶ A PDF library on a network drive

▶ Multimedia titles

▶ CD-ROM titles

▶ Software documentation

▶ Form submission and retrieval applications

▶ Searchable information libraries

▶ Electronic books and manuals

▶ Electronic brochures

. . . .

You're thinking about using Acrobat for preparing a specific type of electronic document. Perhaps your company has a new gadget for computer users — what better way to distribute a brochure than on diskette? Or maybe you have some information you want to make accessible on your Web site?

Many Acrobat users don't realize all the possibilities housed on that Acrobat CD-ROM. You know that you can use it to create attractive documents for one type of application, such as documentation for distributing with your software or shareware applications. But you can also use it for multimedia titles, publishing your own books and manuals. The question is, what can't you do with Acrobat?

This chapter presents a bunch of ideas for using Acrobat. After you finish reading it, see what you can come up with. Then, if you want, take the time to e-mail your ideas to me at hostmaster@dock.net.

Using PDFs to Create Interactive Documents for the World Wide Web

I'm guessing (educated as the guess may be) that a majority of the people who buy this book are planning on publishing PDFs on their or their company's Web site. The new page-at-a-time downloading feature in Version 3 makes PDFs an ideal medium for distributing information across the Internet. (In fact, I use them on an Internet server to provide new users with logon information and other help issues.)

In addition to providing a small, compact medium for distributing complex documents, PDFs are more versatile than standard HTML pages. Because PDFs originate in creator applications, such as desktop publishing software or word processors, your layout options are virtually unlimited.

With PDFs, you can create navigational links in the current PDF, links to other PDFs on the Web (no matter what server they reside on), and even HTML pages anywhere on the Web. This powerful application enables you to link up with information on your own server or servers around the world, providing visitors to your site virtually unlimited volumes of information.

PDFs are fast, versatile, and dynamic (easy to change). For detailed information on designing PDFs for the World Wide Web, check out Chapters 3, 6, 7, 15, and 16.

Using PDFs to Create a Company Library on a Network Drive

Need to get control of the paper blizzard at your company? An electronic document library is the answer. As members of your organization generate documents, you can easily convert the documents to PDFs and place them on a network drive.

The PDF library can then be indexed, searched, and retrieved by anyone with the right privileges on the network. Acrobat provides a number of ways for users to search: by keywords and phrases, by words that sound alike, by words that have the same meaning, by the date a document was created or modified, by author, and much, much more. When users access a document that shows up as part of a search, they are taken directly to the page where the first occurrence of their search term or phrase appears, as shown in Figure 18-1. (Cataloging and searching indexes are discussed in Chapters 13 and 14.)

Figure 18-1:
I searched for the word *cartoon*, and Acrobat displayed a list of documents that contained my search term. Then I selected a document to look at, and Acrobat displayed the first page containing the search term.

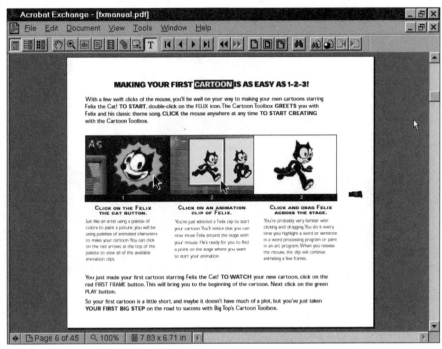

You can also set up Acrobat to automatically create PDFs from existing documents with Distiller. In addition, you can tell Acrobat to update indexes automatically with Catalog. These two features allow you to maintain a company library virtually unattended. (See Chapter 17 to find out more.)

Acrobat's security features — such as the capability to password-protect PDFs — enable you to implement restrictions as to who can access which documents.

Using Acrobat to Create Multimedia Titles

A multimedia title is an interactive electronic document containing multimedia files, such as digital sound and movie clips. Although Acrobat is not a full-featured multimedia authoring program, it can help you create sophisticated titles. It's navigational and multimedia file support are adequate for all but the most exacting multimedia applications. And the capability to hide Reader's menus, toolbars, and other application window objects (see Figure 18-2) makes your titles appear as though they were created in high-end authoring packages.

Figure 18-2:
An Acrobat
multimedia
title with
the Reader
interface
hidden.

You can easily create all kinds of multimedia titles in Acrobat, including:

Word games and quizzes

Courseware

Edutainment

Interactive software documentation

Multimedia brochures

Interactive manuals

Using Acrobat to Create CD-ROM Titles

With the proliferation of inexpensive CD recorders, many people are authoring their own CD-ROM applications. With a minimal investment, some planning, and Acrobat, so can you.

A CD-ROM title is virtually any kind of software that comes on a CD. The term, however, is often restricted to applications designed to run from the CD, such as multimedia games, references, and searchable information text and databases. You can, for example, place your company's manuals and procedures documents on a CD, use Adobe Catalog to make it searchable (see Chapter 13), and distribute it throughout the company.

Anything you can create with Acrobat can be distributed on CD-ROM, including multimedia titles and software documentation.

Using Acrobat to Create Software Documentation

Any type of document traditionally produced on paper can be turned into an easily navigable PDF. Many companies, especially Adobe (and many Macintosh software publishers) already produce their manuals in PDF documents. Companies that distribute trial versions of their software online, for instance, often include PDF documentation. Remember, Reader can be freely copied and distributed, making it easy to provide PDFs as documentation.

Using Acrobat for Form Submission and Retrieval Applications

Whether your company wants to produce a form retrieval and submission application on the World Wide Web or on the company network, Acrobat can act as an easy-to-use front-end for designing, retrieving, completing, and submitting the forms. Form data can be saved in the Acrobat PDF file format, which can be incorporated into several applications with a little behind-the-scenes programming.

You can even use form data retrieval to fill in portions of forms containing critical data, saving time and assuring data integrity, as discussed in Chapter 17.

Using Acrobat to Create Electronic Books and Manuals

Acrobat allows you to take any long document, such as a book or a manual, laid out in PageMaker or QuarkXPress, and quickly turn it into an easy-to-use electronic document. If you read the chapters concerned with navigating PDFs (see Chapters 2 and 6), you already know that finding information in a PDF can be much easier than wading through the table of contents and index of a hard copy document.

PDFs can contain hot links from contents lists that jump the user to the referenced information. Users also can search for specific words and phrases. If the PDF was produced from a PDF-savvy application, such as PageMaker, links between index and table of contents lists and references are created automatically. This saves you from hours of labor creating the links yourself.

Using Acrobat to Create Electronic Brochures

One of my favorites is using Acrobat to create electronic brochures. Granted, you can use a presentation program or multimedia authoring package to create electronic brochures, but neither type of application has the capability to compress text and graphics as effectively as Acrobat — and Acrobat usually does so without requiring you to adjust the default settings. It's difficult to get presentation programs and multimedia titles to fit on a single floppy disk. But not PDFs. You can squeeze a lot of document into a megabyte of disk space. Most brochures you produce for printing can be converted to an interactive, easily navigated PDF with minimal preparation and fuss. For example, I converted a series of six medical brochures to PDFs for access on the Web — in about 30 minutes.

Chapter 19

Ten Troubleshooting Tips
for Creating PDFs

. . . .

In This Chapter

▶ Poor image quality

▶ Distiller won't convert a PostScript file

▶ Fonts look funny or aren't what you expected

▶ Pages from your presentation software have weird borders

▶ Watched folders keep running out of disk space

▶ Distiller Assistant won't run

▶ Your PDFs don't download from the Web a page a time

▶ Users complain that they can't access your PDFs on the Web

. . . .

*I*n most situations, Acrobat hums along without a hitch. Now and then, however, unexpected problems arise. In this chapter, you look at some common mishaps. You find more in TROUBLE.PDF on the Acrobat CD-ROM disk, and still more on the Adobe Web site's Tips and Techniques page. From Exchange (using a computer with Internet access), choose Help⇨Acrobat on the Web⇨Tips and Techniques.

What an Ugly Picture!

What should you do if the images in a PDF don't look as good as you want? Chapters 6 and 16 mention that Distiller compresses and resamples images, especially bitmap images, by default. Sometimes, especially with scanned 24-bit photographs, the compression and resampling are too radical, degrading the image beyond acceptability.

The solution? Don't compress and downsample the image so radically. If this happens to all your images in a particular PDF, you can change the downsample rate in the Distiller Job Options dialog box. By default, the settings for color and grayscale images are ZIP/JPEG Medium. Try setting the quality to ZIP/JPEG Medium High or ZIP/JPEG High. Here's how:

1. **From inside Distiller, choose Distiller⇨Job Options.**

2. **To change the Color Bitmap Images setting, click the Automatic Compression list and select the new setting.**

   To change the setting for grayscale images, do the same under Grayscale Bitmap Images.

3. **Click OK.**

4. **Distill the PostScript file again, as I discuss in Chapter 4.**

Remember that the changes in the preceding procedure affect all the images in the PDF, which makes the file larger. If only one or a few images are degraded and you want to maintain a small PDF file size, resample the offending images in an image editor such as Photoshop, as I discuss in Chapter 16.

Why Won't Distiller Convert the PostScript file to PDF?

You've tried and tried, but Distiller keeps choking on a certain PDF (or several PDFs). What's up? Basically, Distiller can't convert a file in three instances:

- ✔ The file is corrupted or contains a PostScript error
- ✔ The file is not a true PostScript file
- ✔ The file has the wrong file name extension (Windows only)

Corrupted files

File corruption is one of the most prevalent causes for a conversion failure. Sometimes computer files, like rotten apples, go bad. Why? Who knows. If you suspect a bad file, simply print it to a PostScript file again. (You can check a PostScript file by copying it to a PostScript printer. In Windows, for instance, simply copy it to LPT1, or wherever your printer is connected. On a Mac, you need to download the file using a communications program.)

If the file contains offending code, Distiller generates an error log file in the folder in which the PDF would have been generated. The file is given the same name as the PostScript file, but with the .log extension. You can open the log file in your word processor, but I doubt you'll know what to do based on the information in the log.

Try to use PDFWriter to distill the file, try a different PostScript printer driver than the one you used to generate the file.

Counterfeit PostScript driver

A few years ago, lots of PostScript clone printers and devices were available, although this is less of a problem today. The printer drivers for these devices do not always generate compatible PostScript files. If you're using one of these devices, install another printer driver for creating PDFs, such as an Apple LaserWriter driver.

A PostScript file by any other name

In Windows, not all printer drivers create files with extensions recognized by Distiller. Some, for example, create files with .prn extensions. Distiller wants files with .ps or .eps extensions. So change the file name, giving it the proper extension.

What Happened to My Fancy Fonts?

You've created a PDF with decorative banners and headlines, but when you open it, you get only Times or Helvetica. What happened to your Bookman Old Style?

Acrobat relies on a standard font set for generating documents. If you want decorative and other fonts in your creator document to show up in your PDF, you must either embed them in the PostScript file with the printer driver's Download Fonts option or make the fonts available to Distiller through the Font Embedding sheet in the Job Options dialog box. I discuss using this dialog box in Chapter 4.

How Can I Get Rid of the Ugly Borders on My Pages?

When you print to a PostScript file from some presentation programs, such as Microsoft PowerPoint, often the pages contain unsightly borders that are not part of the original slide page. You can get rid of these with the Exchange Crop Pages dialog box, shown in Figure 19-1. Here's how:

1. **With the document open in Exchange in a view that allows you to see the entire page, choose Document➪Crop Pages.**

2. **Use the arrows to crop the pages on all four sides as needed.**

   If you watch closely, you see a small hairline on the side of the page you are cropping. Each time you click, it moves slightly.

3. **Select All to crop all the pages in the document.**

4. **Click OK.**

Figure 19-1:
Use this
dialog box
to crop
unsightly
page
borders.

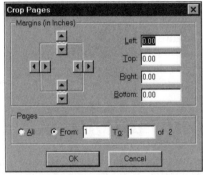

My Watched Folders Keep Running Out of Disk Space

Get another hard disk. Right? A less expensive and easier solution is to perform these basic maintenance operations:

✔ Go through your watched folders now and then and delete obsolete PDFs.

✔ If the PDFs in your library documents expire periodically, use the Delete Files In Out Folder Older Than option in the Distiller Watched Folders dialog box to choose the folder (choose➪Distiller➪Watched Folders).

✔ PostScript files can be huge. Turn on the Deleted option for *After Distilling, the PostScript File Should Be* setting in the Distiller Watched Folders dialog box (choose Distiller⇨Watched Folders).

✔ Purge your indexes regularly, as I discuss in Chapter 13.

✔ Ask for a separate network volume for your PDF library (and hold your breath).

I Can't Run Distiller Assistant Successfully

Distiller Assistant needs to launch Distiller and Exchange at the same time. Between them, they require approximately 20MB of RAM. Your system will also need additional RAM to run the creator application (such as Word or PageMaker). If you don't have enough RAM, you will not be able to use Distiller Assistant.

In addition, Distiller Assistant needs to be set up properly in Windows, as described on page 38 of the *Distiller Online Guide*.

My PDFs Don't Download a Page at a Time from the Web

Bummer! As I mention in Chapter 16, the following conditions must all be present for page-at-a-time byte-serving to work:

✔ The PDF must be created in Acrobat 3 and saved as Acrobat 3 compatible.

✔ The server on which the PDF resides must support byte-serving.

✔ The user's browser must be Netscape Navigator 3 or Microsoft Internet Explorer 3 compatible.

✔ Your user must be using PDF Viewer and Reader (or Exchange) 3.

✔ The PDF must be saved in Exchange as Optimized.

If page-at-a-time is crucial to your application, get everybody upgraded, or move your Web site to a more modern server!

Some of My Users Can't Access My PDFs on the Web

You find a lot of help solving this problem in Chapters 3 and 16. Usually, some users can't open your Web-based PDFs when others can for the follow- ing reasons:

- Your PDFs are Acrobat 3 compatible, but the user is using Reader 2.1 or earlier.
- The user's PDF Viewer plug-in is not installed properly, as I describe in Chapter 3.
- The user's browser does not support PDF viewing. (Get them off America Online and onto a new version of Netscape Navigator, Internet Explorer, or Apple's new Cyberdog.)
- The user's computer does not have enough RAM to run both the browser and the PDF viewer (a common problem on older Macs).

Index

(continued)

(continued)

(continued)

The Fun & Easy Way™ to learn about computers and more!

7/29/96

Windows® 3.11 For Dummies,® 3rd Edition
by Andy Rathbone

ISBN: 1-56884-370-4
$16.95 USA/
$22.95 Canada

Mutual Funds For Dummies™
by Eric Tyson

ISBN: 1-56884-226-0
$16.99 USA/
$22.99 Canada

SUPER STAR

DOS For Dummies,® 2nd Edition
by Dan Gookin

ISBN: 1-878058-75-4
$16.95 USA/
$22.95 Canada

SUPER STAR

The Internet For Dummies,® 2nd Edition
by John Levine & Carol Baroudi

ISBN: 1-56884-222-8
$19.99 USA/
$26.99 Canada

Personal Finance For Dummies™
by Eric Tyson

ISBN: 1-56884-150-7
$16.95 USA/
$22.95 Canada

SUPER STAR

PCs For Dummies,® 3rd Edition
by Dan Gookin & Andy Rathbone

ISBN: 1-56884-904-4
$16.99 USA/
$22.99 Canada

Macs® For Dummies,® 3rd Edition
by David Pogue

ISBN: 1-56884-239-2
$19.99 USA/
$26.99 Canada

SUPER STAR

The SAT® I For Dummies™
by Suzee Vlk

ISBN: 1-56884-213-9
$14.99 USA/
$20.99 Canada

SUPER STAR

Here's a complete listing of IDG Books' ...For Dummies® titles

Title	Author	ISBN	Price
DATABASE			
Access 2 For Dummies®	by Scott Palmer	ISBN: 1-56884-090-X	$19.95 USA/$26.95 Canada
Access Programming For Dummies®	by Rob Krumm	ISBN: 1-56884-091-8	$19.95 USA/$26.95 Canada
Approach 3 For Windows® For Dummies®	by Doug Lowe	ISBN: 1-56884-233-3	$19.99 USA/$26.99 Canada
dBASE For DOS For Dummies®	by Scott Palmer & Michael Stabler	ISBN: 1-56884-188-4	$19.95 USA/$26.95 Canada
dBASE For Windows® For Dummies®	by Scott Palmer	ISBN: 1-56884-179-5	$19.95 USA/$26.95 Canada
dBASE 5 For Windows® Programming For Dummies®	by Ted Coombs & Jason Coombs	ISBN: 1-56884-215-5	$19.99 USA/$26.99 Canada
FoxPro 2.6 For Windows® For Dummies®	by John Kaufeld	ISBN: 1-56884-187-6	$19.95 USA/$26.95 Canada
Paradox 5 For Windows® For Dummies®	by John Kaufeld	ISBN: 1-56884-185-X	$19.95 USA/$26.95 Canada
DESKTOP PUBLISHING/ILLUSTRATION/GRAPHICS			
CorelDRAW! 5 For Dummies®	by Deke McClelland	ISBN: 1-56884-157-4	$19.95 USA/$26.95 Canada
CorelDRAW! For Dummies®	by Deke McClelland	ISBN: 1-56884-042-X	$19.95 USA/$26.95 Canada
Desktop Publishing & Design For Dummies®	by Roger C. Parker	ISBN: 1-56884-234-1	$19.99 USA/$26.99 Canada
Harvard Graphics 2 For Windows® For Dummies®	by Roger C. Parker	ISBN: 1-56884-092-6	$19.95 USA/$26.95 Canada
PageMaker 5 For Macs® For Dummies®	by Galen Gruman & Deke McClelland	ISBN: 1-56884-178-7	$19.95 USA/$26.95 Canada
PageMaker 5 For Windows® For Dummies®	by Deke McClelland & Galen Gruman	ISBN: 1-56884-160-4	$19.95 USA/$26.95 Canada
Photoshop 3 For Macs® For Dummies®	by Deke McClelland	ISBN: 1-56884-208-2	$19.99 USA/$26.99 Canada
QuarkXPress 3.3 For Dummies®	by Galen Gruman & Barbara Assadi	ISBN: 1-56884-217-1	$19.99 USA/$26.99 Canada
FINANCE/PERSONAL FINANCE/TEST TAKING REFERENCE			
Everyday Math For Dummies™	by Charles Seiter	ISBN: 1-56884-248-1	$14.99 USA/$22.99 Canada
Personal Finance For Dummies™ For Canadians	by Eric Tyson & Tony Martin	ISBN: 1-56884-378-X	$18.99 USA/$24.99 Canada
QuickBooks 3 For Dummies®	by Stephen L. Nelson	ISBN: 1-56884-227-9	$19.99 USA/$26.99 Canada
Quicken 8 For DOS For Dummies,® 2nd Edition	by Stephen L. Nelson	ISBN: 1-56884-210-4	$19.95 USA/$26.95 Canada
Quicken 5 For Macs® For Dummies®	by Stephen L. Nelson	ISBN: 1-56884-211-2	$19.95 USA/$26.95 Canada
Quicken 4 For Windows® For Dummies,® 2nd Edition	by Stephen L. Nelson	ISBN: 1-56884-209-0	$19.95 USA/$26.95 Canada
Taxes For Dummies,™ 1995 Edition	by Eric Tyson & David J. Silverman	ISBN: 1-56884-220-1	$14.99 USA/$20.99 Canada
The GMAT® For Dummies™	by Suzee Vlk, Series Editor	ISBN: 1-56884-376-3	$14.99 USA/$20.99 Canada
The GRE® For Dummies™	by Suzee Vlk, Series Editor	ISBN: 1-56884-375-5	$14.99 USA/$20.99 Canada
Time Management For Dummies™	by Jeffrey J. Mayer	ISBN: 1-56884-360-7	$16.99 USA/$22.99 Canada
TurboTax For Windows® For Dummies®	by Gail A. Helsel, CPA	ISBN: 1-56884-228-7	$19.99 USA/$26.99 Canada
GROUPWARE/INTEGRATED			
ClarisWorks For Macs® For Dummies®	by Frank Higgins	ISBN: 1-56884-363-1	$19.99 USA/$26.99 Canada
Lotus Notes For Dummies®	by Pat Freeland & Stephen Londergan	ISBN: 1-56884-212-0	$19.95 USA/$26.95 Canada
Microsoft® Office 4 For Windows® For Dummies®	by Roger C. Parker	ISBN: 1-56884-183-3	$19.95 USA/$26.95 Canada
Microsoft® Works 3 For Windows® For Dummies®	by David C. Kay	ISBN: 1-56884-214-7	$19.99 USA/$26.99 Canada
SmartSuite 3 For Dummies®	by Jan Weingarten & John Weingarten	ISBN: 1-56884-367-4	$19.99 USA/$26.99 Canada
INTERNET/COMMUNICATIONS/NETWORKING			
America Online® For Dummies,® 2nd Edition	by John Kaufeld	ISBN: 1-56884-933-8	$19.99 USA/$26.99 Canada
CompuServe For Dummies,® 2nd Edition	by Wallace Wang	ISBN: 1-56884-937-0	$19.99 USA/$26.99 Canada
Modems For Dummies,® 2nd Edition	by Tina Rathbone	ISBN: 1-56884-223-6	$19.99 USA/$26.99 Canada
MORE Internet For Dummies®	by John R. Levine & Margaret Levine Young	ISBN: 1-56884-164-7	$19.95 USA/$26.95 Canada
MORE Modems & On-line Services For Dummies®	by Tina Rathbone	ISBN: 1-56884-365-8	$19.99 USA/$26.99 Canada
Mosaic For Dummies,® Windows Edition	by David Angell & Brent Heslop	ISBN: 1-56884-242-2	$19.99 USA/$26.99 Canada
NetWare For Dummies,® 2nd Edition	by Ed Tittel, Deni Connor & Earl Follis	ISBN: 1-56884-369-0	$19.99 USA/$26.99 Canada
Networking For Dummies®	by Doug Lowe	ISBN: 1-56884-079-9	$19.95 USA/$26.95 Canada
PROCOMM PLUS 2 For Windows® For Dummies®	by Wallace Wang	ISBN: 1-56884-219-8	$19.99 USA/$26.99 Canada
TCP/IP For Dummies®	by Marshall Wilensky & Candace Leiden	ISBN: 1-56884-241-4	$19.99 USA/$26.99 Canada

For scholastic requests & educational orders please
ll Educational Sales at 1. 800. 434. 2086

FOR MORE INFO OR TO ORDER, PLEASE CALL ▶ 800. 762. 2974

For volume discounts & special orders please call
Corporate Sales, at 415. 655. 3000

Title	Author	ISBN	Price
The Internet For Macs® For Dummies,® 2nd Edition	by Charles Seiter	ISBN: 1-56884-371-2	$19.99 USA/$26.99 Canada
The Internet For Macs® For Dummies® Starter Kit	by Charles Seiter	ISBN: 1-56884-244-9	$29.99 USA/$39.99 Canada
The Internet For Macs® For Dummies® Starter Kit Bestseller Edition	by Charles Seiter	ISBN: 1-56884-245-7	$39.99 USA/$54.99 Canada
The Internet For Windows® For Dummies® Starter Kit	by John R. Levine & Margaret Levine Young	ISBN: 1-56884-237-6	$34.99 USA/$44.99 Canada
The Internet For Windows® For Dummies® Starter Kit, Bestseller Edition	by John R. Levine & Margaret Levine Young	ISBN: 1-56884-246-5	$39.99 USA/$54.99 Canada

MACINTOSH

Title	Author	ISBN	Price
Mac® Programming For Dummies®	by Dan Parks Sydow	ISBN: 1-56884-173-6	$19.95 USA/$26.95 Canada
Macintosh® System 7.5 For Dummies®	by Bob LeVitus	ISBN: 1-56884-197-3	$19.95 USA/$26.95 Canada
MORE Macs® For Dummies®	by David Pogue	ISBN: 1-56884-087-X	$19.95 USA/$26.95 Canada
PageMaker 5 For Macs® For Dummies®	by Galen Gruman & Deke McClelland	ISBN: 1-56884-178-7	$19.95 USA/$26.95 Canada
QuarkXPress 3.3 For Dummies®	by Galen Gruman & Barbara Assadi	ISBN: 1-56884-217-1	$19.99 USA/$26.99 Canada
Upgrading and Fixing Macs® For Dummies®	by Kearney Rietmann & Frank Higgins	ISBN: 1-56884-189-2	$19.95 USA/$26.95 Canada

MULTIMEDIA

Title	Author	ISBN	Price
Multimedia & CD-ROMs For Dummies,® 2nd Edition	by Andy Rathbone	ISBN: 1-56884-907-9	$19.99 USA/$26.99 Canada
Multimedia & CD-ROMs For Dummies,® Interactive Multimedia Value Pack, 2nd Edition	by Andy Rathbone	ISBN: 1-56884-909-5	$29.99 USA/$39.99 Canada

OPERATING SYSTEMS:

DOS

Title	Author	ISBN	Price
MORE DOS For Dummies®	by Dan Gookin	ISBN: 1-56884-046-2	$19.95 USA/$26.95 Canada
OS/2® Warp For Dummies,® 2nd Edition	by Andy Rathbone	ISBN: 1-56884-205-8	$19.99 USA/$26.99 Canada

UNIX

Title	Author	ISBN	Price
MORE UNIX® For Dummies®	by John R. Levine & Margaret Levine Young	ISBN: 1-56884-361-5	$19.99 USA/$26.99 Canada
UNIX® For Dummies®	by John R. Levine & Margaret Levine Young	ISBN: 1-878058-58-4	$19.95 USA/$26.95 Canada

WINDOWS

Title	Author	ISBN	Price
MORE Windows® For Dummies,® 2nd Edition	by Andy Rathbone	ISBN: 1-56884-048-9	$19.95 USA/$26.95 Canada
Windows® 95 For Dummies®	by Andy Rathbone	ISBN: 1-56884-240-6	$19.99 USA/$26.99 Canada

PCS/HARDWARE

Title	Author	ISBN	Price
Illustrated Computer Dictionary For Dummies,® 2nd Edition	by Dan Gookin & Wallace Wang	ISBN: 1-56884-218-X	$12.95 USA/$16.95 Canada
Upgrading and Fixing PCs For Dummies,® 2nd Edition	by Andy Rathbone	ISBN: 1-56884-903-6	$19.99 USA/$26.99 Canada

PRESENTATION/AUTOCAD

Title	Author	ISBN	Price
AutoCAD For Dummies®	by Bud Smith	ISBN: 1-56884-191-4	$19.95 USA/$26.95 Canada
PowerPoint 4 For Windows® For Dummies®	by Doug Lowe	ISBN: 1-56884-161-2	$16.99 USA/$22.99 Canada

PROGRAMMING

Title	Author	ISBN	Price
Borland C++ For Dummies®	by Michael Hyman	ISBN: 1-56884-162-0	$19.95 USA/$26.95 Canada
C For Dummies,® Volume 1	by Dan Gookin	ISBN: 1-878058-78-9	$19.95 USA/$26.95 Canada
C++ For Dummies®	by Stephen R. Davis	ISBN: 1-56884-163-9	$19.95 USA/$26.95 Canada
Delphi Programming For Dummies®	by Neil Rubenking	ISBN: 1-56884-200-7	$19.99 USA/$26.99 Canada
Mac® Programming For Dummies®	by Dan Parks Sydow	ISBN: 1-56884-173-6	$19.95 USA/$26.95 Canada
PowerBuilder 4 Programming For Dummies®	by Ted Coombs & Jason Coombs	ISBN: 1-56884-325-9	$19.99 USA/$26.99 Canada
QBasic Programming For Dummies®	by Douglas Hergert	ISBN: 1-56884-093-4	$19.95 USA/$26.95 Canada
Visual Basic 3 For Dummies®	by Wallace Wang	ISBN: 1-56884-076-4	$19.95 USA/$26.95 Canada
Visual Basic "X" For Dummies®	by Wallace Wang	ISBN: 1-56884-230-9	$19.99 USA/$26.99 Canada
Visual C++ 2 For Dummies®	by Michael Hyman & Bob Arnson	ISBN: 1-56884-328-3	$19.99 USA/$26.99 Canada
Windows® 95 Programming For Dummies®	by S. Randy Davis	ISBN: 1-56884-327-5	$19.99 USA/$26.99 Canada

SPREADSHEET

Title	Author	ISBN	Price
1-2-3 For Dummies®	by Greg Harvey	ISBN: 1-878058-60-6	$16.95 USA/$22.95 Canada
1-2-3 For Windows® 5 For Dummies,® 2nd Edition	by John Walkenbach	ISBN: 1-56884-216-3	$16.95 USA/$22.95 Canada
Excel 5 For Macs® For Dummies®	by Greg Harvey	ISBN: 1-56884-186-8	$19.95 USA/$26.95 Canada
Excel For Dummies,® 2nd Edition	by Greg Harvey	ISBN: 1-56884-050-0	$16.95 USA/$22.95 Canada
MORE 1-2-3 For DOS For Dummies®	by John Weingarten	ISBN: 1-56884-224-4	$19.99 USA/$26.99 Canada
MORE Excel 5 For Windows® For Dummies®	by Greg Harvey	ISBN: 1-56884-207-4	$19.95 USA/$26.95 Canada
Quattro Pro 6 For Windows® For Dummies®	by John Walkenbach	ISBN: 1-56884-174-4	$19.95 USA/$26.95 Canada
Quattro Pro For DOS For Dummies®	by John Walkenbach	ISBN: 1-56884-023-3	$16.95 USA/$22.95 Canada

UTILITIES

Title	Author	ISBN	Price
Norton Utilities 8 For Dummies®	by Beth Slick	ISBN: 1-56884-166-3	$19.95 USA/$26.95 Canada

VCRS/CAMCORDERS

Title	Author	ISBN	Price
VCRs & Camcorders For Dummies™	by Gordon McComb & Andy Rathbone	ISBN: 1-56884-229-5	$14.99 USA/$20.99 Canada

WORD PROCESSING

Title	Author	ISBN	Price
Ami Pro For Dummies®	by Jim Meade	ISBN: 1-56884-049-7	$19.95 USA/$26.95 Canada
MORE Word For Windows® 6 For Dummies®	by Doug Lowe	ISBN: 1-56884-165-5	$19.95 USA/$26.95 Canada
MORE WordPerfect® 6 For Windows® For Dummies®	by Margaret Levine Young & David C. Kay	ISBN: 1-56884-206-6	$19.95 USA/$26.95 Canada
MORE WordPerfect® 6 For DOS For Dummies®	by Wallace Wang, edited by Dan Gookin	ISBN: 1-56884-047-0	$19.95 USA/$26.95 Canada
Word 6 For Macs® For Dummies®	by Dan Gookin	ISBN: 1-56884-190-6	$19.95 USA/$26.95 Canada
Word For Windows® 6 For Dummies®	by Dan Gookin	ISBN: 1-56884-075-6	$16.95 USA/$22.95 Canada
Word For Windows® For Dummies®	by Dan Gookin & Ray Werner	ISBN: 1-878058-86-X	$16.95 USA/$22.95 Canada
WordPerfect® 6 For DOS For Dummies®	by Dan Gookin	ISBN: 1-878058-77-0	$16.95 USA/$22.95 Canada
WordPerfect® 6.1 For Windows® For Dummies,® 2nd Edition	by Margaret Levine Young & David Kay	ISBN: 1-56884-243-0	$16.95 USA/$22.95 Canada
WordPerfect® For Dummies®	by Dan Gookin	ISBN: 1-878058-52-5	$16.95 USA/$22.95 Canada

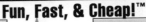

Fun, Fast, & Cheap!™

NEW!

NEW!

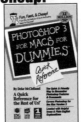

SUPER STAR

SUPER STAR

The Internet For Macs® For Dummies® Quick Reference
by Charles Seiter

ISBN:1-56884-967-2
$9.99 USA/$12.99 Canada

Windows® 95 For Dummies® Quick Reference
by Greg Harvey

ISBN: 1-56884-964-8
$9.99 USA/$12.99 Canada

Photoshop 3 For Macs® For Dummies® Quick Reference
by Deke McClelland

ISBN: 1-56884-968-0
$9.99 USA/$12.99 Canada

WordPerfect® For DOS For Dummies® Quick Reference
by Greg Harvey

ISBN: 1-56884-009-8
$8.95 USA/$12.95 Canada

Title	Author	ISBN	Price
DATABASE			
Access 2 For Dummies® Quick Reference	by Stuart J. Stuple	ISBN: 1-56884-167-1	$8.95 USA/$11.95 Canada
dBASE 5 For DOS For Dummies® Quick Reference	by Barrie Sosinsky	ISBN: 1-56884-954-0	$9.99 USA/$12.99 Canada
dBASE 5 For Windows® For Dummies® Quick Reference	by Stuart J. Stuple	ISBN: 1-56884-953-2	$9.99 USA/$12.99 Canada
Paradox 5 For Windows® For Dummies® Quick Reference	by Scott Palmer	ISBN: 1-56884-960-5	$9.99 USA/$12.99 Canada
DESKTOP PUBLISHING/ILLUSTRATION/GRAPHICS			
CorelDRAW! 5 For Dummies® Quick Reference	by Raymond E. Werner	ISBN: 1-56884-952-4	$9.99 USA/$12.99 Canada
Harvard Graphics For Windows® For Dummies® Quick Reference	by Raymond E. Werner	ISBN: 1-56884-962-1	$9.99 USA/$12.99 Canada
Photoshop 3 For Macs® For Dummies® Quick Reference	by Deke McClelland	ISBN: 1-56884-968-0	$9.99 USA/$12.99 Canada
FINANCE/PERSONAL FINANCE			
Quicken 4 For Windows® For Dummies® Quick Reference	by Stephen L. Nelson	ISBN: 1-56884-950-8	$9.95 USA/$12.95 Canada
GROUPWARE/INTEGRATED			
Microsoft® Office 4 For Windows® For Dummies® Quick Reference	by Doug Lowe	ISBN: 1-56884-958-3	$9.99 USA/$12.99 Canada
Microsoft® Works 3 For Windows® For Dummies® Quick Reference	by Michael Partington	ISBN: 1-56884-959-1	$9.99 USA/$12.99 Canada
INTERNET/COMMUNICATIONS/NETWORKING			
The Internet For Dummies® Quick Reference	by John R. Levine & Margaret Levine Young	ISBN: 1-56884-168-X	$8.95 USA/$11.95 Canada
MACINTOSH			
Macintosh® System 7.5 For Dummies® Quick Reference	by Stuart J. Stuple	ISBN: 1-56884-956-7	$9.99 USA/$12.99 Canada
OPERATING SYSTEMS:			
DOS			
DOS For Dummies® Quick Reference	by Greg Harvey	ISBN: 1-56884-007-1	$8.95 USA/$11.95 Canada
UNIX			
UNIX® For Dummies® Quick Reference	by John R. Levine & Margaret Levine Young	ISBN: 1-56884-094-2	$8.95 USA/$11.95 Canada
WINDOWS			
Windows® 3.1 For Dummies® Quick Reference, 2nd Edition	by Greg Harvey	ISBN: 1-56884-951-6	$8.95 USA/$11.95 Canada
PCs/HARDWARE			
Memory Management For Dummies® Quick Reference	by Doug Lowe	ISBN: 1-56884-362-3	$9.99 USA/$12.99 Canada
PRESENTATION/AUTOCAD			
AutoCAD For Dummies® Quick Reference	by Ellen Finkelstein	ISBN: 1-56884-198-1	$9.95 USA/$12.95 Canada
SPREADSHEET			
1-2-3 For Dummies® Quick Reference	by John Walkenbach	ISBN: 1-56884-027-6	$8.95 USA/$11.95 Canada
1-2-3 For Windows® 5 For Dummies® Quick Reference	by John Walkenbach	ISBN: 1-56884-957-5	$9.99 USA/$12.95 Canada
Excel For Windows® For Dummies® Quick Reference, 2nd Edition	by John Walkenbach	ISBN: 1-56884-096-9	$8.95 USA/$11.95 Canada
Quattro Pro 6 For Windows® For Dummies® Quick Reference	by Stuart J. Stuple	ISBN: 1-56884-172-8	$9.99 USA/$12.95 Canada
WORD PROCESSING			
Word For Windows® 6 For Dummies® Quick Reference	by George Lynch	ISBN: 1-56884-095-0	$8.95 USA/$11.95 Canada
Word For Windows® For Dummies® Quick Reference	by George Lynch	ISBN: 1-56884-029-2	$8.95 USA/$11.95 Canada
WordPerfect® 6.1 For Windows® For Dummies® Quick Reference, 2nd Edition	by Greg Harvey	ISBN: 1-56884-966-4	$9.99 USA/$12.99/Canada

For scholastic requests & educational orders please call Educational Sales at 1. 800. 434. 2086

FOR MORE INFO OR TO ORDER, PLEASE CALL ▶ **800. 762. 2974**

For volume discounts & special orders please call Corporate Sales, at 415. 655. 3000

Windows® 3.1 SECRETS™
by Brian Livingston

ISBN: 1-878058-43-6
$39.95 USA/$52.95 Canada
Includes software.

MORE Windows® 3.1 SECRETS™
by Brian Livingston

ISBN: 1-56884-019-5
$39.95 USA/$52.95 Canada
Includes software.

Windows® GIZMOS™
by Brian Livingston & Margie Livingston

ISBN: 1-878058-66-5
$39.95 USA/$52.95 Canada
Includes software.

Windows® 3.1 Connectivity SECRETS™
by Runnoe Connally, David Rorabaugh, & Sheldon Hall

ISBN: 1-56884-030-6
$49.95 USA/$64.95 Canada
Includes software.

Windows® 3.1 Configuration SECRETS™
by Valda Hilley & James Blakely

ISBN: 1-56884-026-8
$49.95 USA/$64.95 Canada
Includes software.

Internet SECRETS™
by John Levine & Carol Baroudi

ISBN: 1-56884-452-2
$39.99 USA/$54.99 Canada
Includes software.

Internet GIZMOS™ For Windows®
by Joel Diamond, Howard Sobel, & Valda Hilley

ISBN: 1-56884-451-4
$39.99 USA/$54.99 Canada
Includes software.

Network Security SECRETS™
by David Stang & Sylvia Moon

ISBN: 1-56884-021-7
Int'l. ISBN: 1-56884-151-5
$49.95 USA/$64.95 Canada
Includes software.

PC SECRETS™
by Caroline M. Halliday

ISBN: 1-878058-49-5
$39.95 USA/$52.95 Canada
Includes software.

WordPerfect® 6 SECRETS™
by Roger C. Parker & David A. Holzgang

ISBN: 1-56884-040-3
$39.95 USA/$52.95 Canada
Includes software.

DOS 6 SECRETS™
by Robert D. Ainsbury

ISBN: 1-878058-70-3
$39.95 USA/$52.95 Canada
Includes software.

Paradox 4 Power Programming SECRETS,™ 2nd Edition
by Gregory B. Salcedo & Martin W. Rudy

ISBN: 1-878058-54-1
$44.95 USA/$59.95 Canada
Includes software.

Paradox 5 For Windows® Power Programming SECRETS™
by Gregory B. Salcedo & Martin W. Rudy

ISBN: 1-56884-085-3
$44.95 USA/$59.95 Canada
Includes software.

Hard Disk SECRETS™
by John M. Goodman, Ph.D.

ISBN: 1-878058-64-9
$39.95 USA/$52.95 Canada
Includes software.

WordPerfect® 6 For Windows® Tips & Techniques Revealed
by David A. Holzgang & Roger C. Parker

ISBN: 1-56884-202-3
$39.95 USA/$52.95 Canada
Includes software.

Excel 5 For Windows® Power Programming Techniques
by John Walkenbach

ISBN: 1-56884-303-8
$39.95 USA/$52.95 Canada
Includes software.

For scholastic requests & educational orders please call Educational Sales at 1. 800. 434. 2086

FOR MORE INFO OR TO ORDER, PLEASE CALL ▶ 800. 762. 2974

For volume discounts & special orders please ca Corporate Sales, at 415. 655. 3000

"A lot easier to use than the book Excel gives you!"

Lisa Schmeckpeper, New Berlin, WI, on PC World Excel 5 For Windows Handbook

**Official Hayes Modem
Communications
Companion**
by Caroline M. Halliday

ISBN: 1-56884-072-1
$29.95 USA/$39.95 Canada
Includes software.

**1,001 Komputer Answers
from Kim Komando**
by Kim Komando

ISBN: 1-56884-460-3
$29.99 USA/$39.99 Canada
Includes software.

**PC World DOS 6
Handbook, 2nd Edition**
*by John Socha, Clint Hicks, &
Devra Hall*

ISBN: 1-878058-79-7
$34.95 USA/$44.95 Canada
Includes software.

**PC World Word
For Windows® 6 Handbook**
*by Brent Heslop
& David Angell*

ISBN: 1-56884-054-3
$34.95 USA/$44.95 Canada
Includes software.

**PC World Microsoft®
Access 2 Bible,
2nd Edition**
*by Cary N. Prague
& Michael R. Irwin*

ISBN: 1-56884-086-1
$39.95 USA/$52.95 Canada
Includes software.

**PC World Excel 5
For Windows® Handbook,
2nd Edition**
*by John Walkenbach
& Dave Maguiness*

ISBN: 1-56884-056-X
$34.95 USA/$44.95 Canada
Includes software.

**PC World WordPerfect® 6
Handbook**
by Greg Harvey

ISBN: 1-878058-80-0
$34.95 USA/$44.95 Canada
Includes software.

**QuarkXPress
For Windows® Designer
Handbook**
*by Barbara Assadi
& Galen Gruman*

ISBN: 1-878058-45-2
$29.95 USA/$39.95 Canada

**Official XTree
Companion, 3rd Edition**
by Beth Slick

ISBN: 1-878058-57-6
$19.95 USA/$26.95 Canada

**PC World DOS 6
Command Reference
and Problem Solver**
*by John Socha
& Devra Hall*

ISBN: 1-56884-055-1
$24.95 USA/$32.95 Canada

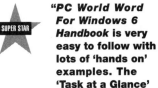

**Client/Server
Strategies™: A Survival
Guide for Corporate
Reengineers**
by David Vaskevitch

ISBN: 1-56884-064-0
$29.95 USA/$39.95 Canada

**"PC World Word
For Windows 6
Handbook is very
easy to follow with
lots of 'hands on'
examples. The
'Task at a Glance'
is very helpful!"**

Jacqueline Martens, Tacoma, WA

**"Thanks for publish-
ing this book! It's
the best money I've
spent this year!"**

*Robert D. Templeton,
Ft. Worth, TX, on MORE
Windows 3.1 SECRETS*

Unauthorized Windows® 95: A Developer's Guide to Exploring the Foundations of Windows "Chicago"
by Andrew Schulman

ISBN: 1-56884-169-8
$29.99 USA/$39.99 Canada

Unauthorized Windows® 95 Developer's Resource Kit
by Andrew Schulman

ISBN: 1-56884-305-4
$39.99 USA/$54.99 Canada

Best of the Net
by Seth Godin

ISBN: 1-56884-313-5
$22.99 USA/$32.99 Canada

Detour: The Truth About the Information Superhighway
by Michael Sullivan-Trainor

ISBN: 1-56884-307-0
$22.99 USA/$32.99 Canada

PowerPC Programming For Intel Programmers
by Kip McClanahan

ISBN: 1-56884-306-2
$49.99 USA/$64.99 Canada

Foundations™ of Visual C++ Programming For Windows® 95
by Paul Yao & Joseph Yao

ISBN: 1-56884-321-6
$39.99 USA/$54.99 Canada

Heavy Metal™ Visual C++ Programming
by Steve Holzner

ISBN: 1-56884-196-5
$39.95 USA/$54.95 Canada

Heavy Metal™ OLE 2.0 Programming
by Steve Holzner

ISBN: 1-56884-301-1
$39.95 USA/$54.95 Canada

Lotus Notes Application Development Handbook
by Erica Kerwien

ISBN: 1-56884-308-9
$39.99 USA/$54.99 Canada

The Internet Direct Connect Kit
by Peter John Harrison

ISBN: 1-56884-135-3
$29.95 USA/$39.95 Canada

Macworld® Ultimate Mac® Programming
by Dave Mark

ISBN: 1-56884-195-7
$39.95 USA/$54.95 Canada

The UNIX®-Haters Handbook
by Simson Garfinkel, Daniel Weise, & Steven Strassmann

ISBN: 1-56884-203-1
$16.95 USA/$22.95 Canada

Learn C++ Today!
by Martin Rinehart

ISBN: 1-56884-310-0
34.99 USA/$44.99 Canada

Type & Learn™ C
by Tom Swan

ISBN: 1-56884-073-X
34.95 USA/$44.95 Canada

Type & Learn™ Windows® Programming
by Tom Swan

ISBN: 1-56884-071-3
34.95 USA/$44.95 Canada

**COMPUTER
BOOK SERIES
FROM IDG**

For Dummies
who want
to program...

**Delphi Programming
For Dummies®**
by Neil Rubenking

ISBN: 1-56884-200-7
$19.99 USA/$26.99 Canada

**Access Programming
For Dummies®**
by Rob Krumm

ISBN: 1-56884-091-8
$19.95 USA/$26.95 Canada

TCP/IP For Dummies®
*by Marshall Wilensky &
Candace Leiden*

ISBN: 1-56884-241-4
$19.99 USA/$26.99 Canada

HTML For Dummies®
by Ed Tittel & Carl de Cordova

ISBN: 1-56884-330-5
$29.99 USA/$39.99 Canada

**Windows® 95 Programming
For Dummies®**
by S. Randy Davis

ISBN: 1-56884-327-5
$19.99 USA/$26.99 Canada

**Mac® Programming
For Dummies®**
by Dan Parks Sydow

ISBN: 1-56884-173-6
$19.95 USA/$26.95 Canada

**PowerBuilder 4 Programming
For Dummies®**
by Ted Coombs & Jason Coombs

ISBN: 1-56884-325-9
$19.99 USA/$26.99 Canada

Visual Basic 3 For Dummies®
by Wallace Wang

ISBN: 1-56884-076-4
$19.95 USA/$26.95 Canada

Covers version 3.

ISDN For Dummies®
by David Angell

ISBN: 1-56884-331-3
$19.99 USA/$26.99 Canada

Visual C++ "2" For Dummies®
*by Michael Hyman &
Bob Arnson*

ISBN: 1-56884-328-3
$19.99 USA/$26.99 Canada

Borland C++ For Dummies®
by Michael Hyman

ISBN: 1-56884-162-0
$19.95 USA/$26.95 Canada

C For Dummies,® Volume I
by Dan Gookin

ISBN: 1-878058-78-9
$19.95 USA/$26.95 Canada

C++ For Dummies®
by Stephen R. Davis

ISBN: 1-56884-163-9
$19.95 USA/$26.95 Canada

**QBasic Programming
For Dummies®**
by Douglas Hergert

ISBN: 1-56884-093-4
$19.95 USA/$26.95 Canada

**dBase 5 For Windows®
Programming For Dummies®**
by Ted Coombs & Jason Coombs

ISBN: 1-56884-215-5
$19.99 USA/$26.99 Canada

scholastic requests & educational orders please
Educational Sales at 1. 800. 434. 2086

FOR MORE INFO OR TO ORDER, PLEASE CALL ▶ 800. 762. 2974

For volume discounts & special orders please call
Corporate Sales, at 415. 655. 3000

Official Hayes Modem Communications Companion
by Caroline M. Halliday

ISBN: 1-56884-072-1
$29.95 USA/$39.95 Canada

Includes software.

1,001 Komputer Answers from Kim Komando
by Kim Komando

ISBN: 1-56884-460-3
$29.99 USA/$39.99 Canada

Includes software.

PC World Excel 5 For Windows® Handbook, 2nd Edition
by John Walkenbach & Dave Maguiness

ISBN: 1-56884-056-X
$34.95 USA/$44.95 Canada

Includes software

PC World WordPerfect® 6 Handbook
by Greg Harvey

ISBN: 1-878058-80-0
$34.95 USA/$44.95 Canada

Includes software.

PC World DOS 6 Command Reference and Problem Solver
by John Socha & Devra Hall

ISBN: 1-56884-055-1
$24.95 USA/$32.95 Canada

NATION BESTSELL

Client/Server Strategies™: A Survival Guide for Corporate Reengineers
by David Vaskevitch

SUPER STAR

ISBN: 1-56884-064-0
$29.95 USA/$39.95 Canada

Internet SECRETS™
by John Levine & Carol Baroudi

ISBN: 1-56884-452-2
$39.99 USA/$54.99 Canada

Includes software.

Network Security SECRETS™
by David Stang & Sylvia Moon

ISBN: 1-56884-021-7
Int'l. ISBN: 1-56884-151-5
$49.95 USA/$64.95 Canada

Includes software.

PC SECRETS™
by Caroline M. Halliday

ISBN: 1-878058-49-5
$39.95 USA/$52.95 Canada

Includes software.

...SECRETS®

IDG BOOKS WORLDWIDE

Here's a complete listing of PC Press Titles

Title	Author	ISBN	Price
BBS SECRETS™	by Ray Werner	ISBN: 1-56884-491-3	$39.99 USA/$54.99 Canada
Creating Cool Web Pages with HTML	by Dave Taylor	ISBN: 1-56884-454-9	$19.99 USA/$26.99 Canada
DOS 6 SECRETS™	by Robert D. Ainsbury	ISBN: 1-878058-70-3	$39.95 USA/$52.95 Canada
Excel 5 For Windows® Power Programming Techniques	by John Walkenbach	ISBN: 1-56884-303-8	$39.95 USA/$52.95 Canada
Hard Disk SECRETS™	by John M. Goodman, Ph.D.	ISBN: 1-878058-64-9	$39.95 USA/$52.95 Canada
Internet GIZMOS™ For Windows®	by Joel Diamond, Howard Sobel, & Valda Hilley	ISBN: 1-56884-451-4	$39.99 USA/$54.99 Canada
Making Multimedia Work	by Michael Goodwin	ISBN: 1-56884-468-9	$19.99 USA/$26.99 Canada
MORE Windows® 3.1 SECRETS™	by Brian Livingston	ISBN: 1-56884-019-5	$39.95 USA/$52.95 Canada
Official XTree Companion 3rd Edition	by Beth Slick	ISBN: 1-878058-57-6	$19.95 USA/$26.95 Canada
Paradox 4 Power Programming SECRETS™ 2nd Edition	by Gregory B. Salcedo & Martin W. Rudy	ISBN: 1-878058-54-1	$44.95 USA/$59.95 Canada
Paradox 5 For Windows® Power Programming SECRETS™	by Gregory B. Salcedo & Martin W. Rudy	ISBN: 1-878058-085-3	$44.95 USA/$59.95 Canada
PC World DOS 6 Handbook, 2nd Edition	by John Socha, Clint Hicks & Devra Hall	ISBN: 1-878058-79-7	$34.95 USA/$44.95 Canada
PC World Microsoft® Access 2 Bible, 2nd Edition	by Cary N. Prague & Michael R. Irwin	ISBN: 1-56884-086-1	$39.95 USA/$52.95 Canada
PC World Word For Windows® 6 Handbook	by Brent Heslop & David Angell	ISBN: 1-56884-054-3	$34.95 USA/$44.95 Canada
QuarkXPress For Windows® Designer Handbook	by Barbara Assadi & James Gruman	ISBN: 1-878058-45-2	$29.95 USA/$39.95 Canada
Windows® 3.1 Configuration SECRETS™	by Valda Hilley & James Blakely	ISBN: 1-56884-026-8	$49.95 USA/$64.95 Canada
Windows® 3.1 Connectivity SECRETS™	by Runnoe Connally, David Rorabaugh & Sheldon Hall	ISBN: 1-56884-030-6	$49.95 USA/$64.95 Canada
Windows® 3.1 SECRETS™	by Brian Livingston	ISBN: 1-878058-43-6	$39.95 USA/$52.95 Canada
Windows® 95 A.S.A.P.	by Dan Gookin	ISBN: 1-56884-483-2	$24.99 USA/$34.99 Canada
Windows® 95 Bible	by Alan Simpson	ISBN: 1-56884-074-8	$29.99 USA/$39.99 Canada
Windows® 95 SECRETS™	by Brian Livingston	ISBN: 1-56884-453-0	$39.99 USA/$54.99 Canada
Windows® GIZMOS™	by Brian Livingston & Margie Livingston	ISBN: 1-878058-66-5	$39.95 USA/$52.95 Canada
WordPerfect® 6 For Windows® Tips & Techniques Revealed	by David A. Holzgang & Roger C. Parker	ISBN: 1-56884-202-3	$39.95 USA/$52.95 Canada
WordPerfect® 6 SECRETS™	by Roger C. Parker & David A. Holzgang	ISBN: 1-56884-040-3	$39.95 USA/$52.95 Canada

IDG BOOKS WORLDWIDE

Order Center: **(800) 762-2974** *(8 a.m.–6 p.m., EST, weekdays)*

Quantity	ISBN	Title	Price	Total

Shipping & Handling Charges

	Description	First book	Each additional book	Total
Domestic	Normal	$4.50	$1.50	$
	Two Day Air	$8.50	$2.50	$
	Overnight	$18.00	$3.00	$
International	Surface	$8.00	$8.00	$
	Airmail	$16.00	$16.00	$
	DHL Air	$17.00	$17.00	$

*For large quantities call for shipping & handling charges.
**Prices are subject to change without notice.

Ship to:

Name _____

Company _____

Address _____

City/State/Zip _____

Daytime Phone _____

Payment: ☐ Check to IDG Books Worldwide (US Funds Only)

    ☐ VISA   ☐ MasterCard   ☐ American Express

Card # _____ Expires _____

Signature _____

Subtotal _____

CA residents add
applicable sales tax _____

IN, MA, and MD
residents add
5% sales tax _____

IL residents add
6.25% sales tax _____

RI residents add
7% sales tax _____

TX residents add
8.25% sales tax _____

Shipping _____

Total _____

Please send this order form to:

IDG Books Worldwide, Inc.
Attn: Order Entry Dept.
7260 Shadeland Station, Suite 100
Indianapolis, IN 46256

*Allow up to 3 weeks for delivery.
Thank you!*

Notes

Notes

Notes

Notes

 # YES!

Please keep me informed about IDG Books Worldwide's
World of Computer Knowledge. Send me your latest catalog.